OTHER TITLES IN THE
PSYCHOLOGY OF POPULAR CULTURE SERIES

The Psychology of The Simpsons:
D'oh!

The Psychology of Harry Potter:
An Unauthorized Examination of the Boy Who Lived

THE PSYCHOLOGY OF SURVIVOR

OVERANALYZE — OVEREMOTE — OVERCOMPENSATE

Leading Psychologists Take an Unauthorized Look at
the Most Elaborate Psychological Experiment Ever
Conducted ... *Survivor*!

EDITED BY

RICHARD J. GERRIG, PH.D.

SMART
POP

An imprint of BenBella Books, Inc.
Dallas, Texas

Smart Pop Books is an imprint of BenBella Books, Inc.
10440 N. Central Expy., Suite 800 | Dallas, TX 75231
www.smartpopbooks.com | www.benbellabooks.com
Send feedback to feedback@benbellabooks.com

Smart Pop and BenBella are federally registered trademarks.

Printed in the United States of America

Library of Congress Cataloging-in-Publication Data
The psychology of Survivor : leading psychologists take an unauthorized look at the most elaborate psychological experiment ever conducted-- Survivor! / edited by Richard J. Gerrig.
       p. cm.
       ISBN
     1-933771-05-4
   1. Survivor (Television program) 2. Reality television programs--Psychological aspects. I. Gerrig, Richard J.

 PN1992.77.S865P79 2007
791.45'72--dc22

                              20070066

Proofreading by Emily Chauviere and Stacia Seaman
Text design and composition by Moxie Studio
Cover design by Todd Michael Bushman

Table of Contents

INTRODUCTION

RICHARD J. GERRIG, PH.D.

Before *Survivor* premiered in May of 2000, the premise had already become familiar. Sixteen strangers would be deposited in a remote area of Borneo; only one (metaphorically speaking, we presumed) would survive. But how exactly would that work? The premise called to mind a whole range of cultural images. We could imagine the slapstick antics of the castaways stranded on *Gilligan's Island*. We could picture the Swiss Family Robinson merrily building their tree house. We could recall the young boys of *Lord of the Flies* descending into violence as human nature overwhelmed the façade of civilization.

As *Survivor* unfolded, some of these reference points proved apt. The show had its slapstick moments as well as a certain amount of merry (and, often, less merry) shelter building. Although the presence of the cameras presumably suppressed the more extreme forms of incivility, there were still an abundance of *Lord of the Flies* moments as contestants searched for ways to assume overt or covert control over their tribemates. However, to demonstrate that truth—or at least "reality"—is, indeed, stranger than fiction, *Survivor's* first season produced a dazzling outcome. In *Lord of the Flies*, Piggy is the most logical, rational boy and he is also wildly unpopular; Piggy, quite famously, does not survive his island ordeal. By contrast, on the first season of *Survivor* the castaway who most nearly embodied the spirit of Piggy—the one and only Richard Hatch—outwitted, outplayed, and outlasted his competitors to become the sole survivor.

Almost as soon as *Survivor* debuted, social scientists began to flaunt their expertise. Why, they were asked, had the show become so popular? How, they were asked, could one play the game to assure victory? The essays in this volume have the benefit of twelve seasons of *Survivor* to provide a longer view on those still urgent questions. The essays establish, to begin with, why social science expertise is so relevant. We have theories that describe and explain how people respond to the stress of extreme conditions and how they manipulate their social standing to achieve the outcomes they desire. We understand how people's behavior is shaped by the interactions of personality and situation.

The authors in this volume draw upon several domains of psychological theory to explain *Survivor*'s popularity. In most cases, the authors are trying to explain their own unflagging loyalty to the show. That's part of what makes this collection such a pleasurable read: the authors' interest in the psychology of *Survivor* is quite personal. These aren't academics dissecting a phenomenon from the safe distance of their ivory towers. These are genuine fans who seek to deploy their expertise to understand their own experiences. There are no dry abstractions here. Each chapter makes its case by citing chapter and verse from the first dozen seasons of *Survivor*.

These authors also use the evidence of those seasons to advance hypotheses about what one might best do to emerge as the sole survivor. The authors must always start with the fact of Richard Hatch's first season victory. However, the essays also document how subsequent contestants have changed the rules of engagement. The essays give quite specific advice about the psychological principles that should be most profitably applied given the current state of the game's evolution. While these authors acknowledge the impact of recent innovations such as Exile Island, the overall sense is that the psychology of *Survivor* has reached a point of stability. Read and learn—and then submit an audition tape.

If you prefer to play *Survivor* from the comfort of home, you should watch the show to see how well we authors of *The Psychology of Survivor* have done. We promise that we will continue to collect data (i.e., we will continue to watch the show) to refine our theories of how *Survivor* functions. We need to get those theories right. Like everyone else, we fear the one misjudgment that will get us voted off the island!

How can we explain why Survivor *is so addictive? Barbara
Ann Schapiro argues that* Survivor *dramatizes the tension
between the needs for affiliation—the need to belong—and self-
interest—the need to achieve one's own goals.* Survivor *may
serve a therapeutic function for viewers who must struggle to
balance these two needs in their own lives.*

Who's Afraid of Being Kicked Off the Island?

The Psychological Appeal of *Survivor*

BARBARA ANN SCHAPIRO, PH.D.

I have been a fan of *Survivor* since it first aired in the summer of
2000. Initially I kept quiet about my addiction to the show, embarrassed that I was so captivated by what many of my friends and academic colleagues considered a new low in schlocky popular television.
This was the beginning of the Reality TV trend, a trend some feared
would only further impoverish a medium already lacking in well-writ-
ten, imaginative programs. Why was it, then, that this show seemed to
lodge itself so firmly in my imagination? I remember waking up one
morning during that first *Survivor* series with scenarios of the previous
night's show running through my head: Was Rich going to betray Rudy?
What should Kelly's strategy be? Would Sue ever forgive her? And what
was wrong with my life that I should even care or be wasting my time
thinking about any of this? After all, as one of my friends observed, the
show is hardly reality, but a manufactured, highly contrived, fake reality.

So what is the appeal of this artificially constructed reality that
Survivor creates? The show has continued to attract strong ratings for six
years now. I am still watching and still questioning my fascination with
it. Those questions, along with my background in psychoanalytic rela-

tional theory, have led me finally to the following hypothesis: Much of *Survivor's* appeal lies in the psychological tension it creates, a tension that mirrors a conflictual state intrinsic to growing up within the family structure. The social reality *Survivor* constructs is at once intensely intimate and intensely competitive, one that demands both trusting interdependence—affiliations, alliances—as well as ruthless self-interest. In order not to be voted off, contestants need to be nice, likable, and attentive to the needs of others. They need to establish bonds and connections. Yet in order to win, bonds must be sacrificed and trusts betrayed in favor of furthering one's own individual success. As such, the show zeroes in on a dialectic between affiliation and self-interest—a dialectic many contemporary psychoanalytic theorists see as deeply ingrained in psychic and relational life.

From birth on, we must negotiate competing desires and demands. As children we are dependent on our caretakers. To avoid being rejected or emotionally abandoned—being kicked off the island, so to speak—we must adjust ourselves to the personalities of our caretakers and do all we can to secure our bonds with them. On the other hand, those bonds will inevitably conflict at times with the expression of our individual narcissism and the need to assert our own selfish needs and desires. We must stay within the good graces of those on whom we depend while also pursuing our own self-interests—interests that may, and often do, conflict with the interests of those others. As relational theorist Stephen Mitchell states, "The self operates in the intricate and subtle dialectic between spontaneous vitality and self-expression on the one hand and the requirement, crucial for survival, to preserve secure and familiar connections with others on the other" (133). As *Survivor* works on this dialectic between affiliation and self-assertion, it hits a deep chord within us. It also plays on fears and fantasies associated with both sides of the dialectic. The show highlights the humiliation of being excluded and rejected by others and of being a social outcast, and it also exposes conflicting attitudes toward aggressive individualism and cut-throat competitiveness. The appeal of the show thus lies less in its "reality" than in the underlying fantasies and conflicts it evokes and allows viewers to experience vicariously.

On the affiliation side of the dialectic, *Survivor* appeals to us because it plays on a deep-seated fear of rejection and humiliation—the fantasy of being kicked off the island. As we are all social animals in need of love and acceptance, I suspect we all harbor this fear to some extent—hence our pleasure in watching others have to confront and deal with it. Insecurities about social acceptance—the need to belong and the fear of banishment—are especially rampant during adolescence. The show reenacts the fierce tribal alliances of high school cliques, where inclusion or exclusion from the in-crowd can feel like a life-or-death matter. Though I do not know the specific ratings figures on teenage viewers of *Survivor*, I do have three nieces between the ages of twelve and seventeen who are addicted to the show. The clique phenomenon is especially intense for female adolescents in our culture, particularly in the middle school years. I certainly remember those years as some of the most miserable in my life, which might contribute to my own peculiar fascination with the show. *Survivor* may in fact serve a therapeutic function as it externalizes anxieties about rejection and exclusion and thus gives public expression to an adolescent angst that is often experienced as privately shameful.

Watching contestants scramble, sometimes desperately, to fit in, find a role, and be accepted by the group can indeed frequently make us cringe. I think of the socially inept Kel in *Survivor: Australian Outback*, pathetically trying to win the others' respect as a hunter, but coming up empty-handed every time. Or Rupert's equally pitiful parting words after being ousted from *Survivor: Pearl Islands*: "I always get hurt trusting people. I want so badly to be accepted, and I never get the acceptance that I want. I don't fit. So much for my dreams." Even Richard Hatch, the winner of the first *Survivor*, who claimed not to be emotionally invested and insisted he didn't care whether the others liked him, sulked after receiving three votes in one Tribal Council and refused for a while to do any more fishing for the tribe. One of the most horrible cringe-making moments occurred during the *Survivor: Australian Outback* reunion show, in which Debb, the first contestant to be voted off, fought back tears as she revealed her mortification at having even to appear on the broadcast. She felt deeply disparaged by the other contestants, by the press, and by the public. You could see Bryant Gumbel and the others squirming on the set, just as I was squirming on my sofa.

National Public Radio commentator Adam Sternberg, in a piece that aired on *This American Life*, argued that both the appeal and the value of reality shows lie precisely in the fact that they do make us cringe. A cringe, he explained, "combines repugnance with identification." We identify with the person experiencing shame or humiliation, for instance, and that identification signals a real emotional connection. This type of connection, Sternberg suggested, is more genuine than what we can experience by watching most network TV. I agree. Indeed the denial of such identification and the split-off projections that can result from defending against shameful feelings within are highly implicated in the psychodynamics of racism, sexism, and other dehumanizing phenomena in our world.

Survivor not only allows us to confront our fears of humiliation and social ostracism, it also makes us examine our feelings about the other side of the dialectic—the aggressive self-assertion, the ruthless, cutthroat competitiveness that our capitalist culture rewards. Contestants who display overt aggression generally do not survive for long. The show's creator/producer Mark Burnett described Joel of *Survivo: Borneo*, for instance, as "wrapped up in achieving alpha male status" (Burnett 41), a strategy that did not serve him well. In *Survivor: Australian Outback*, Jerri, an aspiring actress, stated bluntly that she decided "to play the game from the very beginning in an aggressive manner," and she suffered the consequences: She was despised by the other contestants and by viewers alike. The joke about her was that she not only gave the word "actress" a bad name, but the word "aspiring" as well. She was not diplomatic. She set her sights on Colby, whom she perceived as the physically strongest player, and she essentially disregarded the feelings of everyone else. Musing on camera at one point, she expressed some concern about how the others might be perceiving her, but then blurted, "Basically, I don't give a crap."

Such frank, self-centered nastiness also characterized *Survivor's* most notorious villain to date, Jon Dalton (a.k.a. Jonny "Fairplay") of *Survivor: Pearl Islands*. In a pre-arranged ploy, he baldly lied to his tribemates about receiving news of his grandmother's death. We then hear him cackling privately on camera, "My grandmother's home watching Jerry Springer right now!" Jon's parting words again unabashedly expressed his unscrupulous attitude: "I'm pretty proud of myself. I never gave up, and I didn't play fair, and I didn't plan on it." Jon's strategy reflects the view repeated in a line uttered by a number of contestants throughout the various *Survivor* series: "I didn't come here to make friends." A militant selfishness is in fact necessary to play the game seriously, even if viewers and contestants don't always like to acknowledge it. Such callous self-centeredness alone, however, cannot win the game. Attention must also be paid to affiliations and to securing the trust and alliances of others.

The dynamics of the *Survivor* game nevertheless often demand that those trusted alliances be broken. A guarded duplicity is thus usually necessary in order actually to win. Richard Hatch claimed that it was both his experience with corporate politics and with being a gay man in America that gave him the requisite skills to succeed in the game. As Burnett explains, the *Survivor* environment "was an arena where hiding your true self, sharing secrets with only trusted friends, and existing under constant scrutiny in a tribal environment would determine the winner. No one on the island had lived that life before but Richard" (Burnett 85).

Women and contestants from minority groups outside the mainstream might indeed be conditioned to be especially adept at playing *Survivor's* social game. With a history of being excluded from structured power, women and minorities have for generations had to rely on their ability to observe social interactions and to manipulate quietly and unobtrusively behind the scenes in order to get what they need. Such social observation and relational manipulation perhaps represent a kind of survival knowledge of the disenfranchised. Sandra Diaz-Twine, the winner of *Survivor: Pearl Islands*, attributed her win to her ability to fly under the radar and maneuver quietly in the background. In *Survivor: Panama*, the thirty-five-year-old African-American woman, Cirie Fields, though not the final winner, was generally acknowledged by both viewers and by the other contestants on the reunion show to have been the most accomplished player of the social game. Also voted the most popular player by viewers, she was rewarded with a new car. Cirie was not strong physically, but she lasted far longer than many expected. In a post-show interview, Cirie attributed her success to her work as a nurse:

"I can kind of pick out what each person needs. I don't know if it's from having patients and having to give them what they need. I really believe that helped me a lot. I think that's why people felt so easy and relaxed with me. I would give each person what they needed" (Bloomberg).

Cirie's social sensitivity and affiliation skills were especially acute; she could adjust herself to the personalities of the others and, as she says, give them what they needed in order to secure her alliances with them. At times she resented having to subsume her own needs to theirs: "I felt like Shane's secretary. Whatever he needed, I got for him. And that went for anybody. I hated to get water, but I had to do what I had to do to stay around" (Bloomberg). Yet Cirie was also expert at asserting her own self-interest by strategizing behind the others' backs, by breaking established bonds and alliances and by forming new bonds that would serve her better. Cirie made it to the final four, then ultimately lost a tie-breaking, fire-building Challenge with Danielle at her last Tribal Council. Social skills alone cannot assure a win in the *Survivor* game; athleticism and luck also play critical roles. Yet because Cirie could negotiate so well between affiliation and self-interest, she was recognized as one of the game's most consummate players.

The affiliation/self-assertion dialectic operates particularly within the family structure, and *Survivor* often reflects, and to some degree re-creates, family dynamics. This is most apparent as players of different age generations fall into parent-child roles and relationships. Some of the most intense dyadic relationships to emerge from the first two *Survivor* series were specifically configured in parent-child terms, making the affiliation side of the dialectic especially charged. In *Survivor: Borneo* this was true of the relationships between Richard and Rudy and between Kelly and Sue. The bond between the thirty-eight-year-old openly gay corporate trainer, Richard Hatch, and the homophobic seventy-two-year-old retired Navy SEAL, Rudy Boesch, was especially incongruous. Yet Burnett notes that "Rudy and Richard had become so close that members of the crew were comparing them to Darth Vader and Luke Skywalker, wondering aloud if Rudy weren't actually Richard's father" (Burnett 85). Richard even claimed that "Rudy was like his father, only more open-minded" (Burnett 172). In Burnett's book, Rudy's identifying quote is "I don't need none of that affection" (Burnett 17), yet he clearly formed a strong, loyal bond with

Richard. Indeed, toward the end, when he and Richard were among the final four left, the possibility that Richard might ultimately betray him provoked Rudy to threaten dramatically, "If he goes back on his word about our partnership, I've got friends who'll come after him" (Burnett 209). Although contestants are constantly reminding each other that it is only a game they are playing—the objective being to Outwit, Outplay, and Outlast—the alliances and loyalties that form in the course of playing the game take on a life of their own and create a competing pressure. The issue of trust and betrayal is most acute when the bond between players gets structured, as it was in the case of Richard and Rudy, in parent-child terms.

A similar though far more volatile case developed in the relationship between Kelly, a twenty-two-year-old river guide, and the thirty-eight-year-old truck driver, Sue. One of the most riveting, and excruciating, moments of *Survivor: Borneo* was Sue's virulent diatribe against Kelly in the final episode as she ranted about why she would never vote for Kelly to win. Sue's sense of betrayal by Kelly, the "rat," as she called her, was so raw and bitter it was difficult to watch. "If Kelly was lying in the street, dying," she proclaimed, "I'd walk past without giving her so much as a drink of water." I remember wondering at the time where all this aggressive fury toward Kelly was coming from—it seemed so wildly excessive. True, Sue had had an alliance and a friendship with Kelly, and Kelly had gone behind Sue's back to try to form an exclusive pact with Richard, but that sort of betrayal was typical of the game. Burnett's book, however, by again emphasizing the parent-child dynamic of the Kelly-Sue relationship, helped shed some light on the emotional intensity of their alliance. Kelly, with her tattoos and pierced tongue, was very much the rebellious child, yet also, according to Burnett, a child much in need of a mother-figure, and Sue fulfilled that role for her. The two apparently spent long hours together which viewers did not see (over a hundred hours of tape are edited down for each hour that is broadcast), with Sue taking Kelly under her maternal wing. Burnett believes that in order to feel empowered herself, Kelly needed to vote "her symbolic mother off the island" (Burnett 88). Sue could not forgive her for this. Again, when affiliations between contestants become familial in nature, betrayals are experienced with an overdetermined intensity.

In *Survivor: Panama*, the fierce rivalry between the forty-six-year-old retired Navy fighter pilot, Terry, and the twenty-four-year-old yoga instructor, Aras, prompted Jeff Probst on the reunion show to comment, rather fumblingly, that "there was a lot of sort of . . . 'father/son' would maybe be a way to say it" in terms of their relationship. Aras's frustration at repeatedly losing to Terry in the Immunity Challenges occasionally erupted in angry outbursts, insults, and shouting matches. An Oedipal dynamic may not only help account for the intensity of the rivalry, but also for an underlying guilt that prompted Aras ultimately to apologize to Terry, and to shake hands and reaffirm his respect for him. While Terry, after voting for Aras's ouster numerous times at Tribal Council, ultimately affirmed his bond with Aras by voting for him to win in the final contest with Danielle.

A similar dynamic may help explain one of the most bizarre moves by a *Survivor* player in the history of the series thus far. The last Immunity Challenge in *Survivor: Palau* between the final three contestants—Tom, Ian, and Katie—consisted of an endurance Challenge in which contestants each had to hold on to a navigation buoy as it bobbed on the waves. After Katie dropped out at five hours, a duel ensued between the forty-one-year-old firefighter, Tom, and the twenty-three-year-old dolphin trainer, Ian. Earlier, Tom had learned that Ian had planned to betray him. After almost twelve hours of holding on to these buoys, through a rainstorm and into the chilly night, Ian finally told Tom that he would drop off if Tom promised to take *not him* but Katie to the final two! How does one understand such seemingly irrational self-sacrifice? Clearly for Ian, the affiliation side of the dialectic in his inner world at that moment must have felt more urgent and more compelling than asserting his own self-interest. The bond with the father-figure Tom and the need to regain Tom's respect and friendship (as well as that of Katie, whom he had betrayed earlier as well) must have seemed far more vital than winning a million dollars.

Survivor: Australian Outback also featured some symbolic parent-child relationships, with two contestants similarly sacrificing individual advancement in favor of the relational bond. The most obvious such relationship was that between the perky twenty-three-year-old shoe designer, Elisabeth, and Rodger, the fifty-three-year-old Kentucky farmer. Rodger spoke explicitly about his tender regard for Elisabeth in terms of a father's feelings toward a daughter, and Elisabeth was equally direct about her affection for Rodger as a kindly paternal protector. Rodger and Elisabeth lasted longer after the merge (with most of their original tribe members gone) than many had predicted, because their very niceness was seen as a liability. As Jerri explained her vote for Elisabeth at one Tribal Council, "Because you are such a likable person it is a definite threat." When it became clear toward the end, however, that one of the two would be the next to go, Rodger sacrificed himself for Elisabeth, urging the other tribe members to vote for him rather than her. The public seemed to admire this. According to a poll on the official *Survivor* Web site at the time, Rodger was the most popular and well-liked contestant on that series, followed closely by Elisabeth. In one episode, however, Elisabeth revealed that she too had a ruthless side. Speaking to the camera about her relationship with Tina, she stated, "Tina and I have become close. I mean, *outback* close. Close enough to get the dirt you want on someone else. Close enough to let you advance ahead of the person you are trying to get close to." Yet we never saw Elisabeth actually deceiving Tina or betraying her alliances—she remained the loving and grateful daughter toward Rodger to the end— and thus she maintained her reputation as nice and likable.

A more interesting and subtle parent-child dynamic in *Survivor: Australian Outback*, however, involved the relationship between the twenty-six-year-old Texan, Colby, and the forty-year-old nurse, and ultimate winner of the game, Tina. Although their relationship, unlike Elisabeth and Rodger's, was never explicitly cast in such terms—Tina is a bit young to be Colby's actual mother—one wonders if the dynamic was not unconsciously in play. Throughout much of the show Colby seemed to be following Richard Hatch's dictum that to form emotional attachments and loyalties was not really to play the game. Colby told the camera at one point, "If you trust somebody, it's your own fault. You're a fool for not playing the game. The only one I've trusted is myself." He had no trouble spurning and deceiving the thirty-year-old Jerri. Yet when he won immunity in the final episode and so had to choose between Tina and Keith to be his sole competitor at the last Tribal Council, he sacrificed a near-certain win by selecting Tina. Keith was much disliked by the other castaways, and Colby was well aware of this fact. He even told us on camera that he knew he could beat Keith, but that he wasn't sure he even had a fifty-fifty chance against Tina.

So why did Colby sacrifice self-interest in favor of his affiliation with Tina? As the series progressed, Colby seemed to be struggling with a sense of himself as a "good" person. Using a Texan metaphor, he spoke of his wearing both black and white hats, and the black hat he associated specifically with "selfishness." Choosing Tina, he said, was "not selfish." He believed she was a better and more deserving person than Keith. Yet I wonder: If Tina had been someone of his own generation, would he have had such scruples or experienced such conflict about acting selfishly? Tina, as an older woman, could well have held maternal associations for Colby, making the conflict between his relational allegiances and his narcissistic strivings particularly intense. Colby's actual mother, in fact, made an appearance on the show (as a result of Colby's winning one of the reward Challenges), and it was clear that the two had an unusually close relationship. He described his mother as his "best friend" and said that they talked on the phone every day.

Also of interest was the audience reaction to Colby's choice. While Rodger's sacrifice was seen only as kind and generous, and resulted in his winning the popularity poll, Colby's selfless act, from what I gathered from talk shows and magazines, seemed to have generated primarily ridicule and contempt. *Newsweek* ("Newsmakers") quipped that "the hunky Texan had plenty of brawn . . . but a lack of brains" (*Newsweek* 67). Perhaps because Rodger was never seen as a serious contender, he escaped the derision that Colby provoked. Or perhaps Colby's deferring to a mother-figure sparked anxieties about maternal power and emasculation. Our culture may pay lip service to self-sacrifice, but it really only rewards and respects winners.

Like Colby, Tina also seemed to be experiencing tension—especially toward the end of *Survivor: Australian Outback*—between her selfish, aggressive, competitive side and her interpersonal affiliations and sense of herself as a good, caring, or nurturing person. At one point in the middle of the series, she explained her voting philosophy: "I want this to be on an individual basis. I want the good people to win." Yet she repeatedly voted against the "good" people—betraying her friend

Maralyn early on, and voting with her tribe to oust Alicia before the less-deserving Jerri. In the last episode, having made it to the final three, Tina began making frequent references to the importance of family in her life. "This experience," she said, "taught me how much family means. I have been so focused on independence. Now I just want to go nurture my family." Her family and its importance in her life came up again in her final appeal to the Tribal Council Jury.

All of Tina's harping on family and nurturance seemed to me some-how defensive, triggered perhaps by anxieties about her independence or about her betrayals and selfish pursuit of victory. This same tension in relation to Tina was raised yet again by Bryant Gumbel in the live reunion show following the contestants' return from the Outback. "We saw the sweet mother out there," he said to her in the closing minutes of the program, "but you've also been described by someone here as ruthless. Which is it?" She paused, then replied, "In the middle, a little of both." Watching Tina, like the other contestants, struggle to balance the competing sides of her nature accounts, I believe, for much of the appeal of the show. In varying degrees, we all are involved in a similar balancing act.

BARBARA ANN SCHAPIRO, PH.D., is a professor of English at Rhode Island College with a specialty in psychoanalysis and literature. She is the author of *The Romantic Mother: Narcissistic Patterns in Romantic Poetry* (Johns Hopkins, 1983), *Literature and the Relational Self* (NYU, 1994), and *D. H. Lawrence and the Paradoxes of Psychic Life* (SUNY, 1999). She is also co-editor with Lynne Layton of *Narcissism and the Text: Studies in Literature and the Psychology of Self* (NYU, 1986). Barbara remains a *Survivor* fan and is no longer embarrassed by it. She has even convinced her husband, after some initial resistance, to watch with her. He now shares her addiction.

ACKNOWLEDGMENTS

This essay is a revised and updated version of an article that originally appeared in *Journal for the Psychoanalysis of Culture and Society* 7.2 (Fall 2002): 274–279. Parts of that original essay are reprinted here with permission of the journal and Ohio State University Press.

REFERENCES

Burnett, Mark with Martin Dugard. *Survivor: The Official Companion Book to the CBS Television Show*. New York: TV Books, 2000.

Fields, Cirie. Interview by David Bloomberg. "'Un-fricking-believable!' An Interview with *Survivor: Exile Island*'s Cirie." RealityNewsOnline, 16 May 2006. <http://www.realitynewsonline.com/cgi-bin/ae.pl?mode=1&article=article6162.art&page=1>

Mitchell, Stephen A. *Hope and Dread in Psychoanalysis*. New York: Basic, 1993.

"Newsmakers": *Newsweek*, 14 May 2001, 67.

Sternberg, Adam. *This American Life*. National Public Radio. WBUR, Boston. 15 Apr. 2001.

Brad Wolgast and Mario J. Lanza provide a history of how standards for ethical play have evolved over the first dozen seasons of Survivor. *They demonstrate that early players who embraced strategy over emotion were scorned—despite their successes. Norms have now shifted so that "successful" play almost completely dominates ethical concerns. For Wolgast and Lanza, this shift toward "heartless mercenaries" has diluted* Survivor's *appeal.*

The Rise of the Heartless Mercenary

Sole Survivor? Or Sociopath?

BRAD WOLGAST, PH.D., AND MARIO J. LANZA

(Note: In this chapter we do not attempt to diagnose *Survivor* players with an actual personality disorder. We are simply taking small pieces of their edited TV characters and making vast leaps in the clinical diagnostic realm. And though we had a great time doing it, we sincerely hope that none of these players come after us, or our puppies, with a machete one day. Especially Brian Heidik.)

One of the most important steps in a child's development is the ability to learn how to empathize with others. This stage can begin as early as age two (Feldman 1997) and, in many ways, is as important as learning to walk or talk. Because if a child misses this stage, and somehow never learns how to relate to other people, he or she faces the very real prospect of one day developing into a sociopath.

What is a sociopath? Well, according to Hare (1995), sociopaths (or psychopaths, as he calls them) are "predators who use charm, manipulation, intimidation, and violence to control others and to satisfy their own selfish needs." These are people who seemingly have no positive connection to the world (or society) around them. They exhibit only the most limited human emotions, and even then are basically only putting on an act by essentially mimicking what they *think* would be the normal adult response to a given situation. It is because of this mimicry that sociopaths will often be able to cooperate with other people. True, they may be doing it only to have their own personal needs met, but on the surface it would appear that they can actually be part of a group. Deep down, however, there is very little actual human interaction going on. The only reason a true sociopath would cooperate would be to get something out of it for personal gain.

The most troubling aspect of sociopathology is the fact that sociopaths demonstrate no concern for the well-being of others, nor do they feel remorse or guilt. Even worse, they will usually display a complete disregard for the consequences of their actions. They have no experience of empathy for the suffering of others, as they feel that they are too special or too smart to conform to the laws and mores of society; it is for this reason that sociopaths are often predisposed to become criminals (or used-car salesmen).

So is it true that if a person lacks basic human empathy, he or she is destined to become a career criminal? Of course not. Resiliency research shows that there are plenty of other variables able to provide support and context for a person to develop connection with other people. But empathy remains, in many ways, the most important factor. The ability to understand and relate to those around you is extremely crucial in what every human culture would consider a healthy adult life, and its absence from the development of a normal child can lead to chronic difficulty in connecting with others, or worse. After all, it's no coincidence that nearly every serial killer from the past twenty years has at some point been diagnosed as a sociopath.

Why bring up sociopathy in a chapter on *Survivor*? Easy. Because *Survivor* is a game that forces the average person to think and act like a heartless and emotionless sociopath.

No, *Survivor* doesn't turn people into criminals or serial arsonists. And, so far, no *Survivor* player has yet been arrested for hacking people up at the local summer camp. But there's no denying the fact that *Survivor* is an inherently cruel game: a game that attempts to undo years of social conditioning in a normal human psyche. Because, honestly, in what other game are you expected to systematically eliminate your friends until you, and only you, remain standing? And in what other game are you expected to think of those around you as human chess pieces, to be moved and discarded when you no longer feel they are needed?

You guessed it; we're not talking about Battleship. We're talking about *Survivor*. We're talking about arguably the single creepiest game show ever designed. After all, it's the only competitive game show on prime-time TV that rewards those who can act, talk, charm, and lie like serial killer Ted Bundy (who would actually be pretty good at *Survivor*, all things considered).

Survivor wasn't always like this, however. It wasn't always the "do anything to win" contest that we now see every Thursday. In fact, most people forget that the first season of *Survivor* was a lot different, and is almost unrecognizable when compared to the show we know and love today.

In the early days of *Survivor*, the line between being a good player and being an outright sociopath was very well-defined. This line may have been different for each individual player, but it was still very much defined. Players knew exactly what line they were unwilling to cross, they knew exactly how far they would go to get the million dollars, and it became one of the most fascinating aspects of the first few installments of *Survivor*.

We watched, season after season, as players such as Gabriel Cade (*Survivor: Marquesas*), Sean Kenniff (*Survivor: Borneo*), and Gretchen Cordy (*Survivor: Borneo*) struggled with their own ethics and tried to adapt to a game in which you were required to vote out your friends. We watched their inner turmoil, and we were fascinated by it, because this was one of the purest psychological experiments ever put before a mainstream television audience. How far are you willing to go, and how able are you to turn on your friends? In fact the subtitle for the first four *Survivor* seasons might as well have been "Outwit, Outplay, and Undermine Your Pals" because that's very much the dilemma that players found themselves up against.

In the early days of *Survivor*, the focus of the storyline was about ethics just as much as it was about strategy. A lot of fans tend to forget this fact, but *Survivor* was once a social experiment just as much as it was a game show. It was a clever experiment designed to test one's character under extreme stress, while at the same time being an open-ended abstract game with few defined rules for the players to obey. In fact, for the most part the players were expected to decide their *own* rules, and few things were as fascinating that first season as watching player after player struggle to determine what his or her ethics were supposed to be. Should I play for the team all the way? Should I join an alliance? Are alliances even fair? Would I feel good about myself if I won that way?

Yes, it may seem archaic now, but at one point in time the concept of joining an alliance was seen to be little more than outright cheating. Back in the first season, the words "voting bloc" were spoken through angry gritted teeth, and any mention of the idea around camp was bound to get you glares of disgust. "A voting bloc? In a social game where you have to learn to get along? What fun is that?" That's the exact argument that most players used during the first season of *Survivor*. They didn't want to join an alliance because it wasn't considered an honorable way to win.

This type of thinking may sound quaint now, but it was a very valid and accepted viewpoint among players in the first season's cast. Most players were unwilling to go the alliance route. It went against *everything* they'd been taught about good sportsmanship, ethics, and gamesmanship, and thus, was a line in the sand they were unable, or unwilling, to cross. Joining an alliance was seen as a cowardly way to win, and all parties involved (audience, players, producers) seemed to be on the same page in regard to this subject. In fact, the producers were so convinced about this that they hadn't even *considered* the fact that players might actually band together to get further in the game. Mark Burnett wrote in his season one book that he hadn't planned for that sort of outcome in the slightest. The idea of "alliances" hadn't crossed his mind for even a second.

So who gets the credit for coming up with the first *Survivor* alliance? That's right; it was Richard Hatch, the puppet master of the *Borneo* season. Richard was smart, he was a meticulous planner, and right off the bat he saw that alliances were the way to win this thing. He knew an easy way to victory when he saw one, so he jumped right into his plan with the greatest of zeal. Richard formed a four-person alliance made up of like-minded players, they coasted all the way to an easy victory, and Richard became the first-ever *Survivor* millionaire.

Was Richard universally loved and respected for being the first player to figure out how to win the game? Um, not so much. In fact, Richard Hatch may have actually been the most unpopular *Survivor* winner of all time. The reason for this is that a good deal of the *Survivor* fan base felt that Richard had cheated. People were furious that he would take such a "cowardly" path to victory. Armchair psychologists were horrified that he had turned a social experiment into a strategic game of chess. They were aghast that he had turned people into pawns for his own benefit. In fact, some experts even classified Richard's win as one of the darkest days on TV, simply because he had taken the sociopath's route to easy victory. They were particularly worried about the ease with which he had systematically dismantled his competition, and they feared that it would set a bad example for the impressionable children watching at home. Because what would happen if America somehow canonized Richard for the ruthless way in which he had approached the game? Wouldn't that be a very bad thing for society in the long run?

So Richard won *Survivor*, and Richard was now routinely alluded to as a cold-hearted emotionless sociopath. *Survivor* fans hated him. Psychologists were frightened by him. Sociologists were practically apologizing for him. Meanwhile, Richard Hatch (the king of *Survivor*) was sitting there in interviews, protesting this treatment vociferously, and defending his actions as loudly and as often as he could.

"I didn't do anything wrong!" he would protest. "How can you say I played the game unethically? All I did was create a numbers bloc out of strategic necessity. I used strategy in a strategic game, and now everybody is coming down on me for it. Why on earth was that such a wrong thing to do?"

Richard Hatch was legitimately baffled by the angry reaction to his win, and who can blame him? Because if you look back at Richard's actions during *Borneo*, you will see that his statements are true. He was never particularly unethical during the game. Nor was he especially cruel. In fact, the worst thing you can say about his actions in Borneo is that Richard was probably a little too cocky. But in no way was he a dangerous and unethical sociopath.

No, if you wanted to see a real *Survivor* sociopath, you'd have to wait four seasons to watch *Survivor: Thailand.*

MISTER FREEZE

Survivor: Thailand was the season where we were introduced to the most cold-hearted player of them all, one-time used-car salesman and former porn actor Brian Heidik. And he was an entirely different beast altogether from Richard Hatch. Heidik came into *Survivor* with the personality of a detached gunslinger, he ran through the competition with little display of emotion, and at no point in the game did he display any sense of guilt or remorse over the way he had dispatched his friends. It was the easiest win in *Survivor* history, and in many ways it was also the most frightening. Because what Brian did was essentially show us the way that a sociopath thinks. He betrayed friends. He showed no regret. He showed no empathy. He showed no emotion. It was business from day one, and Brian showed no mercy to anyone who dared stand in his way.

The most interesting thing about Brian's win was that it was met largely with apathy. You would expect that the audience would have been outraged by Heidik's complete indifference toward his tribemates in general, but for the most part the audience didn't really seem to care. It was almost as if they didn't know what to make of Brian; as if his cold, flat affect made people unable to relate to him as a human being. And for this reason Brian Heidik remains one of the most forgettable *Survivor* winners of all time. When an emotionless, unempathetic cyborg wins a million dollars using cold, hard business, few people stand up to applaud or hiss. They just shrug indifferently, move on to the next season, and hope that the next *Survivor* winner is somebody they will be more able to relate to.

Richard Hatch and Brian Heidik were both top-notch practitioners of the unemotional side of *Survivor* strategy. They were two of the very few players from the first five seasons who had the ability to separate logic from emotion, and treat every other player like they were disposable pawns on an imaginary chessboard. And in many ways, this ability to detach made Richard and Brian two of the best *Survivor* players of all time. They both won the game easily, neither had any serious competition along the way, and both were heralded by hardcore strate-gists as two of the only players who ever really understood the game. In fact, among armchair *Survivor* experts, Richard Hatch and Brian Heidik are held in the highest of strategic esteem, even to this day. And this is specifically because they had the ability to play and think like a sociopath.

One interesting parallel between Brian and Richard is the fact that neither one was all that popular among his fellow players. Even though Brian and Richard both won the game, even though they both outwitted, outplayed, and outlasted, other Survivors have never described them as being particularly nice or likable people. In fact, it could be possible that no *Survivor* alumnus has *ever* spoken a nice word about Brian Heidik. If you read interviews and chat transcripts from other Survivors, you will notice over time that Brian's name is never mentioned, not by any of them. Ever. Among *Survivor* alums, Brian Heidik is quite possibly the least respected player in the history of the show. And that's stunning when you realize he was actually a winner!

So Richard Hatch and Brian Heidik both won *Survivor*. Richard Hatch and Brian Heidik both won without the slightest bit of competition. Yet Richard Hatch and Brian Heidik were never really embraced by fellow players afterward, or by the general television audience overall.

IS THIS A COINCIDENCE?

In a game like *Survivor*, the most successful players will always be the ones who can separate emotion from strategy. In fact, it is a game designed to test that very trait. How capable are you of stabbing your best friend in the back? How easily can you lie to people right to their faces? And how far are you willing to go to outwit, outplay, and outlast? These are the most obvious questions that come up in *Survivor*, because this is a game designed to test ethics and personal character. It's a char-acterological litmus test on a thirty-nine-day scale. And, again, it's designed to reward you for the ability to think and act like a sociopath.

In other words, of course it's no coincidence that Brian and Richard were not especially popular. The best *Survivor* strategists are inevitably going to be disliked after the game is over—that's just the way that sociopathy works. This is the inherent flaw in the game of *Survivor*, and it's amazing that it has never come back to bite the show in the rump. It's also amazing that the producers didn't foresee this problem when they first sat down to design the game. After all, wouldn't they be the first to realize that most of their winners were inevitably going to be disliked?

In direct contrast to cyborgs Richard and Brian, the most interesting (and fascinating) *Survivor* players throughout the years have been the ones who weren't particularly all that good. These were the players who were unable to separate emotion from the cold, hard facts of the game, and these were the players who inspired the most widespread appeal. Why? Because watching an ordinary human being struggle with ethics is a dilemma we all can relate to. This behavior is wholly relatable to viewers at home, and this in turn is what brings in a large and diverse television audience. We watch the players struggle with feelings of guilt, betrayal, and torn loyalty, and we think about what we would do if faced with the same situation. We sit there at home watching ethical people being forced to make unethical choices, and this leads to, in large part, the psychological appeal that has always been an aspect of the show.

In the early days, there were plenty of players like this: relatable everyday people who were not particularly skilled in how to play the game. These were the players who could not vote out a friend in the final three (Colby Donaldson), would not join an alliance because it somehow seemed unfair (Gretchen Cordy), would not cast legitimate votes because they didn't want to hurt anybody's feelings (Sean Kenniff), or were totally ruled by emotion and would make impulsive, irrational decisions just because they felt it "in [their] gut" (Lex van den Berghe). These players might not have won a million dollars, but they were fascinating precisely because they had this inherent strategic weakness. Their flaws made them appear human, their humanity made them appear real, and this in turn made them much more relatable than Brian or Richard. We as a TV audience could never relate to emotionless gunslingers who marched through the game without a care. But we could relate to people who struggled with their consciences. And in the greater scheme of social psychology, wouldn't that be considered a good thing? Wouldn't it be much more troubling if the audience could relate to the sociopathic thinkers like Richard or Brian? And wouldn't you be worried if America had taken in Brian Heidik like a favorite son?

This is the way that *Survivor* worked for the first five seasons. Sure, the cold-hearted mercenaries might do well strategically, but for the most part they were never really embraced by the audience. Oh, the audience might respect the fact that a sociopath had won, but their victories were never really the touchy-feely fan favorite moments that the producers probably would have liked. In fact, the most fan-friendly winner of the first five seasons, *Africa's* Ethan Zohn, was largely considered to have won because he was "lucky." Fans didn't like Ethan because he was the best player in Africa. No, fans liked Ethan because he genuinely seemed to be a nice guy. Women adored him because he was likable, he was an introvert, and he was cute. In fact, you really couldn't have found a more popular winner than Ethan, and this is despite the fact that he wasn't even all that great at the game of *Survivor*. Although, come to think of it, maybe that's precisely why Ethan Zohn was so popular. Maybe the fact that he was the complete opposite of Richard Hatch had more to do with it than we thought. . . .

ENTER CESTERNINO

This is where we come to Rob Cesternino. You may remember Rob Cesternino as the "mastermind" from the sixth season of *Survivor*, set in the Amazon. Rob was a twenty-four-year-old computer whiz from New York who knew the game of *Survivor* inside and out, and he would one day be known as "the player who changed the game of *Survivor* forever."

Right from the start, Rob was a very different breed of *Survivor* player. We had literally never seen someone of his kind on the show before, and it started and ended with his unique *Survivor* background.

Why was Rob so incredibly different? Well for starters, he had almost zero camping experience. He was not the sort of "outdoorsy adventure enthusiast" that the producers normally cast on the show. In fact, Rob was exactly the opposite. He wasn't outdoorsy, nor was he particularly in shape. In fact, by most accounts Rob was a guy who never even liked to leave the house. He was just a twenty-four-year-old kid who lived at home, who studied *Survivor* like he was preparing for a test, and who came on the show just to prove he had this thing all figured out. In other words, Rob Cesternino was officially the first "armchair *Survivor* expert" ever to be cast on the show. He stood up off his couch at home one day, he reported for duty in the middle of the Amazon, and he proceeded to cut a trail of *Survivor* carnage that, to this day, people still talk about with reverential awe.

Rob came to the Amazon prepared. Rob had definitely done his strategic homework. And he had figured out (ahead of time) that the game of *Survivor* was not about being in the dominant alliance, and it was not about always being the one in control. In Rob's mind, the player running the game was the player who was always going to be targeted. Everybody else would want this person's head on a platter, and Rob realized very quickly that there was no visible advantage to being this guy. So Rob set out to turn this game upside-down, simply by never being the guy who was standing at the head of the pack.

Rob had also figured out that *Survivor* had nothing to do with loyalty (or outdoor ability, for that matter). Nor did it have anything to do with riding your alliance to the end. No, in Rob's mind the easiest way to get to the end was to jump from alliance to alliance, always taking the best deal possible. In this manner you could keep your options open, and always keep yourself away from the dreaded vote. Rob didn't care about *Survivor* loyalty. He didn't care a thing about making friends. And he didn't care about being true to the people who trusted him. All Rob cared about was giving himself some flexible options, and always taking a good deal when it was presented to him. And in this manner he would alliance-jump his way to a million-dollar check.

Does Rob's strategy sound particularly unique? Not really. Nowadays any *Survivor* fan knows that the best way to win is always to keep your options open. You have to give yourself multiple paths to the end of the game, you should never look a gift horse in the mouth, and you shouldn't feel guilty if you have to abandon your original plans. This is the way that *Survivor* is played now, and we have come to accept this as strategic fact.

But it wasn't always like this. In fact, before Rob Cesternino, alliance-hopping would have been the fastest way to get voted out of the game. It would have branded you a traitor for life, and there's no possible way you ever could have won a final vote. After all, remember what happened to

Shii Ann Huang in Thailand? Traitors never prospered before Rob Cesternino. Before he came along, this sort of tactic never would have succeeded.

Anyway, here comes Rob Cesternino in the Amazon to dispel every stigma attached to being a *Survivor* "traitor." Because not only did Rob turn his back on his allies, he did it multiple times, and he actually did it with glee. Rob loved nothing more than switching the game around when he didn't feel comfortable with what was going on. And in doing so, he "unwrote" every rule in the *Survivor* rulebook. Loyalty to your friends in the alliance? Not important! Sticking to promises you made early in the game? That's for fools! Rob treated every player like a human chess piece, he had no compassion or mercy for anybody who stood in his way, and, most important, he did it behind the façade of being a goofy kid from Long Island who was just happy to be here and wanted to make everybody laugh.

This last part of the Cesternino package is the piece that was most significant, because it disarmed the other players and kept them from seeing Rob as the most dangerous player in the game. Because if you just gave him a quick once-over, you would see a player who was particularly unremarkable. Rob Cesternino was just an immature kid who lived at home with his parents. He was a wannabe stand-up comedian who could reel off corny jokes at the drop of a hat. In fact, Rob didn't appear to be the least bit dangerous if you just looked at his bio on paper. And it was this "wolf in sheep's clothing" disguise that was probably the single most effective weapon in Rob's formidable arsenal. He was able to dominate the game, and he was able to get away with it because he came in the perfect package for a sneaky *Survivor* mastermind. Nobody was the slightest bit frightened of Rob because Rob was just a kid. And everybody knew there were bigger fish to fry than this joke-telling twenty-four-year-old clown.

Rob Cesternino dominated the game in the Amazon until the final three, and then he turned around and met with the general public. And was Rob hated and despised like earlier *Survivor* masterminds Brian and Richard? Of course not! Rob Cesternino was met with virtual adoration. He wasn't just well-liked; in many ways he was positively worshipped. Fans practically deified him right there at the reunion show. They adored this new *Survivor* "mastermind" for what he had done in the Amazon. They adored how much he had brought to their favorite show. And they adored the way he had "finally showed the world how you were supposed to play *Survivor*." In fact, it's safe to say that Rob was a legend before he ever showed up at the *Amazon* reunion.

Rob Cesternino was received entirely differently than Brian Heidik and Richard Hatch, and the psychology behind this response was absolutely fascinating. Because here you had three people who had done essentially the exact same thing (turned *Survivor* into a game of human chess), yet one was loved while the other two had been cast out in shame. Heck, even Jeff Probst was raving about Rob Cesternino, calling him "the smartest player never to win," and this was in reference to a player who had played dirtier than anybody who had ever played the game before him. And yes, that includes Richard Hatch and Brian Heidik. Rob Cesternino was beloved, yet Rob Cesternino had used dirtier tactics than either of them! And this is where the big question inevitably comes up: Why was the reaction so much different to Rob Cesternino? What was the factor that allowed him to get away with things that nobody previously had been allowed to get away with?

Most *Survivor* experts would agree that in addition to his charm and disarming humor, Rob's age probably had something to do with it. He was well-liked, in large part, because he was so young, as well as being so eager to make people laugh. This kid was not a cocky corporate trainer who liked to parade around naked (Richard), nor was he a cold used-car salesman who would one day be arrested for shooting a puppy with an arrow (Brian). No, Rob was just a genuinely funny young kid who could get you to laugh simply by opening his mouth. You immediately liked him the first time he started talking, you genuinely rooted for him despite his sociopathic game play, and it marked the first time ever that we had a player who could personify the difference between "game play" and "personality." Because one look at Rob Cesternino told you he wasn't a trained social assassin. He was just a kid who had figured out how to play *Survivor*. No one expected him to be a heartless villain after the game and, indeed, he wasn't. Rob was just a normal, humble, genuinely likable kid. And this was the factor that set him apart from the previous *Survivor* masters.

After the *Amazon* season, Rob did a lot of interviews explaining how people were supposed to approach a game like *Survivor*. He did it in a very logical, systematic way, he did it through humor, and he demonstrated very clearly that you don't have to be a heartless sociopath in real life to be good at this game. In fact, you don't even have to be a bad guy at all. One's game play can be entirely independent from one's out-of-the-game personality, and this was a lesson that the general *Survivor* audience had never really accepted before. People had always assumed that the best *Survivor* players would somehow be scumbags in real life, but with Rob there was a curious difference. Rob made it somehow okay to be a good *Survivor* player, so long as you did it with style and a sense of humor. And in one fell swoop, Rob Cesternino managed to kill the stigma that had long been attached to being a successful *Survivor* strategist.

What was Rob Cesternino's legacy in *Survivor* history? Well for starters, he made it possible for every player after season six to play the game without guilt. Starting from *Pearl Islands* on, the players became smarter, more strategic, more dangerous, and much more willing to switch alliances. Rob converted almost every single player into a heartless mercenary Cesternino-type clone, and he did it by removing the stigma that had previously been attached. No longer would "traitors" be seen as scumbags destined to lose. No longer would "being good at *Survivor*" be something that suggested unsavory assumptions about a person's character. Rob taught players that it was okay to look beyond that. He taught players that they could ignore their social conditioning, they could ignore their inherent feelings of empathy, and that they should treat this game like the chessboard that it really is. In fact, Rob was such an influential player that he completely changed the way that people looked at the game. Every post-Cesternino season has been a cut-throat one, and every player has had improved strategic ability. Players got smarter after *Amazon*, players got better after *Amazon*, and Rob Cesternino is the man you can thank (or blame) for nearly all of that.

AT WHAT COST, THE CESTERNINO ERA?

Hearing that "*Survivor* players have gotten better" suggests that something good has happened for the show. After all, if the competition and the talent are better overall, that can only lead to a better product, right? Isn't that the way that all competitions work? The better the talent, the more superior the game. Right?

Unfortunately this was not a good thing for *Survivor*. In fact, it was the single most devastating thing ever to happen to the game. Because the minute Rob Cesternino killed the stigma of the *Survivor* winner, the show lost a lot of its heart and soul. After all, what's the fun of watching trained snipers try to out-sociopath one another? It is a horribly drastic change from the way *Survivor* started out in season one. Where is the social experiment in that? Where are the important ethical dilemmas? What fun is it when every player suddenly has no qualms operating like your everyday, garden-variety sociopath?

As we stated before, *Survivor: Borneo* was as much a social experiment as it was a strategic game show. It was essentially a giant psychology experiment designed to test the character and ethics of people exposed to extreme stress. It started out as a hypothetical game of "what if?" and this aspect of the show went a long way toward explaining its over-whelming appeal. Back then viewers at home could put themselves in the players' shoes, and it wasn't hard to do. After all, we weren't watch-ing strategic masterminds trying to outwit one another. We weren't watching *Survivor* experts using tried-and-true strategies that they knew were going to work. What we saw (and liked) were flawed human beings like ourselves who were thrust into a chaotic and immoral game, and the ethical dilemmas it brought out in all of them. We saw normal human social conditioning being put to the test, we saw a situation that was designed to make people think like sociopaths, and we debated the next day if we would have done what the players had done on the island. In fact, in many ways the first season of *Survivor* was almost interactive. We literally felt like we could be the ones who were out there on the island, and it's why the show was so fascinating to so many people. It was com-pelling precisely because it was so darn relatable.

But this is where the show changed drastically after Rob Cesternino—because when Rob showed the players how to excel, he also showed them how to be much less interesting to an everyday viewing audience. Rob taught future players how to ignore the *Survivor* stigma. He converted future players from flawed everyday humans into heartless mercenary strategists. And it's how he single-handedly managed to kill the show *Survivor*.

Survivor hasn't been a watercooler topic for a long time, and probably never will be again. Because that's what happens when you end up with players who aren't relatable to a TV audience. You may end up with better players (from a strategic standpoint), but they are missing the humanity and "spark" that much weaker players from earlier seasons would have possessed. And this is exactly why the first few *Survivor* seasons look so crude and barbaric (yet warm and refreshing) compared to the slickly produced strategy-fests we're apt to see today.

Survivor stopped being a national phenomenon around the time of *Survivor: Pearl Islands* in the fall of 2003. And this happened to be the first *Survivor* season after Rob Cesternino had played the game. The correlation between the two cannot possibly be ignored.

Did Rob Cesternino ruin the game of *Survivor*? Well, that probably depends on your definition of the word "ruin." But *Survivor* ceased being a test of ethics some time ago. Players nowadays "play the game" from day one, they come into the game ready to deceive and undermine, and you can trace it all back to the teachings of Rob Cesternino. This explains why some fans refer to *Survivor* seasons as being either B.C. (before Cesternino) or A.C. (after Cesternino). Because, in nearly every manner possible, the two *Survivor* eras are almost like completely different shows.

Rob Cesternino often gets credit for saving *Survivor* from becoming predictable. Yet at the same time he altered the game by obliterating its original humanity. He is not the only person who could have done this. Indeed, if it hadn't been him, it would have been someone else. But since Rob was the right person at the right time, he's the one who has to take the fall. With great power comes great responsibility, and what he did was like throwing an open flame onto a pile of gunpowder. He's the one who made everything explode.

Rob taught people how to play the game, he showed them the path to success, and then he sat back and watched as his minions did as he taught. And you'd be hard-pressed not to see the parallels to another classic sociopath, Charles Manson. In fact the parallels between the two cult leaders are downright eerie. Like Manson, Rob Cesternino might not have done the dirty deed himself, he might not have changed the game completely on his own, but he was directly responsible for the actions of his "disciples" down the road. And that makes him just as guilty and culpable of malfeasance, at least in the eyes of the law.

In summary, the game of *Survivor* has changed a lot in twelve seasons. It started as a social experiment disguised as a game show, yet along the way it morphed into a game show disguised as a social experiment. There was once a negative stigma attached to being a successful player, but nowadays the only negative stigma is for unsuccessful players. And while some may tout this as a good thing, in the end all it has done is make the players that much less relatable. Is it still a fun show to watch? Of course. But you're fooling yourself if you think *Survivor* has any more social relevance. All we're doing now is watching *When Sociopaths Attack!*

BRAD WOLGAST (who received his Ph.D. from Temple University) learned the basics of group dynamics under the stress of the outdoors as a backpacking guide in New Mexico, and later across the country. He thought he had struck research gold when an advisor recommended he use a survival analysis for a research project. Not knowing this statistical method, he said, "No problem, I analyze that show every week. But how do we use that for a research project?" Well, now we know. Brad would like to thank the hard-working Daniel Strunk, Ph.D., without whom this wouldn't have been written, and his two favorite *Survivor* fans, Henry and Claire.

MARIO J. LANZA is a well-known writer and humorist whose "*Survivor* Strategy" column was one of the most widely read on the Internet between the years 2001 and 2004. He was recently called "one of the foremost *Survivor* experts in the world" by *Survivor: Amazon* contestant/sociopath Rob Cesternino. Mario has read every book on serial killers ever written, and he's also done extensive research on criminal psychopathology. In fact, at one point in his life he wanted to work for the FBI as "one of those *Silence of the Lambs* guys." This didn't quite pan out, but he does claim he can spot a sociopath 100 yards away. When he's not writing about *Survivor*, Mario enjoys baseball, horror movies, being creeped out by Brian Heidik, and empathizing with other humans. And he's thrilled that his bio is just a little bit longer than Brad's. You can read Mario's other *Survivor* writings at http://members.aol.com/AllStarHawaii.

REFERENCES

Feldman, R. S. *Development Across the Life Span*. Upper Saddle River, NJ: Prentice Hall, 1997.

Hare, Robert D. "Psychopaths: New Trends in Research," *The Harvard Mental Health Letter* (September 1995).

Survivor contestants must use their brains' cognitive resources to outwit their opponents. Karyn M. Frick enumerates the brain regions and functions that underlie that capacity to out-wit. She argues that Survivor *is rough on brains. The stressors of* Survivor—*including hunger and fatigue*—*may have a dramatic negative impact on neural functioning. This is your brain on* Survivor!

The Neuroscience of Survivor

Why the "Sole Survivor" Might Have the Most Resilient Brain

KARYN M. FRICK, PH.D.

Outwit. It's the first of the three tenets upon which *Survivor* is built, and is perhaps the most important. The other principles of the *Survivor* mantra, Outplay and Outlast, both involve elements of physical strength. Strength can enable an individual to outplay rivals in Challenges and better endure the harsh physical conditions of the game. But the strong do not always survive. If physical strength was *the* critical element in an individual's ability to win the title of "Sole Survivor," then past winners such as Sandra Diaz-Twine or Jenna Morasca should have been gone long before the final vote. Rather, *Survivor* is a game of wits—quickly judging with whom to make alliances and carefully deciding when to honor and break them, trying to make friends or win respect without betraying your strategy, and, if you win the final Immunity Challenge, carefully selecting the best person to take to the final two. Thus, when discussing the "psychology" of *Survivor*, it is important to consider how the human mind deals with such an intensely mentally and physically draining experience.

In modern neuroscience, what we refer to as the "mind" is really the byproduct of the activity of millions of neurons in the brain. It is the brain that forms attachments, feels emotion, and calculates the odds in our favor. As such, this chapter will focus on the contributions of certain portions of the brain to the game of *Survivor*. What are the critical regions of the brain that may contribute to determining who wins and who loses? How are these regions affected by elements of the game such as stress, lack of sleep and food, and age? Because we, as viewers, can never know what it is truly like to experience the game ourselves, and because CBS is unlikely to ever let neuroscientists measure brain activity during the course of the game, the best we can do is to examine the existing scientific literature for clues about how the brain might fare under such arduous circumstances. Unfortunately, the field of social neuroscience, the study of how the brain processes complex social situations, is in its infancy. Therefore, scientists still have a rather rudimentary knowledge of the specific neural processes that mediate complicated social concepts such as loyalty and group affiliation. However, several brain regions are critical for aspects of these behaviors, so this essay will extrapolate from there. Before we get started, however, it is important to review briefly how the brain works.

A CRASH COURSE IN BRAIN FUNCTION

The basic unit of the nervous system is the neuron. Neurons consist of three main parts—the *cell body*, *dendrite*, and *axon*. The *cell body* is the storehouse of the neuron—it contains a nucleus housing DNA and other structures that keep the cell alive. Neurons differ from other cells in our bodies because they have the ability to transmit information rapidly. Information enters neurons via the *dendrite*. This information can take multiple forms—for example, a change in the permeability of the membrane that encases a neuron or a cascade of chemical changes inside a dendrite. Either way, if the sheer volume of information eventually reaches a certain threshold, then an electrical potential is generated that passes down the dendrite, through the cell body, and then down the *axon*, the portion of a neuron that sends out information. When the potential reaches the end of the axon, chemical messengers are released which cross the narrow space separating the neuron from its neighbors (the *synapse*), and bind to receptors on the post-synaptic surface of these adjacent neurons, thereby propagating the information from neuron to neuron.

Individual neurons are grouped into structures that form anatomically and functionally distinct regions of the brain. Most neurons in a brain region are involved in the same psychological function. For example, neurons in the occipital cortex at the back of the brain are all involved in some aspect of vision. Neurons in the hippocampus are all involved in memory formation. Individual brain regions, then, are further integrated into brain systems, or circuits. For example, the occipital cortex can't "see" by itself. It receives information from the eyes through the thalamus in the center of the brain. The hippocampus forms memories in conjunction with several cortical areas, including the prefrontal cortex at the front of the brain. In addition, it also can influence memories made by other regions of the brain—for example, emotional memories formed by the amygdala. Thus, brain regions are not islands unto themselves; each interacts with other regions to allow us to interact with the world.

For the purposes of *Survivor*, we will limit our discussion to three regions of the brain: the *prefrontal cortex*, *hippocampus*, and *amygdala* (Figure 1).

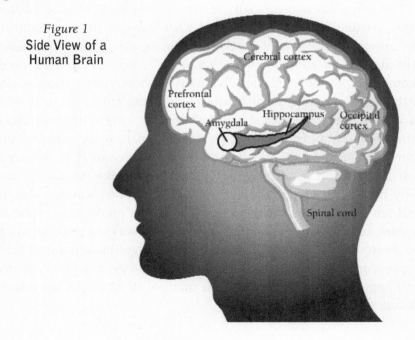

Figure 1
Side View of a
Human Brain

The *prefrontal cortex* is likely to be involved in all psychological aspects of the game. It is a region of the cerebral cortex located right behind your forehead and is responsible for most of the high-level cognitive function (termed "executive function") that makes humans unique among animals. This region is critical for making decisions and judgments, knowing right from wrong, focusing attention, inhibiting socially inappropriate behavior, calculating odds, projecting into the future, and forming short-term memories. Humans with damage to the prefrontal cortex typically exhibit crass and inappropriate behavior, are very impulsive and risk-taking, and have difficulty forming new memories and focusing their attention.

The *hippocampus* is critical for forming memories in which relationships among elements (e.g., locations or objects) must be integrated to form a context. For example, the hippocampus helps to make the mental maps of your environment that you use to navigate through the world. The hippocampus is also important in helping you to learn new information—patients with damage to the hippocampus and related cortical regions have difficulty remembering new names, faces, and factual information.

The *amygdala* is principally involved in forming emotional memories, particularly those associated with fear and threat. Removal of the amygdala prevents animals from being able to associate fearful stimuli (e.g., a shock) with other non-fearful stimuli that predict them (e.g., a tone). Similarly, humans with amygdala damage show little emotion and have difficulty recognizing emotions in the faces of others. They also respond much less to fear- or threat-inducing stimuli. The hippocampus helps the amygdala make sense of these stimuli by providing information about the context in which the fearful situation occurred. This information helps us to be fearful only in the context in which the fearful stimulus was encountered, and not at all times. Interactions between the prefrontal cortex, hippocampus, and amygdala allow us to further shape our thoughts and memories, for example, in helping us to judge the amount of fear to express in various situations, the likelihood that a previous event will happen in the future, and the amount of attention necessary to devote to various tasks.

Now that we have a basic understanding of some brain regions that are vital to the game, let's consider how *Survivor* might affect these structures and the psychological processes that they mediate.

DECISIONS, DECISIONS

From the moment *Survivor* contestants congregate to start filming the show, the game, and the psychological stress associated with it, begins. A group of strangers must immediately begin to size each other up, and form opinions about who they like, whom they can trust, and who they perceive as a threat to them in the game. Tribal affiliations typically lead to the strongest alliances (e.g., the powerful Richard-Rudy-Sue-Kelly alliance from season one), but as the game wears on and tribes merge, managing alliances and interpersonal relationships becomes more difficult. Making the right decisions, calculating the correct odds, and accurately judging the reactions of other players to breaks in alliances and loyalties, become absolutely critical to surviving.

All of these important skills involve the prefrontal cortex. In addition, the hippocampus helps keep track of events of the game and the amygdala aids in perceiving threats to one's position in the tribe. So how might the stresses of the game affect the functioning of these brain regions? Acute stress, such as that experienced when encountering a bear in the woods, typically enhances brain function. The rush of endorphins to the brain heightens the senses, and allows one to act quickly and vividly remember the event. However, chronic stress, the stress experienced over time, can profoundly interfere with psychological and brain function. In animal studies, chronic stress reduces the number and length of dendrites (so-called *dendritic arborization*) on neurons in the prefrontal cortex and hippocampus, thereby reducing information intake. In the prefrontal cortex, these alterations can reduce cognitive flexibility (Liston et al. 2006), and hinder the ability of an individual to change strategy when the rules or situation changes (e.g., when tribe members switch or tribes merge). In the hippocampus, stress-induced reductions in dendritic arborization impair the ability to form accurate memories about events or facts (see Kim and Diamond 2002 for review). Interestingly, stress produces greater dendritic arborization in the amygdala, which may serve to heighten anxiety and fear (Radley and Morrison 2005), and may lead a player to make a bad decision due to paranoia.

Of particular relevance to *Survivor* may be studies of patients with post-traumatic stress disorder, or PTSD, a disorder in which people repeatedly relive traumatic events in their lives. These patients have an atrophied hippocampus and deficits in hippocampal-dependent memories. They also exhibit reduced blood flow to the prefrontal cortex, and their symptoms suggest a hyper-responsive amygdala. Although *Survivor* does not produce enough stress to cause PTSD, the game is designed to produce constant stress. For example, players have been frequently surprised by sudden switches in tribe members or, as in *Survivor: Pearl Islands*, sudden reintroduction of members that were previously voted out. These stresses likely take their toll on the prefrontal cortex, hippocampus, and amygdala. Altered functioning of these brain regions could lead players to become more anxious or forgetful, or impair executive function. For example, for goat farmer Tom Buchanan of *Survivor: Africa*, the goat herding reward Challenge should have been a piece of cake, but somehow he was not able to apply his skills well to the task and his tribe lost. In addition, hesitation in making decisions about alliances can be costly, like when Christy Smith from *Survivor: Amazon* was voted out because she was hesitant to commit to Rob Cesternino's fledgling alliance. The ability of an individual to handle stress prior to the game will likely determine how much the psychological stress affects them. As such, it would appear that those crowned "Sole Survivor" previously had excellent strategies for managing anxiety and stress in their daily lives.

SLEEPING IN THE ELEMENTS

Sleeping on *Survivor* appears, from the viewer's perspective, to be very challenging. Of course, there are the relatively minor inconveniences—sleeping in groups, and not having comfort items such as pillows, blankets, or mattresses (unless they're won). However, the elements themselves pose significant challenges for sleep. For example, torrential downpours and exposure to rats, snakes, and bugs can make sleeping all but impossible. Perhaps most harrowing of all was the experience of Survivors from Africa, who had to sleep in shifts to guard their camps against lions. As such, it's really quite amazing that the contestants get any sleep at all. But anyone who has found it hard to think after a poor night's sleep knows the importance of a good night's sleep to proper psychological functioning.

Unlike stress, chronic sleep deprivation does not lead to long-term alterations in the brain; however, lack of sleep does appear to have deleterious short-term consequences on cognitive function. For example, it reduces the ability to pay attention (often resulting in accidents on the road and elsewhere) and form new memories. Sleep deprivation prevents an individual from thinking clearly, thus interfering with prefrontal cortex-dependent cognitive processes (e.g., making judgments, forming strategies). One theory also holds that sleep is critical for memory formation; while we're unconscious and oblivious to external stimulation, our hippocampal neurons are busy replaying the events of the day and storing that information (Wilson and McNaughton 1994). This theory garners some support from evidence that sleep-deprived individuals have a more difficult time remembering things. Nevertheless, individuals with serious sleep disorders still manage to learn and remember new information, so not all remembering is dependent on sleep.

How might sleep deprivation affect the play on *Survivor*? A lack of sleep from the conditions inherent to the game should have detrimental effects on cognitive functions subserved by the prefrontal cortex and hippocampus. These effects would likely be subtle and vary from day to day, depending on how well each individual is able to sleep in camp. On its own, a lack of sleep is unlikely to significantly change how a player deals with the game. However, sleep deprivation in combination with the other stresses of the game could lead contestants to make bad decisions that compromise their position in the tribe. For example, exhaustion due to lack of sleep and hunger may have prevented Nick Brown from formulating a strategy to stay in the Barramundi tribe on *Survivor: Australian Outback*.

RICE, RICE, AND MORE RICE

Without question, one of the most important challenges that *Survivor* contestants face is food availability. In some seasons, the tribes have been provided with rice. In others, they have been given no food at all. Being able to provide food for the tribe can, at least temporarily, afford protection from being voted out at Tribal Council. The *Survivor* diet typically consists mainly of starchy food (rice, taro, manioc flour) with some protein (fish, rats, chicken) and, occasionally, coconuts and fruit. Contestants who make it to the end of the game experience significant weight loss, so much so that seeing them again when the final vote is revealed can be shocking. In Australia, the final four were given a scale to weigh themselves. Colby Donaldson and Keith Famie lost twenty-five and twenty-seven pounds, respectively, and Elizabeth Filarski (now Hasselbeck) lost twelve pounds. The eventual winner, Tina Wesson, lost sixteen pounds to tip the scales at an emaciated ninety-nine pounds. Similarly, *Survivor: Amazon* winner Jenna Morasca also weighed just ninety-nine pounds by the final four, reflecting a loss of nineteen pounds. Out of desperation for a certain kind of food, Jenna and her tribemate Heidi Strobel produced one of *Survivor's* most memorable moments by stripping naked for peanut butter and chocolate. Although beneficial for the waistline, does this kind of semi-starvation impair psychological function?

Chances are that it does. Glucose is one of the main fuels used by the body to produce energy. In the brain, neurons depend on glucose to make the copious amounts of energy they consume. Although the brain consists of only 2 percent of our total body mass, it accounts for approximately 50 percent of the body's total glucose metabolism (Fehm, Kern, and Peters 2006). Because neurons cannot store glucose, they can be vulnerable to significant fluctuations in glucose availability.

Relatively few studies of starvation in adults have been carried out, given ethical issues surrounding such treatment. Thus, it is somewhat difficult to draw parallels to *Survivor* from the existing scientific literature. Perhaps the most insight into this issue can be drawn from studies of patients with anorexia nervosa. Anorexic patients experience a significant reduction in the volume of the hippocampus and several areas of the cerebral cortex, including the frontal cortex, as well as an increase in the volume of fluid-filled spaces in the brain (Connan et al. 2006; Krieg et al. 1988; Swayze et al. 2003). Further, reduced cerebral metabolism in the prefrontal cortices of anorexic patients has been associated with impaired verbal learning, attention, and executive function (Ohrmann et al. 2003). Decision-making in tasks that tap the ability to balance immediate reward with future negative outcomes is also impaired in anorexic patients (Cavedini et al. 2004). Although anorexic patients experience semi-starvation for much longer periods than *Survivor* contestants, the data do suggest that severe nutrient loss can influence neural function in adults. As such, the lack of food experienced during the game may influence how well an individual's brain is able to process stimuli. Clearly, reward Challenges that lead to increased food intake are beneficial for both the mind and body, which may be why most rewards involve food or tools for acquiring food.

ARE OLDER CONTESTANTS AT A PSYCHOLOGICAL DISADVANTAGE?

Statistics indicate that the chances of winning *Survivor* decrease with age. Of the contestants in the final two through season twelve, 50 percent were in their twenties, 25 percent were in their thirties, 16.7 percent were in their forties, and 8.3 percent were in their fifties. Of the first twelve winners, five each were in their twenties and thirties, and two were in their forties. None were fifty or older. Surely, one factor behind these data is declining physical strength. But can declining neural function also account for this effect?

For contestants in their sixties and beyond, the answer may be "yes." Typically, alterations in cognitive function start to appear around age sixty (Schaie 1994). These changes are considered "normal" aging, or aging not associated with a neurological disease such as Alzheimer's disease. Normal aging is associated with an impaired ability to remember new information—e.g., new facts and events, the order of events, multiple items at a time, and the source of new information (see Woodruff-Pak 1997 for review). Spatial memory, the ability to use a mental map of the environment to navigate around the world, can also be severely impaired (Evans et al., 1984). Executive functioning may also be reduced, causing difficulty learning new strategies, planning, making decisions, and dividing attention (Woodruff-Pak 1997). These alterations are easily traced to deterioration in the prefrontal cortex and hippocampus, which are particularly vulnerable to aging.

On average, the brain's ability to process and store information starts to decline in the early sixties (Woodruff-Pak 1997). At the most basic level, the brain shrinks in size and fluid-filled spaces expand. Brain regions such as the prefrontal cortex experience a reduction in volume and metabolic activity. In aging humans, hippocampal size can significantly predict future decline in memory, with a smaller hippocampus in the late sixties leading to greater memory loss in the early seventies (Golumb et al. 1996). Although neuron loss with aging is much less widespread than previously thought, neurons shrink in size and lose both dendrites and synapses. The resulting reduction in the ability to receive and transmit information is significantly correlated with impaired cognitive function in aging subjects (Rosenzweig and Barnes 2003). Furthermore, animal studies report numerous changes in the neurotransmitters that neurons use to communicate. For example, deficits have been noted in the ability of neurons to synthesize and release neurotransmitters, to generate sufficient numbers of receptors to bind them, and to produce enough enzymes to properly degrade them. In particular, age-related alterations in neurons that release the neurotransmitter acetylcholine in the hippocampus have been associated with memory loss in normal aged subjects and patients with Alzheimer's disease (Muir 2000). Changes associated with another neurotransmitter, dopamine, in the prefrontal cortex and hippocampus lead to impaired short-term memory and executive function (Arnsten and Goldman-Rakic 1985; Luine et al. 1990).

In sum, normal aging is associated with numerous alterations in many different brain systems, which all can result in compromised cognitive function. Thus, it would seem that these age-related changes would automatically put older players at a disadvantage. However, the changes outlined above describe the mean, or average, of study populations. One of the main characteristics of any aging population is variability—that is, not all individuals age at the same rate. Thus, many elderly are as mentally sharp as younger individuals. In fact, one of the benefits of aging that is often ignored by society is the wisdom that accumulates from life experience. Although younger players might have the physical and neurobiological edge, older players should benefit from years of experience dealing with people in complex social situations. As such, older players might be construed to have an advantage in outwitting their younger counterparts.

As with all of the factors discussed thus far, the effect of age on a contestant will depend greatly on the individual. Although advanced age may put the average player at a disadvantage, the possibility that an extraordinary older individual could win the game is not out of the question—witness Rudy Boesch's third place finish on *Survivor: Borneo*. However, even Rudy's popularity couldn't save him on *Survivor: All-Stars*, as he was the first survivor voted out of his tribe due to his age and perceived weakness. Nevertheless, an older player with the right combination of physical strength, social skills, and strategy usage could certainly win the game.

CONCLUSIONS

What may we conclude about *Survivor*'s effects on neural functioning? Of all of the reality game shows, *Survivor* is perhaps the toughest on its contestants. Other shows in this genre involve similar psychological stressors (e.g., *Big Brother*) or physical challenges (e.g., *Fear Factor*). However, the combined effect of psychological stressors, difficult environmental conditions, lack of food and sleep, and extreme physical challenges make *Survivor* a very difficult game to win. The conditions even forced one strong young man, Osten Taylor from *Survivor: Pearl Islands*, to quit the game in exhaustion. In this essay, I have attempted to review how some of these factors might affect neural functioning in *Survivor* players. Individually, increasing age and/or chronic exposure to psychosocial stressors, semi-starvation, and sleeplessness can profoundly affect neural structure and function. In combination, these elements may significantly affect an individual's performance. For example, the ability of players to judge the motivations of others or make decisions in their best interests could easily be impaired due to peer pressure, exhaustion, or hunger. Perhaps the "Sole Survivor" is the player whose brain is most resilient to the stresses of the game and, therefore, is able to make the best decisions and judgments.

Indeed, *Survivor* is a very interesting psychological experiment. When I first heard that CBS was planning to strand willing participants on a desert island to see who could outlast the others, I thought this was a particularly cruel idea for a show. But for some reason, I watched, and got hooked. The fact that people are so eager to compete on *Survivor* (and indeed, to compete more than once), suggests that the challenges posed by the game are a primary attraction for players. Certainly, the $1 million prize is enough to lure contestants, but it is far easier to win $1 million on other shows. Rather, being able to claim the title of "Sole Survivor," having outwitted and outplayed the other contestants, and outlasted the elements, is the pinnacle in bragging reality TV rights and should be worthy of our respect as such.

KARYN M. FRICK, PH.D., is an associate professor of behavioral neuroscience in the Department of Psychology at Yale University. She received her B.A. from Franklin and Marshall College, and her M.A. and Ph.D. in psychology from The Johns Hopkins University. Her research focuses on the neurobiology of learning and memory, with particular interest in how hormones, aging, and the environment affect these processes. She spends way too much time watching reality TV, including *Survivor*, and still feels that Boston Rob should have won *Survivor: All-Stars* (at least he got the girl!).

REFERENCES

Arnsten, A. F., and P. S. Goldman-Rakic. "Catecholamines and Cognitive Decline in Aged Nonhuman Primates." *Annals of the New York Academy of Sciences* 444 (1985): 218–234.

Cavedini, P., T. Bassi, A. Ubbiali, A. Casolari, S. Giordani, C. Zorzi, and L. Bellodi. "Neuropsychological Investigation of Decision-making in Anorexia Nervosa." *Psychiatry Research* 127 (2004): 259–266.

Connan, F., F. Murphy, S. E. J. Connor, P. Rich, T. Murphy, N. Bara-Carill, S. Landau, S. Krljes, V. Ng, S. Williams, R. G. Morris, I. C. Campbell, and J. Treasure. "Hippocampal Volume and Cognitive Function in Anorexia Nervosa." *Psychiatry Research: Neuroimaging* 146 (2006): 117–125.

Evans, G. W., P. L. Brennan, M. A. Skorpanich, and D. Held. "Cognitive Mapping and Elderly Adults: Verbal and Location Memory for Urban Landmarks." *Journal of Gerontology* 39 no. 4 (1984): 452–457.

Fehm, H. L., W. Kern, and A. Peters. "Chapter 7: The Selfish Brain: Competition for Energy Resources." *Progress in Brain Research* 153 (2006): 129–140.

Golumb, J., A. Kluger, M. J. de Leon, S. H. Ferris, M. Mittelman, J. Cohen, and A. E. George. "Hippocampal Formation Size Predicts Declining Memory Performance in Normal Aging." *Neurology* 47 (1996): 810–813.

Kim, J. J., and D. M. Diamond. "The Stressed Hippocampus, Synaptic Plasticity and Lost Memories." *Nature Reviews Neuroscience* 3, no. 6 (2002): 453–462.

Krieg, J. C., K. M. Pirke, C. Lauer, and H. Backmund. "Endocrine, Metabolic, and Cranial Computed Tomographic Findings in Anorexia Nervosa." *Biological Psychiatry* 23, no. 4 (1988): 377–387.

Liston, C., M. M. Miller, D. S. Goldwater, J. J. Radley, A. B. Rocher, P. R. Hof, J. H. Morrison, and B. S. McEwen. "Stress-Induced Alterations in Prefrontal Cortical Dendritic Morphology Predict Selective Impairments in Perceptual Attentional Set-Shifting." *Journal of Neuroscience* 26, no. 3 (2006): 7870–7874.

Luine, V., D. Bowling, and M. Hearns. "Spatial Memory Deficits in Aged Rats: Contributions of Monoaminergic Systems." *Brain Research* 537, no. 1–2 (1990): 271–278.

Muir, J. L. "Acetylcholine, Aging, and Alzheimer's Disease." *Pharmacology Biochemistry and Behavior* 56, no. 4 (2000): 687–696.

Ohrmann, P., A. Kersting, T. Suslow, J. Lahlee-Mentzel, U. S. Donges, M. Fiebich, V. Arolt, W. Heindel, and B. Pfleiderer. "Proton Magnetic Resonance

Spectroscopy in Anorexia Nervosa: Correlations with Cognition." *NeuroReport* 15, no. 3 (2004): 549–553.

Radley, J. J., and J. H. Morrison. "Repeated Stress and Structural Plasticity in the Brain." *Ageing Research Reviews* 4, no. 2 (2005): 271–287.

Rosenzweig, E. S., and C. A. Barnes. "Impact of Aging on Hippocampal Function: Plasticity, Network Dynamics, and Cognition." *Progress in Neurobiology* 69, no. 3 (2003): 143–179.

Schaie, K. W. "The Course of Adult Intellectual Development." *American Psychologist* 49, no. 4 (1994): 304–313.

Swayze, V. W., A. E. Andersen, N. C. Andreasen, S. Arndt, Y. Sato, and S. Ziebell. "Brain Tissue Volume Segmentation in Patients with Anorexia Nervosa Before and After Weight Normalization." *International Journal of Eating Disorders* 33, no. 1 (2003): 33–44.

Wilson M. A., and B. L. McNaughton. "Reactivation of Hippocampal Ensemble Memories During Sleep." *Science* 265, no. 5172 (1994): 676–679.

Woodruff-Pak, D. S. *The Neuropsychology of Aging.* Oxford, UK: Blackwell Publishers, 1997.

When we watch Survivor, *we often believe that contestants'
behavior reveals the quirks of their personalities. Kevin J.
Apple and Melissa J. Beers review classic social psychological
research that demonstrates the powerful ways in which situations and social roles constrain behavior. Apple and Beers generate advice for both contestants and viewers for how they
might factor social psychological forces into their experience
of* Survivor.

The Power
of the Situation

KEVIN J. APPLE, PH.D., AND MELISSA J. BEERS, PH.D.

THE POWER OF THE SITUATION

Ever since the first episode aired, we have loved watching *Survivor*. As
social psychologists, we particularly enjoyed watching ordinary people
being placed in extraordinary situations and observing what happens. In
fact, social psychologists study how ordinary people behave in different
situations—with many surprising results. Drawing on social psychology
research, we have some advice to help future players of *Survivor*s avoid
the classic mistake of trusting their fellow tribe members too much. The
majority of people voted off are usually shocked because they believed
they could trust their competitors. It is understandable that contestants
made this error during the first season, but why would the majority of
contestants, season after season, be so surprised that someone betrayed
them? The game, after all, is about betrayal.

Social psychologists study how individuals' thoughts and behaviors
are influenced by others. In a game like *Survivor*, players are constantly trying to predict how the other players will respond in the game.
How will they vote? Can they be trusted? How will they perform in the

game's Challenges for rewards or immunity? Every player—as well as every viewer—engages in a little "armchair psychology" as the game unfolds, trying to determine the players' motivation and predict what they will do next. But how accurate are these predictions? Social psychologists have tried to answer this question with more than fifty years of research on attribution—the process of attributing meaning to why events happen the way they do. This research is particularly relevant to the game of *Survivor*. How much of a player's behavior is due to the kind of person he or she is, and how much is due to the situation he or she is in? And what advice does the field of social psychology offer players in the game? We begin with a review of some classic social psychological studies that pit the person against the situation—with some often unexpected results.

THE PERSON VS. SITUATION DEBATE

Researchers have debated about which is more powerful in predicting future behavior: one's personality or one's circumstances? This debate can easily be applied to *Survivor*. When we observe the players of *Survivor*, do we notice that their personalities predict their style of game-playing? Or is it something about the situation that causes them to behave as they do? When asked these questions, most laypeople tend to believe in the power of personality. For example, the majority of people attribute season one winner Richard Hatch's cunning game style to his manipulative personality. Similarly, many attribute Tina Wesson's (winner of season two) or Ethan Zohn's (winner of season three) success in their respective seasons to their more "laid-back" personas. As social psychologists, however, we cannot discount the importance of the situations in which these Survivors found themselves.

Although people may not like to think so, situational pressures can often override personality or preferred behaviors. Perhaps the most dramatic example of the power of a situation is provided in a series of clever experiments conducted by Stanley Milgram (1963). Imagine you were a participant in this study by Milgram:

You read an advertisement in a local paper for a psychology experiment. According to the ad, the study will not take long and you will be paid for your time. When you arrive at the research laboratory, you discover that you will participate in a study on learning with another person. Specifically, the study is about the effectiveness of punishment on learning word-pairs. By drawing lots, the experimenter randomly assigns you to be the "teacher," and the other participant becomes the "learner." As the teacher, you are placed in a separate room from the learner and you communicate with him via a microphone. You are told to read a list of word-pairs to the learner, then you have to "quiz" the learner to see how well he remembers the pairs. For each wrong answer he gives, you are asked to deliver an electric shock. For the first wrong answer, the learner gets a mild fifteen-volt shock. However, for each subsequent wrong answer the shock increases in intensity by fifteen volts. Although you are concerned about this, the experimenter assures you that there is no risk to the learner, and that it's important for the experiment to follow these procedures exactly. The experimenter sits at a nearby table and observes as you carry out the instructions.

The learner starts out getting the answers correct, but he does make occasional mistakes. You comply with the experimenter's instructions and give increasingly intense shocks. At the learner's twentieth mistake, you deliver a 300-volt shock. After this painful shock, the learner bangs on the wall and begs for the experiment to end. The experimenter seems unfazed and presses you to continue, saying, "The study must go on." After additional mistakes, the learner screams in agony, begging for the experiment to stop. Still, the experimenter says, "Go on, teacher—the experiment must continue." As the experiment wears on, the learner complains about heart pain, screams in anguish, and finally refuses to answer any more questions. You turn, beseechingly, to the experimenter for guidance. He calmly explains that you have no choice but to continue; the learner's failure to respond counts as a wrong answer, and you must continue administering shocks. Not only should you continue delivering shocks to the maximum level—450 volts—but you must continue to give the unresponsive learner shocks at that level for each wrong answer or non-response.

While hearing about this study, you may have asked yourself what you would do in this situation. And, if you are similar to our students, you probably think that you would be very unlikely to follow the experimenter's instructions. When most people hear about this research procedure, they are quick to insist that if they were participating in such a study they would stop shocking the learner fairly early in the process. Regularly, when we share this study with our students, informal class polls reveal that they believe they would stop shocking the learner as soon as he bangs on the wall and complains about the pain. Actually, even Milgram himself did not anticipate that so many participants would obey the experimental instructions. In fact, when he described the study that he intended to perform to a number of his colleagues, the consensus among them was that less than approximately 1 percent of subjects—only a "sadistic few"— would follow the instructions completely.

Although the participants in this study had different personalities and came from different socio-economic and educational backgrounds, the majority of participants behaved similarly in response to the commands of an authority figure. In fact, 65 percent of the participants were fully obedient and kept shocking the learner until they reached 450 volts. No one, not even Milgram himself, expected such a response.

From their reactions during the experiment and from their conversations with Milgram after the study ended, the participants believed they were hurting the learner and possibly aggravating his heart condition. However, they did not realize that the learner was a paid confederate. That is, the learner was only pretending to be hurt, and the screams and protests were carefully staged and arranged in advance by Milgram. No one actually received shocks in this experiment, and all participants were carefully and thoroughly debriefed at the conclusion of the experiment so that they knew the learner was actually unharmed. Still, participants found themselves to be quite surprised at how completely they followed the experimenter's directions.

Just as Milgram's participants found themselves behaving in surprising ways because of their situation, many *Survivor* players also find themselves behaving in surprising ways. For example, after the merge in season one, Kelly confessed to the camera that she could not believe she was betraying her new friends from the other tribe. Of course, the stakes of the game are not life-threatening; however, the Survivors often find themselves telling lies, betraying friends, and making and breaking alliances.

Milgram's shocking study (no pun intended) is often used as an example of the power of the situation. The situation—in this case, the experiment—was so powerful that people from all walks of life behaved in a similar manner, and were obedient to the authority figure represented by the experimenter. Through careful analysis, Blass (2004) reviewed obedience studies done between 1963 and 1985 in both the United States and other countries. For each of these studies, Blass noted what percentage of participants completely obeyed the experimenter. The obedience rate did not change dramatically over time. That is, as society changed, the average obedience rate remained about the same. Researchers in other countries have also found comparable obedience rates. Blass concluded that if Milgram's study were repeated today, the results would be similar. The implications for a game like *Survivor* are clear: Although players may believe they know whom they can trust, they may not fully appreciate the power that the situation may hold over them and their fellow players. Although they may enter the game thinking they know what to expect of their own—and other players'—behavior, the game's constant twists and turns frequently create high-pressure situations that override personal preferences.

Decades of social psychological research have repeatedly demonstrated the power of the situation. Another compelling example comes from a study by Darley and Batson (1973), who studied situational and personal predictors of helping. In the study, seminary students were either told to rush across campus to deliver a speech or were told they had plenty of time to get across campus before giving the speech. On their way, a confederate (a person working with the experimenters) was planted along the path, slumped in a doorway—clearly in need of help. The primary question of interest was: would the seminary students stop to help the person in the street? In this experiment, the power of the situation was dramatic. When in a hurry, the majority of students did not offer assistance. Ironically, this remained true even if the seminary students were in a hurry to give a talk about the parable of the "Good Samaritan." As you may remember, the "Good Samaritan" stops to help someone in need, even at great expense to himself. Personality variables such as religiosity (internal or external) were unable to predict the participants' behavior.

Based on these research studies, many social psychologists have argued that personality does not predict behavior (Mischel and Peake 1982). Global personality traits do not predict specific behaviors (especially when there are strong situational demands). For example, the global trait of conscientiousness will not predict whether you will pay your next electric bill on time. Instead, situational constraints such as amount of money in your bank account or availability of stamps will be better predictors. Many social psychologists argue that information about someone's personality is not useful when trying to make future predictions. Thus, from a social psychological perspective, personality is a less important consideration in determining how people play *Survivor* than the situational constraints introduced during the game.

Today, psychologists are no longer vigorously debating the Person vs. Situation controversy (Newman 2002). Most psychologists recognize that both personality and the power of the situation work together to predict behavior. However, the "armchair psychologist" is often prone to making mistakes or errors in attribution and may not always fully appreciate the impact of the situation. People are often unaware of how much their behaviors change as a result of being in different situations.

SOCIAL ROLES

The co-authors of this paper are parents, spouses, and college professors, and we behave differently in each of these roles. In fact, when students see us interacting with our families, they are often surprised to see us behave so differently. It is not surprising that our social roles can shape our behavior; however, social psychologist Philip Zimbardo and his colleagues were astonished by the extent to which this can occur (Haney, Banks, and Zimbardo 1973).

Zimbardo recruited male college students to participate in a simulated prison for two weeks. The researchers gave each of the participants extensive psychological tests to ensure that they were normal adults without any psychological disorders. Zimbardo randomly assigned some of these students to be prisoners, and the rest of the participants to be guards. The prisoners and guards wore distinct uniforms (not unlike the *Survivor* "buff").

To help everyone adapt to the assigned roles, Zimbardo made the simulated prison as realistic as possible. He converted a basement laboratory to look like a jail. He also arranged for the prisoners to be picked up in a police car. Once the prisoners arrived in the simulated jail, they were given prison ID numbers to replace their names.

Everyone took on his role as if it were a real-life responsibility. The prisoners became apathetic and depressed, and the guards became quite cruel. They made prisoners clean toilets by hand, and they took away toilet privileges, forcing prisoners to go the bathroom in a bucket. They deprived prisoners of sleep by having hourly line-ups to make sure that no prisoner escaped. For the prisoners, the conditions were arguably worse than the conditions the Survivors have dealt with when playing the game. When Zimbardo saw the cruelty of the guards and the poor shape in which the prisoners were, he ended his study eight days earlier than planned.

The contestants on *Survivor* are also being asked to play roles. And, comparable to Zimbardo's participants, they allow their social roles to shape their behaviors. Once they accept the role of contestant in a game, their behavior begins to change. For example, Rupert Boneham (*Survivor: Pearl Islands*) stole the shoes of members from the other tribe during the first episode of his season. Rupert admitted that he was simply getting into the role of a "pirate" based on the theme for that season's game. Outside of his role as a contestant on *Survivor*, we doubt that Rupert would consider stealing as an acceptable behavior. However, Rupert acted in line with a social role. Over the years, multiple contestants have admitted that they are "playing a game," and they are there to win. These contestants are demonstrating that they are really into their roles. For example, Rob Mariano (*Survivor: All-Stars*) claimed he was "just playing a game" when he betrayed his friend Lex van den Berghe. Ironically, Lex made a similar claim when he betrayed his friend Ethan earlier in the season. We doubt that Rob and Lex regularly betray their friends and acquaintances; however, they both got caught up in their roles as contestants in a game.

OUR ADVICE TO FUTURE *SURVIVOR* PLAYERS

Our best advice to future contestants is not to underestimate the power of the situation. Although future players may be tempted to trust the other players on their team, they need to realize that the situation will likely overpower the other players' personalities. In addition, the roles the contestants will play will also overpower their personalities. Thus, our advice is to try to pay close attention to the players' situations. In fact, we believe that Richard Hatch (season one) did exactly that. He picked three other people to be in his alliance. The people he chose (Rudy, Sue, and Kelly) were not in a good situation early in the game. For example, Rudy and Sue were both quite outspoken, and they had made statements that upset the other members of the tribe. In fact, it was likely that Rudy and Sue were in danger of being voted out. We believe that Richard used the situation of these players to his advantage. Because these contestants knew they were in danger, joining the alliance with Richard made sense. We believe that Richard intentionally formed his alliance with people he would never be friends with outside of the game. Thus, he was ignoring their personalities. For example, as a homosexual, it is unlikely that Richard would otherwise ever have become friends with someone like Rudy, who had strong homophobic attitudes.

After twelve seasons of *Survivor*, one might think our advice of not trusting people is obvious. However, when one plays *Survivor*, this advice may not be so easy to take. The heat, exhaustion, and lack of food make it difficult for people to use the cognitive resources necessary to truly understand the situational constraints. Because so many previous players have made this mistake, they really should not be surprised when they are voted out. Yet they are surprised because they made the mistake of trusting the other tribe members, even though the situation makes it unlikely for anyone to be trustworthy.

ADVICE FOR VIEWERS

Most of us will be viewers of the show, instead of players. But even as viewers, it is also important that we pay attention to situational constraints. When watching the show, it is easy for us to believe we would behave differently than many of the contestants—just like it is easy for us to believe that we are not capable of hurting someone by giving them painful electric shocks or humiliating someone by not letting them go to the bathroom. The participants in Milgram's obedience studies and Zimbardo's prison study also did not believe they were capable of hurting others. In reality, we cannot tell how we will behave unless we are in the situation. So, instead of being overly critical of a contestant making what we perceive to be a foolish move, we need to remember that anyone else may have made that same choice in that situation. We should also remember that we do not know how the contestants behave in their normal, everyday lives. We are watching people in extreme conditions, and the game of *Survivor* can certainly bring out the worst in its players.

KEVIN J. APPLE, PH.D., is an assistant department head and associate professor at the Department of Psychology at James Madison University. He enjoys teaching a wide variety of classes including general psychology, research methods, and the psychology of the Holocaust. His main research interests include both the intergroup bias and methods for assessing classroom learning. When not teaching classes or doing research, he is most likely spending time with his wife and two children or watching a reality television show. His favorite *Survivor* player is Ethan Zohn. Kevin admires Ethan for being a fierce competitor who played the game with integrity.

MELISSA J. BEERS, PH.D., is senior lecturer and Psychology 100 Program Coordinator at The Ohio State University, where she teaches several courses, including social psychology, statistics, and a graduate course in the teaching of psychology. She is also vice president of the Strategic Research Group (SRG), a research firm based in Columbus, Ohio, as well as a wife and very proud mother of a four-year-old son. Her favorite *Survivor* player is "Boston" Rob Mariano, who really knows how to take advantage of the power of the situation.

REFERENCES

Blass, T. *The Man Who Shocked the World: The Life and Legacy of Stanley Milgram*. Cambridge: Basic Books, 2004.

Darley, J. M. and C. D. Batson. "From Jerusalem to Jericho: A Study of Situational and Dispositional Variables in Helping Behavior." *Journal of Personality and Social Psychology* 27 (1973): 100–108.

Haney, C., C. Banks, and P. Zimbardo. "Interpersonal Dynamics in a Simulated Prison." *Institutional Journal of Criminology and Penology* 1 (1973): 69–97.

Milgram, S. "Behavioral Study of Obedience." *Journal of Abnormal and Social Psychology* 67 (1963): 371–378.

Mischel, W. and P. K. Peake. "Beyond Deja Vu in the Search for Cross-Situational Consistency." *Psychological Review* 89 (1982): 730–755.

Newman, L. S. "What is a 'Social-Psychological' Account of Perpetrator Behavior? The Person Versus the Situation in Goldhagen's Hitler's Willing Executioners." *In Understanding Genocide: The Social Psychology of the Holocaust*, edited by L. S. Newman and R. Erber, 2002.

At the beginning of each season of Survivor, *viewers watch a new group of contestants warily taking stock of each other. Gary Lewandowski, Jr., and Benjamin Le suggest that contestants succeed to the extent that they are able to manage first and subsequent impressions. Contestants safeguard their progress in the game both by manipulating the impressions they make and by detecting their opponents' manipulations.*

Outwitting to Outlast

The Role of Impression Management on *Survivor*

GARY LEWANDOWSKI, JR., PH.D., AND BENJAMIN LE, PH.D.

No man is an island, entire of itself.
—JOHN DONNE

This quotation, taken from *Devotions Upon Emergent Occasions* (1624), emphasizes the interconnectedness and reliance on others that is inherent in human existence. While this idea is generally applicable to our daily lives, it carries special relevance when you are in a remote location competing with other people for a million dollars! The game of *Survivor* presents a unique social situation in which members of a tribe must possess physical skills as well as interpersonal skills to be successful. Ultimately, the ability to outplay, outwit, and outlast the other opponents is largely based on contestants' abilities to read other people's intentions accurately and to convey properly their own. Psychologists refer to these processes as *impression formation* and *impression management*.

FIRST IMPRESSIONS ARE FAST IMPRESSIONS

From the moment we first meet another person, we form impressions about that person. In fact, this process happens almost instantaneously (Bar, Neta, and Linz 2006). For this reason, the first interaction with a fellow tribe member on *Survivor* is extremely important because it lays the foundation for future interactions with that person. Despite their rapid acquisition, our first impressions are relatively accurate. For example, one study had participants provide personality ratings for a stranger after viewing a five-minute video clip (Funder and Colvin 1998). Even after just five minutes, participants' ratings were very consistent with the self-ratings of the person in the video clip. First impressions based on very limited exposure, or "thin slices" of information, are also stable over time. To test this, Nalini Ambady and Robert Rosenthal (1993) had raters evaluate a silent thirty-second clip of a professor's lecture. These ratings were then used to predict student evaluations of the professor's quality at the end of the semester. Remarkably, the ratings based on the thirty-second video clip paralleled the rating given after a fifteen-week semester! Follow-up studies showed that even thinner slices of behavior, clips of two and five seconds, yielded similar degrees of accuracy. These studies show that it only takes a brief period of exposure to form an accurate impression. In *Survivor*, the impressions that contestants form about each other on Day One are likely to be very accurate and, therefore, guide their interactions for the rest of the game. When contestants arrive for the first day wearing business suits or high heels, their styles of dress are likely to create very different impressions than if they were wearing workout clothes or overalls.

THE POWER OF FIRST IMPRESSIONS

A long-held assumption is that first impressions are lasting impressions. As such, there may be a primacy effect wherein the first information one learns has more influence on one's overall impression than information acquired later. A classic study provided participants with a list of the same adjectives describing an individual, with the only variation being the order in which the traits were presented—from positive to negative or negative to positive (Asch 1946). Participants were then asked to evaluate their perception of the individual described by the traits. Results showed that perceptions were more favorable when exposed to positive traits first and more negative when exposed to negative traits first, even though both lists were identical except for their order. This demonstrates that individuals have a propensity for maintaining first impressions, despite subsequent contradictory information. First impressions are especially important for succeeding on *Survivor*. At the very beginning of the game it is unwise to be excessively bossy or appear too competitive. For example, Jolanda, who outwardly appeared to have potential as a strong female tribe member, was voted out immediately in the *Survivor: Palau* season because she was overly directive early on in the game.

BASIS FOR IMPRESSIONS

Impressions of others form quickly, and these initial impressions weigh on ensuing evaluations. These impressions can be influenced by small amounts of information or from seemingly unrelated sources, such as physical features and perceived similarity to the self. The nature of most social situations is such that we learn about a person's outward physical characteristics first, and then discover elements of his or her personality afterward. When contestants first meet on *Survivor*, the first hints they have about what other contestants are like are based on physical appearance characteristics, such as physical attractiveness, style of dress, gender, and age.

Attractiveness/Appearance: One of the most powerful pieces of information on which we base impressions is physical attractiveness. When judging a person's attractiveness, people tend to agree on who is "hot," and who is not (Langlois, Kalakanis, and Rubenstein 2000). This phenomenon holds true even when members of one culture rate members of another culture. Assessments of another contestant's attractiveness are important because people have a strong tendency to associate physical beauty with positive personality qualities. In a classic social psychology study, Karen Dion, Ellen Berscheid, and Elaine Walster (1972) showed participants pictures of people who were rated by a set of judges to be of high, medium, and low attractiveness. Based on the picture alone, participants were asked to infer personality characteristics and life outcomes about the person in the picture. They found that the people in the more attractive pictures were seen as being warmer, more sexually responsive, more sensitive, kinder, more interesting, stronger, more poised, more sociable, more nurturing, and more outgoing. This effect, known as the "what-is-beautiful-is-good" stereotype, is based solely on how attractive a picture is!

If thinking someone is attractive leads us to think that that person is stronger and more sociable, as this phenomenon suggests, it might make us more likely to want to form an alliance with him or her. Evidence of this can be seen in the romantic alliances between tribe members. In two of the most notable occurrences, Rob and Amber in *Survivor: All-Stars* and Jennifer and Gregg in *Survivor: Palau*, attractive females have formed alliances with attractive males. These types of alliances are virtually non-existent among less-attractive tribe members. However, being good-looking can also lead to the formation of negative impressions. For example, in *Survivor: Palau* Kim Mullen, a former Miss USA contestant, was ultimately voted out because she was seen as lazy around camp. It is likely that this impression was intensified by a combination of her beauty and her affinity for giving herself facials.

There are other characteristics about a person's appearance, aside from physical attractiveness, that help guide our impressions. For example, when first meeting someone, we are immediately aware of the other person's gender, age, style of dress, and—once conversation starts—any accent he or she might have. Of these, age and gender are perhaps the most powerful pieces of information. In any season of *Survivor*, it is common for male contestants to remark on how the females struggle with Challenges, while a female contestant will usually suggest that some of the male contestants are underestimating her abilities because of her gender. Similarly, in each season, one of the older tribe members will claim an advantage over others due to life experience, while a younger tribe member will claim an advantage due to physical prowess and additional energy. While both age and gender are related to attractiveness, they are ultimately important because of what they tell us about the type of person someone is.

Similarity: Information about gender, age, and where a person is from are important because they let us know whether someone is like us. The basic fact is that we like others who are similar to us, and the more similar, the better (Byrne and Nelson 1965). If you were a younger male contestant from the South, with whom would you be more likely to trust and ally yourself: 1) an older woman from Massachusetts, or 2) a young guy from Arkansas? It's a no-brainer. Because the younger guy is more similar to you, he is also more familiar, so you would likely feel like you already know more about him. In contrast, you wouldn't know as much about what motivates an older woman from Massachusetts or how to relate to her as easily.

The influence that similarity has on *Survivor* is easy to see. When alliances form, they are primarily gender- and age-based. A set of males will form a bond, as will one of females. Likewise, the older tribe members tend to stick together, while the younger tribe members form their own bonds. This tendency was highlighted in the *Survivor: Panama* season where the game started with four tribes that were created based on age and gender groupings that persisted throughout the game (e.g., the male alliance between Terry, Dan, Nick, and Austin).

USEFULNESS OF FIRST IMPRESSIONS

Although there is evidence that early impressions are stable over time, it seems that a better and more accurate way to form impressions would be to develop them gradually. By taking this approach, we would make data-based decisions about which tribe members are going to be allies and, alternatively, who is likely to stab us in the back. However, waiting to form an impression detracts from the initial utility that having a "sense of someone" might provide. Our early impressions (even those formed within seconds) provide us with information that we can then use to make predictions about others' behaviors and motives.

Specifically, the information we gather activates a *schema*—a mental process that helps individuals classify and arrange information (Bartlett

1932). Schemas are utilized to explain ambiguities and reduce inconsistencies that can arise when faced with new situations or things (Kelley 1950). That is, schemas are shortcuts that help provide a sense of order and familiarity that enables us to make predictions about others more quickly and with more confidence. By using schemas, we have access to a knowledge base about a person, rather than needing to accumulate information more slowly over time.

For example, during *Survivor: Guatemala*, when the two tribes were redistributed, Stephenie had to make a decision about whom from the other tribe she could trust to be part of her alliance. Based on earlier interactions with Judd, Stephenie knew he was from New York. That limited information activated a plan for Stephenie that led her to believe that he would be upfront, honest, and would feel a sense of closeness with her because she was from New Jersey. Based on her schema about people from New York, Stephenie made predictions about how open Judd would be to building an alliance. Ultimately, Stephenie proved to be correct in her decision. The activation of this schema alone likely would not have produced a strong alliance; however, because both Judd and Stephenie recognized a level of similarity between them, an alliance was formed.

The usefulness of forming impressions and the usefulness of schemas is based on a very key assumption: a person is forming his or her impression validly, based on accurate and honest interactions with the other person. However, as can easily be seen in the interactions between contestants on *Survivor*, accurate and honest interactions among contestants are rarities.

IMPRESSION MANAGEMENT

From a very young age, people become aware of the impression formation process, and realize that these impressions are often formed using limited amounts of information. Why else would young children be concerned about what clothes they are wearing to school, if their lunchbox is cool, or why they are the only kid wearing Velcro® shoes? We learn from a young age that very superficial things about us have the ability to mold the impressions others form. This carries over into adulthood and motivates desires for wearing the latest fashions, driving stylish cars, and living in luxurious houses. Why go through all the trouble? Simply because we know these things provide information to others about what we are like. Certainly Bob and Mary Jones are nice people because they look nice, live in a nice neighborhood, and belong to the country club. While this may or may not be true, these are types of assumptions that people tend to make. While our material possessions and status symbols influence others' impressions of us in a general sense (at least in the United States), people also have the ability to shape impressions on a more specific level.

Psychologists refer to a person's purposeful attempt to influence others' thoughts and perceptions through the control of information as *impression management* (Leary and Kowalski 1990). When controlling the information others have about us, we have to account for things that we say and for our behaviors. Studies of behavior in public settings have shown that people are more likely to wash their hands after using the bathroom if there is another person in the room (Munger and Harris 1989). This suggests that people are not concerned about being unsanitary but are concerned about others *thinking* they are unsanitary. Similarly, another study examined the eating habits of men and women in various social situations and found that people eat less when in the presence of an opposite-sex partner than with same-sex partners (Pliner and Chaiken 1990).

While being attractive and similar to others can promote good first impressions, neither one of these characteristics is much under the contestants' control. There are a few more specific strategies that *Survivor* contestants have employed to gain favor with another person through purposeful manipulation of information and actions. In the game of *Survivor*, having the support of other contestants is immensely important for two reasons. First, you need to build alliances to stay alive in the game. Getting people to like you helps achieve that. Second, in order to be the "Sole Survivor" a contestant will have had to break an alliance at some point, typically through deception. For this reason it is crucial to manage impressions so that you can be friends with someone, then vote him or her off the island and still have his or her support in the final Tribal Council. So what are some of the impression management strategies commonly used on *Survivor*?

Deception and Deceit: In addition to altering their behaviors, people also control the types of information they disclose to others. Sometimes this is done through blatant deception because a person is concerned about how he or she will be perceived. For this reason, when sharing information about their personalities or pasts, people will rarely mention any negative qualities they might have, or they will withhold information that they suspect others would find troublesome. For example, no one would ever come right out and say "Nice to meet you, I've been arrested three times, and I hate children, puppies, and kittens." In fact, that person would most likely never mention these facts.

A perfect example of this was in *Survivor: Guatemala* when ex-NFL quarterback Gary Hogeboom did not reveal his former profession. His reasoning, perhaps understandably so, was that if the other contestants knew his former job they would assume he didn't need the prize money associated with winning *Survivor*. Rather than take that chance, he decided to tell everyone that he was a landscaper. This was a good choice on his part because landscaping is consistent with schemas for jobs that a man with Gary's physical dimensions might have—people would be less convinced if he said he was a seamstress or a sumo wrestler—and it creates the impression of someone who is hardworking and not afraid of physical labor (good qualities to have around the tribe). By making the choice to mislead others, Gary did a masterful job of managing impressions and advancing in the game. A more despicable example of deceit was seen in *Survivor: Pearl Islands* when, in an attempt to win sympathy from fellow tribe members, Jon (a.k.a. "Jonny Fairplay") had a friend reveal that his grandmother had passed away. It was later revealed after the show that his grandmother was alive and well and not even terribly old.

Self-promotion: The most common strategy contestants use is self-promotion. Much like the approach that a person takes in a job interview, those using self-promotion champion their own cause by extolling their virtues, demonstrating their abilities, and minimizing their shortcomings (Giacalone and Rosenfeld 1986). Contestants in *Survivor* get a chance at self-promotion in its most straightforward form during every Challenge. Whether it involves standing on a pole, traversing an obstacle course, or solving a puzzle, each person's abilities are on display for all to see. In fact, the most skilled person in a Challenge is granted immunity and gets to carry a symbol of that accomplishment over the next few days. Imagine if you had something like that around the office! Contestants can capitalize on a strong performance by recounting their accomplishments to other tribe members back at camp as a way to further reinforce their utility to the tribe for the next Challenge. Self-promotion can also be used by highlighting existing skills. In the case of Rudy Boesch, the former Navy SEAL from *Survivor: Borneo* and *Survivor: All-Stars*, previous military experience made him an asset to his tribe. Rudy realized this and made his background known to promote himself.

However, as in the case of Blake (a.k.a. "Golden Boy") from *Survivor: Guatemala*, self-promoters run the risk of overdoing it. In this instance, Blake's self-promotion annoyed fellow tribe members who perceived his behavior to be excessive (especially his stories concerning past conquests). Thus, rather than creating a favorable impression, it led to the opposite impression of him as being arrogant, overly confident, and a nuisance who should be voted out of the group.

Tom, the firefighter, and ultimately the winner from *Survivor: Palau*, was a much savvier contestant and was aware of this risk. In an early discussion with Ian, Tom acknowledged the risk of continually winning the individual Challenges and of doing so well in the team Challenges. His reasoning was that people would recognize what a strong contestant he was, which would make him a threat, causing the tribe members to proceed to vote him out. Although it took a while to unfold, his concern was later realized when discussion among the remaining members of Koror centered on voting him out because of his strength. In fact, voting out the stronger members is such a common strategy that it may be better to lie low and use another impression management strategy.

Supplication: Supplication is a counterintuitive, yet guileful, strategy that is the antithesis of self-promotion. This strategy involves a person purposefully acting as if he or she were incapable, overly tired, sick, or otherwise needy (Friedlander and Schwartz 1985). The goal of this strategy is not necessarily to gain the adoration of others, but instead to gain their help and resources. This most commonly happens in *Survivor* when contestants openly remark about how tired, hungry, or stressed out they are. While this may legitimately be the case, it is also possible that they are exaggerating their circumstances in order to gain extra resources (i.e. more food or more time to rest) to help them perform better in future Challenges.

A more purposeful use of supplication is when a player takes the "don't vote me off, I would never be a threat to you" angle. This approach was used most notably in *Survivor: Guatemala* by Lydia, a small, unimposing woman who seemed wholly incapable of winning any Challenge. However, despite her obvious limitations, Lydia was a tribe favorite and was perceived as non-threatening in the Challenges. This approach worked so well that she made it to the final four, despite being arguably the weakest physical player. Even then, she continued to highlight her shortcomings and emphasized how she wasn't a threat. Ultimately, Lydia was voted off because she was enormously well-liked, which gave her a very strong chance of winning if she made it to the final two. Similarly, Cirie from *Survivor: Panama* was a player with virtually no skills who was also very well-liked. Others recognized that she was no physical threat, and that helped her get to the final four. However, her lack of skill caught up with her when she lost the fire-making tie-breaker to Danielle. Through "not playing the game" she was not voted off by others, but, in the end, the game played her.

Ingratiation: Those using supplication look to more powerful people around them for help. Ingratiation does much of the same (Jones and Pittman 1982). This strategy involves a weaker member allying him- or herself with a stronger person through flattery, excessive agreement, compliments, and general attempts to "kiss up." This is the classic example of the sycophant who gains favor, and ultimately power, by riding the coattails of someone else. A great example of this was *Survivor: Palau's* Katie who, despite her lesser skills, orchestrated a path to the top. Instead of the more traditional route of winning Challenges and being a strong contestant, the noticeably weak Katie built an alliance with Tom and Ian, who were two of the stronger contestants that season. It was readily acknowledged by both Tom and Ian that Katie was a weaker contestant, but in their interactions she would mention how well they were doing, how well the three-way alliance was working out for everyone, and how they were probably going to win (saying this to both Tom and Ian separately, of course!). This strategy was fairly successful, but ultimately this impression management strategy was seen as less emblematic of what a winner should be, compared to Tom's strategy of self-promotion. Thus, the final vote of the season between Tom and Katie went decidedly in favor of Tom (six to one).

To a lesser degree, Amber used ingratiation in both of her *Survivor* appearances. In *Survivor: Australian Outback*, she partnered with Jerri. Unfortunately for Amber, Jerri was not well-liked, and once she was voted off, Amber quickly followed. Amber learned from her mistake in *Survivor: All-Stars*, but still used ingratiation by allying with a stronger player in Rob Mariano. This was much more effective during the All-Stars season largely because of Rob's skill as a player. In several instances, Rob interceded on Amber's behalf to keep her in the game, which ultimately led to her taking home the million-dollar prize. In fact, the alliance between them was so strong that it developed into a romantic relationship on the show and an eventual marriage.

Intimidation: The final strategy for managing impressions is also the most ruthless. Intimidation is an impression management strategy that relies on creating fear among those around you by acting in a dangerous, menacing, threatening manner (Tedeschi and Norman 1985). This tactic is very much akin to a well-known quotation by Niccolo Machiavelli: "It is better to be feared than loved, if you cannot be both." Intimidation has been used by contestants, but largely in small doses due to the high likelihood of others forming negative impressions. It is hard to be a tyrant when your fate in the game rests on the votes of others. Jerri Manthey's behavior in *Survivor: Australian Outback* is a good example of this. Due to her dominating personality, she frequently experienced conflict with other tribe members and, though she survived eight votes at Tribal Council, her intimidating style was ultimately why she was voted out. Perhaps because of this, Jerri took a kinder and gentler approach to her appearance on *Survivor: All-Stars*, enabling her to last longer.

A good example of the use of intimidation in a positive way was when Richard Hatch, in the very first season of *Survivor*, let everyone know that the million-dollar check already had his name on it. Despite not being well-liked throughout the season, Richard eventually was crowned the "Sole Survivor." Also in the first season, Susan used intimidation in her infamous "Rats and Snakes" speech in which she compared Richard and Kelly to the two most common animals on the island. She then proceeded to explain to Kelly that she would not offer her water if she were dying of thirst and would let vultures eat her remains with a clear conscience. Such statements certainly conjure up fear in one's opponents, and produce intimidation. Because the season was over, it was a perfectly safe time to use the intimidation strategy, and it was likely the main reason she earned a spot on *Survivor: All-Stars*. During *Survivor: All-Stars*, Rob Mariano (a.k.a. "Boston Rob") was largely considered a diabolical manipulator who was respected and feared—two key indicators of using intimidation as an impression management strategy. For him, though, it backfired, and he was voted off due to his perceived lack of caring for other people.

In the end, a contestant's success on *Survivor* is inextricably tied to his or her ability accurately to form impressions of other contestants and manage others' impressions of them. Only through mastering both sides of the process can a person hope to form necessary alliances, break those alliances by voting people off, and finally gain the favor of the Jury in order to get the votes necessary to outplay, outwit, and outlast the other contestants to be the "Sole Survivor."

AUTHORS' NOTE

It is important to point out that the impression management issues discussed here relate only to interactions among contestants on the show. Due to the editing that takes place prior to broadcast, the impressions of the audience at home are also managed to a large degree.

GARY LEWANDOWSKI, JR., PH.D., originally from Fairless Hills, PA (a suburb of Philadelphia), received his bachelor's degree from Millersville University of Pennsylvania. He received his master's and Ph.D. in social/health psychology from the State University of New York at Stony Brook in Long Island, NY. He is currently an assistant professor of psychology at Monmouth University (the alma mater of former *Survivor* contestants Katie Gallagher and Stephenie LaGrossa) in West Long Branch, NJ. His research focuses on romantic relationships, including interpersonal attraction, relationship maintenance, and break-ups.

BENJAMIN LE, PH.D., is a native Californian and currently an assistant professor of psychology at Haverford College (PA), after having completed his undergraduate degree at Grinnell College and Ph.D. in social psychology at Purdue University. His research is on commitment, emotions, and social networks in close relationships. Le has not yet applied to be on *Survivor*, for fear of being rejected.

REFERENCES

Ambady, N. and R. Rosenthal. "Half a Minute: Predicting Teacher Evaluations from Thin Slices of Nonverbal Behavior and Physical Attractiveness." *Journal of Personality and Social Psychology* 64, no. 3 (1993): 431–441.

Asch, S. E. "Forming Impressions of Personality." *Journal of Abnormal and Social Psychology* 41 (1946): 258–290.

Bar, M., M. Neta, and H. Linz. "Very First Impressions." *Emotion* 6, no. 2 (2006): 269–278.

Bartlett, F. C. *Remembering*. Cambridge, England: Cambridge University Press, 1932.

Byrne, D. and D. Nelson. "The Effect of Topic Importance and Attitude Similarity-Dissimilarity on Attraction in a Multistranger Design." *Psychonomic Science* 3, no. 10 (1965): 449–450.

Dion, K., E. Berscheid, and E. Walster. "What Is Beautiful Is Good." *Journal of Personality and Social Psychology* 24, no. 3 (1972): 285–290.

Friedlander, M. L. and G. S. Schwartz. "Toward a Theory of Strategic Self-Presentation in Counseling and Psychotherapy." *Journal of Counseling Psychology* 32, no. 4 (1985): 483–501.

Funder, D. C. and C. R. Colvin. "Friends and Strangers: Acquaintanceship, Agreement, and the Accuracy of Personality Judgment." *Journal of Personality and Social Psychology* 55, no. 1 (1988): 149–158.

Giacalone, R. A. and P. Rosenfeld. "Self-Presentation and Self-Promotion in an Organizational Setting." *Journal of Social Psychology* 126, no. 3 (1986): 321–326.

Jones, E. E. and T. S. Pittman. "Toward a General Theory of Strategic Self-Presentation." In *Psychological Perspectives on the Self*, edited by J. Suls. Hillsdale, NJ: Erlbaum, 1982.

Kelley, H. H. "The Warm-Cold Variable in First Impressions of Persons." *Journal of Personality* 18 (1950): 431–439.

Langlois, J. H., L. Kalakanis, and A. J. Rubenstein. "Maxims or Myths of Beauty? A Meta-Analytic and Theoretical Review." *Psychological Bulletin* 126, no. 3 (2000): 390–423.

Leary, M. R. *Self-Presentation: Impression Management and Interpersonal Behavior*. Madison, WI: Brown & Benchmark Publishers, 1994.

Leary, M. R. and R. M. Kowalski. "Impression Management: A Literature Review and Two-Component Model." *Psychological Bulletin* 107, no. 1 (1990): 34–47.

Munger, K. and S. J. Harris. "Effects of an Observer on Handwashing in a Public Restroom." *Perceptual and Motor Skills* 69 (1989): 733–734.

Pliner, P. and S. Chaiken. "Eating, Social Motives, and Self-Presentation in Women and Men." *Journal of Experimental Social Psychology* 26, no. 3 (1990): 240–254.

Tedeschi, J. T. and N. Norman. "Social Power, Self-Presentation, and the Self." In *Self and Identity*, edited by B. R. Schlenker. New York: McGraw-Hill, 1985.

Survivor is stressful—that conclusion appears well beyond doubt. Anne Moyer unpacks the major categories of stressors that affect contestants' experiences and documents their likely impact. Moyer also examines the ethics of Survivor. *She considers whether the castaways should endure these stressors to entertain the rest of us—even with the hope of a million dollar prize.*

Stress and Coping and Survivor

ANNE MOYER, PH.D.

Psychologists have long been concerned with stressors—those stimuli that tax our psychological resources, upset our social position or ties, and drain us physically. How do stressors "get under the skin" to affect mental and physical health? How might they be met with resilience in some people and breakdowns in others? *Survivor* offers a forbidden island of insights for researchers that cannot be (ethically) produced in laboratory paradigms or even elegant field experiments. The castaways endure extreme stressors and adopt coping strategies—both to endure the conditions they are subjected to, and to succeed in the game. Although today's psychologists could likely learn much from studying responses to such extreme stressors, they could never induce such conditions as part of a research study.

A good part of what psychological researchers have learned about stressors and coping with extreme conditions comes from sources other than contemporary laboratory studies with human subjects. One source is earlier studies whose methods could not be used today. These classic studies were conducted before our current ethics codes were developed. One study revealed, for instance, that research participants

71

would deliver what they were led to believe were harmful shocks to another person to a greater extent than ever expected (Milgram 1963). All that was required was an authority figure who insisted that they do so. Such studies also showed that the identities of well-adjusted undergraduates simply told to serve as prison guards and prisoners would dissolve thoroughly into their roles as their behavior devolved to brutish actions and helplessness, respectively (Haney, Banks, and Zimbardo 1973). More important, these studies also revealed that people might be harmed emotionally by being placed in such extreme situations, even by researchers whose questions were undoubtedly directed by pro-social concerns, or who had no intention for conditions to go so far awry. The participants in the obedience study exhibited signs of nervous tension—sweating, trembling, stuttering, nervous laughter, and even seizures. This prison experiment had to be terminated early and five of the "prisoners" were released due to acute emotional disturbances. Moreover, the research subjects involved in both of these studies were sobered if not wounded by the resulting knowledge of what they were personally capable of. Ethical codes of research conduct evolved in response to these classic studies. They are upheld by institutions conducting investigations with human subjects in most developed countries.

Ethical constraints do not prevent researchers from studying responses to extreme but naturally occurring stressors, however. These are a second source of our understanding about stressors' effects. We have been able to squeeze lemonade from such bitter events as manufacturing-plant layoffs and to distill knowledge from disasters as horrific as hurricanes and earthquakes, and even terrorist attacks.

Finally, stress research owes much to work conducted with animals. Although behavioral research with animals is also governed by ethical codes, the parameters of what animals are permitted to be subjected to are somewhat wider. This discrepancy in what is considered ethical to do with humans versus with animals in research is accepted by mainstream professional psychological organizations. These bodies carefully stipulate that the costs to animals used in research must be justified and minimized. Nevertheless, many individual psychologists find animal research objectionable. They would not be willing to conduct this type of work in order to answer questions about stress and coping. Thus, from the point of view of psychological researchers, reality TV represents a veritable fantasy world—in terms of the pressures that humans may be observed responding to.

SOCIAL STRESS

What I wasn't prepared for was the loneliness and isolation of being stuck in the middle of Africa and Panama with no friends, no family, no couches.
—ETHAN, *Survivor: Africa* and *Survivor: All-Stars*

One of the techniques used in research to induce stress in social animals such as monkeys is reorganizing their social groupings. Inducing social stress involves re-housing animals living in groups of four or five on a monthly basis with three or four animals that they were not previously living with. This is arduous for them because it involves repeatedly re-establishing dominance hierarchies. Similarly, the parameters of the game of *Survivor* continuously shift—from working as a team against another tribe, to maintaining one's individual viability in a merged tribe, to currying the favor of a jury of players that one likely contributed to voting out of the game. Humans are social animals also, and with each shift in the game of *Survivor*, the strategic and social constraints of the situation are altered, meaning the castaways must adapt and skillfully use different social coping strategies.

In studies involving monkeys, those subjected to repeated social upheavals engage in significantly more affiliative behaviors in their new groupings than monkeys housed in stable conditions (Cohen, Kaplan, Cunnick, Manuck, and Rabin 1992). Researchers suppose that these behaviors—sitting closely, passively touching, and grooming—serve to buffer the stress of losing one's sense of one's place in a group and one's familiars. Indeed, affiliative behaviors in these monkeys are also associated with fewer stress-related adverse effects on their immune systems. Similarly, in *Survivor*, forming alliances has rather spontaneously become a predominant and extremely important gamesmanship tactic. Interestingly, forming alliances has very little to do with an individual player's ability in terms of the stated objectives of the game—outwitting, outplaying, and outlasting the competition. It likely has much more to do with social competence. In fact, in the merged-tribe phase of the game, strength may count against a player because competitors can view it as threatening. Could it be that, in addition to the strategic advantage that it confers, forming alliances is a natural response to the stress of the competition and that players crave the comfort of companionship?

In addition, socially skillful players may capitalize on this natural compulsion to affiliate. Monkeys studied in laboratories whose status within a social group is more subordinate, and therefore stressful, spend more time in body contact with other monkeys, often fearfully scanning their environment (Shively et al. 2005). Furthermore, dominant monkeys are more frequently groomed by other monkeys, perhaps as a way to keep their aggression at bay.

Another socially strategic tactic is gossiping about others. We witness castaways incessantly talking behind each others' backs. This certainly works in the interest of forming and strengthening strategic alliances, but gossiping also has been demonstrated to serve as social glue, even under ordinary circumstances where gamesmanship is not so salient. Most people gossip regularly. Psychologists believe that when we share enticing tidbits of information it helps us to form trusting relationships and solidify social bonds. We humans may be prone to engage in this type of interaction because, evolutionarily, it was adaptive to have as much information as possible about others in our social networks— whether they were rivals or potential allies or mates. In the smaller social groups in which humans evolved, understanding the minds of others in our social networks was essential in meeting the challenges of the day. These challenges were similar to those of the Survivors, functioning in a small group of others for protection but also competing with them for scarce resources. Thus, information is important in gaining and perhaps taking power from others who have higher social status. Gossip is also thought to be useful in conveying and testing the social mores of a group. When we talk about other people's behavior we get perspective on how others in our social network feel about it and learn what is and is not acceptable, which is adaptive to fitting in.

PHYSICAL STRESS

I couldn't wait to come home and eat for hours.
—JENNA, *Survivor: Amazon* and *Survivor: All-Stars*

In addition to the strategic and social challenges of the game of *Survivor*, the game is also physically grueling. The castaways are often deprived of the basics of physical subsistence: shelter, water, and food. This motivates them to improvise as best they can to obtain these necessities in primitive conditions and to succeed in the reward Challenges, which themselves are often physically challenging. Physical stressors, such as food deprivation, also alter psychological factors such as motivation and irritability, and can increase impulsive and aggressive behaviors. As alluded to before, what psychologists know about the consequences of such extreme physical stressors often comes from studies conducted decades ago. With respect to food deprivation, a classic research study using conscientious objectors during World War II was conducted to understand the biology of human starvation and the effectiveness of different diets on re-feeding people who had gone hungry during the years of the conflict (Franklin, Schiele, Brozek, and Keys 1948).

Thirty-six young men who were committed to non-violence and refused to serve in the war, largely because of their religious beliefs, volunteered to be part of this study. Most lost more than 25 percent of their body weight after undergoing six months of eating a reduced-calorie diet. They were given foods such as potatoes, turnips, and bread, similar to those that civilians in Europe had subsisted upon at the time of the war. This is quite like the single-staple carbohydrate diet of rice, maize, or manioc that Survivors consume. The research subjects, like the castaways, experienced fatigue, weakness, and apathy as a result of their semi-starvation conditions. They were also affected psychologically, becoming short-tempered, emotionally unstable, depressed, obsessed with food, and engaging in odd rituals surrounding food. One of the men, who was subsequently dropped from the study by the researchers, was caught eating scraps from the garbage. This parallels what viewers witness in *Survivor* when players have resorted to eating rats and chicken feed, paying $320 Australian in a food auction for a cheeseburger, unhesitatingly trading their only shelter for some rice and fishing hooks, or stripping for a gob of peanut butter and some chocolate.

The conscientious objectors also reported losing their sex drive as a result of their semi-starvation. Although they were enticed by being housed on a university campus where they would be in close proximity to young women, they likely did not anticipate that their focus on food would eclipse their interest in the opposite sex. Jenna and Heidi (*Survivor: Amazon*) and Jerri (*Survivor: Australian Outback*) have been accused of using their sexuality to manipulate other players, and couples Amber and Rob (*Survivor: All-Stars*) and Jenna (*Survivor: Amazon*) and Ethan (*Survivor: Africa*) have formed as a result of the show—but the absence of this sort of strategic play for the majority of players may be a result of the conditions that likely make other players less susceptible to such wiles. Whereas in other reality shows, such as *The Real World*, hooking up is often a prominent feature, in *Survivor* the sexual element is often limited to the physical attractiveness of the contestants chosen, the warm settings that promote skimpy clothing, and scandals that may occur after contestants have left the show.

PSYCHOLOGICAL STRESS

Well, that was a shock, especially since I asked Brian directly if I should plan on coming back tonight. I was given an emphatic "Yes" and "Where's your confidence?" So I guess of the three knives that are in my back right now, that one smarts the most.
—HELEN, *Survivor: Thailand*

Psychologically, succeeding in gamesmanship represents another stressor for the *Survivor* contestants. Is it better to cooperate with or cheat one's tribemates? Some would suggest that lying skillfully pays off. It did for Chris, the winner of *Survivor: Vanuatu*, who deceived tribemates that he promised he would not vote against. Creating the deception that his grandmother had died also got a lot of mileage for Jon (*Survivor: Pearl Islands*). This type of strategic gamesmanship has been studied in detail by psychologists in the laboratory in the form of a paradigm termed Prisoner's Dilemma. In this scheme, the situation is likened to two suspects in a crime being questioned separately by a prosecutor. If either suspect confesses, the charges will be dropped against the confessor and the accomplice will be prosecuted to the full extent of the law. If both confess, both will be prosecuted but offered early parole. If neither confesses, they will both be prosecuted for a lesser crime. Thus, the dilemma for each suspect is that, regardless of what the other suspect does, it is best to confess, *but* the outcome is worse when *both* confess than when both do not. In addition, each individual's best outcome results when they do not confess, but, if their partner also does not confess, their personal outcome is worse than if they had confessed. In the laboratory, research subjects participate in variations of this setup (for instance, with a parallel scheme of monetary rewards) over a series of trials. Thus, on subsequent trials players have the opportunity to "punish" or "reward" their opponent for "defecting" (analogous to not confessing) or "cooperating" (analogous to confessing).

It appears that Survivors are in a similar dilemma when they interact with other members of the tribe. For instance, if a player badmouths or forms an alliance against a particular tribe member, he may certainly gain, because this might sway other tribe members to vote with him against that particular tribe member. However, the risk that a player takes in doing this is, if his behavior incurs that tribe member's wrath, that tribe member and others may end up voting against him, either at Tribal Council or as a Jury member. One contestant, however, managed to exempt himself from this dilemma: Sean (*Survivor: Borneo*) used an "alphabet voting" strategy based on the alphabetical order of the players' names. By doing so, he may have sheltered himself from the cycle of reward and punishment voting by other tribe members, even though his strategy, conveniently, meant voting against former members of the opposing team in the merged tribe. On the other hand, by using the alphabet-voting strategy, rather than, say, deciding to flip a coin at each vote, Sean allowed his voting to be entirely predictable, making himself vulnerable to players who knew when "their number was up."

I was so over having people in my face 24/7.
—SCOUT, *Survivor: Vanuatu*

The castaways are also exposed to psychological stressors once they leave the show by continuing to be subject to public scrutiny. Indiscretions, tangles with the law, faults, and failings are widely trumpeted. Some former contestants have capitalized on their fame by parlaying it into commercial appearances, book deals, acting jobs, centerfolds, and televised weddings. However, the flipside for others has been the intrusion of heckling, hate mail, sex-tape scandals, and even posttraumatic stress. Psychologists thoroughly screen potential contestants before they are considered for the show, and they are also involved in debriefing and counseling contestants once they have been voted off and when the show airs. Still, psychologists are wary about the impact that being on a reality series can have on the players, and the position that psychologists place themselves in ethically when they serve as consultants to reality TV shows.

One question is where the responsibility of the psychologist ends and that of the show's producers begins. Ethically, psychologists must respect the rights and dignity of individuals, but contestants often lose their dignity as part of the show and must agree to waive some of their rights to enter the competition. In *The Contender,* a reality series involving boxing, a contestant committed suicide after the series had been filmed but before it had premiered. Although most accounts purport that his death had little to do with his involvement in the show, this tragic outcome may give pause to psychologists involved in screening potential contestants for reality TV.

It's a million dollars. . . . Challenge me mentally, physically, it don't matter!
—CHRIS, *Survivor: Vanuatu*, audition tape

Some may acknowledge that the game puts the players at risk of suffering the consequences of stressors, but maintain that the possible rewards of significant prize money make these risks worth it. This is, of course, one of the main incentives for players to leave their homes, families, and jobs and challenge themselves to the rigors of the game—and to be filmed while doing so. From the point of view of psychological researchers, however, such rewards cannot be appropriately offered in the research situation, especially if they might be used to induce potential research participants to do things that are unnecessarily arduous, stressful, or risky. It is permissible for research participants to be compensated for their time, and to some extent to be paid more for being involved in more taxing studies. However, there is great concern that offering incentives that are too high would be coercive and exploitative if it encouraged people to subject themselves to things that were against their best interests. This is another reason why contemporary researchers cannot induce extremely stressful conditions in their studies. Even if it were possible ethically to subject people to extreme conditions, it is unlikely that anyone who is psychologically healthy would volunteer for such an experiment without the prospect of a large reward. The young men who signed up for the semi-starvation study were somewhat unique in that they were firmly committed to alternatives to going to war, wanted to prove their mettle, and felt that they were contributing to an important cause. When interviewed years later about their involvement, these men were emphatic that if they had the choice they would do it all over again.

Some would argue that, for individuals who freely make the choice to be part of a reality series and endure its rigors, but win a lot of prize money, the payoff is worth it. This is up to the judgment of the individual winners. In contrast, psychologists, who have studied the effects of good and poor fortune on people's well-being, might caution that such compensation may not be as rewarding as it seems. People who come into large sums of money, such as lottery winners, certainly report positive outcomes as a result, such as an improved and stable quality of life (Eckblad and von der Lippe 1994). Nevertheless, the adage that money can't buy happiness was substantiated in a classic study that followed up lottery winners (Brickman, Coates, and Janoff-Bulman 1978). This investigation found that a few years later, lottery winners were about as happy as they had been before and that their level of happiness was no different than people who had never won the lottery. We see this same pattern with everyday wealth. More recent research shows that income is indeed related to well-being, but only weakly (Kahneman, Krueger, Schkade, Schwarz, and Stone 2006). In general, humans are poor at forecasting their emotional reactions to future events. Thus, people who sign up for a reality series may not accurately anticipate what their actual reaction to winning might be.

> It's been the most amazing experience of my entire life.
> —JENNIFER, Survivor: Palau

The good news for the majority of Survivor contestants, who will not get to take home the million dollars, is that people are particularly bad at anticipating how well they will cope with and recover emotionally from negative events (Wilson and Gilbert 2005). This is thought to be the result of a number of defense mechanisms that humans engage in, often unconsciously. These include our natural ease in explaining or making sense of events that happen to us. When an event, positive or negative, makes sense to us, this drains it of its emotional power, limiting its ability to give us pleasure or to wound us. Similarly, people also have a tendency to want to view themselves as consistent, rational, coherent beings whose beliefs and attitudes are in line with how they behave. Because they are motivated to reduce any "dissonance" or discrepancies in their beliefs and behavior, there is a tendency to adjust their beliefs as a result of behaving in a way that is not consistent with them (Festinger and Carlsmith 1959). Thus, when people have voluntarily endured rigorous and stressful events, perhaps without a payoff, they come to believe that there was indeed some benefit for doing so. In their final words to the camera, Survivors who are voted out of the game typically refer enthusiastically to benefits other than winning—such as learning a lot, having a great experience, getting to know exceptional people, keeping their integrity, or even getting to go home. Psychologists who may have feared for the castaways can only view this human resilience in the face of such demanding challenges with fascination and optimism.

ANNE MOYER earned her Ph.D. from Yale University and is an assistant professor at Stony Brook University. She studies psychosocial issues surrounding cancer and cancer risk. She is also interested in research methodology and methods of synthesizing research. As a social and health psychologist, she is fortunate to be able to refer to her fascination with reality TV as "research."

REFERENCES

Brickman, P., D. Coates, and R. Janoff-Bulman. "Lottery Winners and Accident Victims: Is Happiness Relative?" *Journal of Personality and Social Psychology* 36 (1978): 917–927.

Cohen, S., J. R. Kaplan, J. E. Cunnick, S. B. Manuck, and B. S. Rabin. "Chronic Social Stress, Affiliation, and Cellular Immune Response in Nonhuman Primates." *Psychological Science* 3 (1992): 301–304.

Eckblad, G. F. and A. L. von der Lippe. "Norwegian Lottery Winners: Cautious Realists." *Journal of Gambling Studies* 10 (1994): 305–322.

Festinger, L. and J. M. Carlsmith. "Cognitive Consequences of Forced Compliance." *Journal of Abnormal and Social Psychology* 58 (1959): 203–210.

Franklin, J. C., B. C. Schiele, J. Brozek, and A. Keys. "Observations of Human Behavior in Experimental Semistarvation and Rehabilitation." *Journal of Clinical Psychology* 4 (1948): 28–45.

Haney, C., C. Banks, and P. Zimbardo. "Interpersonal Dynamics in a Simulated Prison." *International Journal of Criminology and Penology* 1, no. 1 (1973): 69–97.

Kahneman, D., A. B. Krueger, D. Schkade, N. Schwarz, and A. A. Stone. "Would You Be Happier if You Were Richer? A Focusing Illusion." *Science* 312 (2006): 1908–1910.

Milgram, S. "Behavioral Study of Obedience." *Journal of Abnormal and Social Psychology* 67 (1963): 371–378.

Shively, C. A., T. C. Register, D. P. Friedman, T. M. Morgan, J. Thompson, and T. Lanier. "Social Stress-associated Depression in Adult Female Cynomolgus Monkeys (Macaca Fascicularis)." *Biological Psychology* 69 (2005): 67–84.

Wilson, T. D. and D. T. Gilbert. "Affective Forecasting: Knowing What to Want." *Current Directions in Psychological Science* 14 (2005): 131–134.

The drama of Survivor *often flows from the contestants' intense displays of "attraction and animosity." Amanda Dykema-Engblade argues that contestants experience unusual levels of physiological arousal. That enduring arousal has consequences that help explain the intensity of* Survivor *emotions. That enduring arousal also makes it quite likely that contestants will misunderstand the origins of those particular emotions.*

Lights! Camera! Attraction?

The Association between Arousal and Heightened Emotions on *Survivor*

AMANDA DYKEMA-ENGBLADE, PH.D.

What makes for great reality television? Really great reality shows could be described as disasters from which you just cannot turn away. But what are the elements of these televised train wrecks that cause us to slow down on our way past, craning our necks to see just a little more of the mess for just a little longer? It's not blood and gore, but the human drama that pulls us in. Both interpersonal attraction and animosity play pivotal roles in that drama. Thus, a relevant question concerning *Survivor* is the following: are the levels of attraction and animosity displayed on *Survivor* (or other reality shows) more intense than what everyday (non-televised) people experience during the course of "normal life"? This is really an empirical question best answered through the use of experimental methodology. However, since Mark Burnett is unlikely to give us full access to his next cast, we will have to settle for a post-hoc strategy instead.

Survivor contestants go to extremes when it comes to loving or loathing each other. Why might this be the case? One explanation for the range and intensity of emotions displayed on the show is arousal (of the physiological variety—sweaty palms, racing heart, rapid breathing,

83

etc.). Psychologists have been studying the role physiological arousal plays in our lives for years. Thanks to this research, we know that emotions can be intensified by arousal. We also know that as human beings, we often make mental mistakes when we are trying to pinpoint the cause of our arousal—something psychologists refer to as misattribution of arousal. We can apply this research to *Survivor* and shed some light on the range and intensity of emotions that are experienced on the show.

DEFINITIONAL CONSIDERATIONS

To understand the prevalence of arousal on *Survivor*, it is necessary to define and expand on this term. When I discuss arousal in this chapter I am referring to sympathetic arousal, which is determined by activity in the *sympathetic nervous system* (part of the peripheral nervous system). In general, the sympathetic nervous system is responsible for speeding things up (e.g., heart rate, blood pressure, and breathing). You may have heard this referred to as a "fight or flight" response. Your sympathetic nervous system kicks in under a number of conditions: For example, think of how your heart races after a near-collision with another automobile. Or, imagine how your body feels just before a public speaking event. According to Wade and Tavris (2006) the sympathetic nervous system ". . . acts like the accelerator of a car, mobilizing the body for action, and output of energy" (104).

Emotions, on the other hand, are more complex. Psychologists generally define emotions as consisting of three parts: physiological changes, thoughts, and a behavioral expression of the emotion. Emotions include such complex feelings as fear, joy, disgust, sadness, surprise, contempt, and anger. Most researchers believe that biology plays a role in emotions, and that such emotions are universal (Wade and Tavris 2006). In other words, it does not matter whether you are on Vanuatu or the Pearl Islands, happy is happy and sad is sad.

SOME THEORIES ON AROUSAL AND EMOTION

Schachter and Singer's (1962) two-factor theory of emotion can tell us a lot about feelings of attraction and animosity. These two researchers argued that physiologically, all of our emotions are similar. For example, whether you are angry or in love, you will probably experience sweaty palms and a racing heart, despite the fact that we experience these emotions in such different ways. So what keeps us from confusing anger and lust? According to Schachter and Singer, we look for cues in our environment to tell us how we should label our arousal. If your heart is racing and you are breathing rapidly, and a bear is in pursuit, you should probably label this physiological response as fear. On the other hand, if your heart is racing and you are breathing rapidly, and you are seated next to Brad Pitt (or Jeff Probst or Ethan!), you would likely label this physiological response as attraction. The two-factor theory suggests that physiological responses alone are unable to generate true emotional responses; the process of labeling these responses, referred to as *cognitive appraisal*, also plays a role.

In a study conducted to test the two-factor theory, Schachter and Singer (1962) injected people with epinephrine (also known as adrenaline), a drug that is known to produce a racing heart and labored breathing. Half of the participants were informed about the drug's side effects (i.e., racing heart, labored breathing) while the other half were not told what to expect. Those who were not told what to expect were heavily influenced by the presence of an angry or euphoric research accomplice. In other words, people who knew what to expect from being injected with epinephrine attributed their physiological response (racing heart, labored breathing) to the drug. These participants probably thought, "Okay, my heart is racing and I feel excitable, but this makes sense because these are the side effects of epinephrine." On the other hand, participants who were uninformed about the side effects looked for cues in their environment to explain their physiological response. These participants probably thought something along these lines: "Okay, my heart is racing and I feel excitable and there is a man singing and dancing the hula on a table; I must be happy" or "Okay, my heart is racing and I feel excitable and there is a man slamming his fist on a table and yelling; I must be angry."

Related to the two-factor theory is *misattribution of arousal* or *excitation transfer* (e.g., Schachter and Singer 1962; Zillmann et al. 1972). The notion behind misattribution of arousal is that you attribute your arousal to the wrong source. Politicians and political conventions capitalize on this idea. At many political conventions, "feel good" music is playing, confetti is dropping from above, and people are wildly waving rally signs, singing, and cheering. Chances are you are feeling pretty good being surrounded by such an uplifting and contagious atmosphere. In this situation, the source of your arousal is likely all the peripheral events (music, confetti, rally signs) at the convention. However, you might mislabel the source of your arousal as good feelings toward the political candidate. In this instance, excitement from being a part of the group has transferred to the candidate. The hit show *The Bachelor* offers another example of misattributing the source of one's arousal. Are the bachelors or bachelorettes really all in love with the same person? Or are they just pumped up about being on national television, traveling all over on a romantic getaway, and competing with each other? During the first episode of each season it is common to see contestants who are sent away in tears after only speaking with the bachelor/bachelorette for five minutes. One man even fainted while waiting to hear if he had been selected by the beautiful bachelorette. Do they really think they just lost their soulmate, or are they misattributing the source of their arousal? This, however, is a discussion for another chapter altogether.

Dutton and Aron (1974) designed a study to empirically test Schachter and Singer's theory. These researchers had male participants cross either a shaky suspension bridge (high-arousing activity; sound like a *Survivor* Challenge?) or a sturdy bridge (low-arousing activity). Halfway across the bridge, participants were approached by an attractive research accomplice who asked them to complete a survey. After making it across, participants who crossed the shaky suspension bridge reported more attraction toward the female research accomplice (and wrote stories that contained more sexual content) than those participants who crossed a sturdy bridge. Presumably, male participants believed the female confederate to be the true source of their arousal. Imagine their thoughts going something like this: "Wow! My heart is racing. It must be because of that cute psychologist giving surveys! She is hot! I bet she is into me!"

In other experimental work, White and colleagues (1981) aroused male participants in one of three ways: having the participants run in place, listen to a comedy routine, or listen to a (improvised) gruesome killing. Regardless of the source of the arousal, participants expressed more interest in a physically attractive female than did a control group of males—apparently because they misattributed their residual arousal as love (or attraction).

There is also evidence to suggest that arousal intensifies any emotion (e.g., Allen et al. 1989). Thus, if you are in love and take the object of your affection on a roller coaster ride, you should feel the emotion of love even more intensely after the ride than you did before. Allen and colleagues (1989) have shown that people stepping off a piece of exercise equipment report higher levels of attraction toward an opposite-sex person than an individual not physiologically aroused from working out. This appeared to be the case even when participants were aware that the source of their arousal stemmed from working out. Likewise, if you are angry with someone you should feel even angrier after working out. Whatever emotion you are experiencing, that emotion is exacerbated when you are physiologically aroused. This is known as the *response facilitation model* and can occur even if one is aware of the source of her or his arousal (Allen et al. 1989). For readers familiar with social facilitation (the strengthening of one's dominant response when in the presence of people [Zajonc 1969]), response facilitation is an analogous concept (the strengthening of one's emotion when aroused). To apply response facilitation to the political convention described above, if you already feel positively toward the candidate then the infectious convention atmosphere should only serve to strengthen those previously existing feelings.

To recap, the response facilitation perspective (Allen et al. 1989) argues that arousal intensifies whatever emotion you are currently experiencing, while misattribution of arousal (Schachter and Singer 1962) should only occur when an individual is unaware of the true source of her or his arousal.

AROUSAL ON *SURVIVOR*

So by now you are probably wondering: what does all this have to do with the television show *Survivor*? Forget political conventions and roller coasters; just tell me why Jerri can't get along with anyone! And more important, why did Amber and Rob fall in love during *Survivor: All-Stars*? Let's take some of the research outlined above and apply it to *Survivor*.

ATTRACTION

The link between arousal and emotion is one of many potential explanations for why people are attracted to one another in real life and on *Survivor*. Many theories of attraction have been proposed to explain how and why we become attracted to others, including such ideas as physical proximity (you like them because they work in the cubicle next to you and you see them a lot) and similarity (you like them because you both like watching *Survivor*) (Myers 2005). While these theories have their merits, when it comes to *Survivor*, arousal seems like the most likely culprit.

The most blatant demonstration of attraction on the show was the relationship (or alliance) between "Boston Rob" and Amber (*Survivor: All-Stars*). (There was speculation that Greg and Colleen [season one, *Survivor: Borneo*] also had a relationship, but they both deny it.) For those researchers studying arousal and emotions, Amber and Rob's relationship might not come as such a big surprise. A more in-depth explanation of the excitation transfer theory is appropriate here. This theory uses the general framework of the two-factor theory (Schachter and Singer 1962) but specifically explains the development of attraction. The excitation transfer theory (Zillman 1971) posits that the physiological response accompanying an arousing activity and/or experience does not dissipate immediately but instead gradually diminishes, resulting in "arousal residue." During the period of arousal residue a person who encounters another emotional situation may misattribute her or his (residual) emotions to the current situation. Consequently, the subsequent emotional situation might be perceived more intensely than it would otherwise. The arousal decays slowly and transfers to the new event/situation (Tannenbaum and Zillman 1975). In other words, people misattribute the residual arousal to the current source rather than the originating source.

Recall from *Survivor: All-Stars* when Boston Rob won a reward Challenge, was presented with a brand-new truck, and was told that he could select another contestant to accompany him to the drive-in movies in his new truck. As a surprise to no one, Rob chose Amber. When the two arrived at the drive-in "theater," host Jeff Probst informed them that he had another surprise in store: he led Amber around some bushes to reveal a new car for her, too. Naturally, Amber was thrilled about receiving a new car—she hugged Rob, and they both shouted and jumped around together. Shortly after the Challenge (an arousing activity in and of itself) and receiving the new cars, Rob and Amber snuggled into the back of Rob's new truck. Amber and Rob were all smiles and reported that they were having the best time and were really enjoying one another's company. The physiological response to winning a reward Challenge and then receiving new cars likely did not cease immediately. Indeed, one would expect the arousal associated with such excitement to remain for quite some time. One of two things might have happened in this case: one, Rob and Amber were misattributing their arousal from the Challenge and the new cars (originating source) as love and/or attraction toward each other (excitation transfer theory/misattribution of arousal); or, two, the residual arousal caused them to experience their current state of love/attraction more intensely even though they were aware that the true source of their arousal was a consequence of the Challenge (response-facilitation).

Rob and Amber had many other arousing situations during the show to strengthen their emotional experiences. They were the last two Survivors remaining on the island (the camera revealed them holding hands), they were constantly engaged in Challenges (reward and Immunity), and they were involved in elaborate schemes that included making several different groups believe that they were in an alliance with them. At one point during the season, Amber expressed concern to Rob about trying to maintain alliances with so many different people.

One could also make the case that misattribution of arousal or response facilitation might occur independent of winning reward (or Immunity) Challenges and cars. Indeed, it is not too difficult to imagine that simply being a contestant on the show is an arousing experience all on its own. Contestants are required to live amongst a group of relative strangers while in a foreign land. As if that were not enough, Survivors engage in constant competition (Immunity and reward Challenges) all while being video recorded around the clock so that a national audience can scrutinize all their actions. Is your heart racing yet? No? Well, there is always the added incentive of trying to win a million dollars, and the arousal elicited by all the snakes, rats, spiders, and other critters that call the *Survivor* sites home. The combination of all of these events is enough to raise anyone's blood pressure.

Walster (1971) and Berscheid and Walster (1974) argued that high arousal will produce emotions of love as long as a person attributes her or his "state" to passion. When cues in the environment allow for a "passion-appropriate label," a person's emotion is likely to be labeled as love. After "starring" in *Survivor*, Amber and Boston Rob went on to do interviews with Jay Leno and David Letterman, and they appeared on *The View* (of course, they did not get to host the show like Elisabeth Hasselbeck [*Survivor: Australian Outback*]). They were also featured in magazines such as *People* and *TV Guide*. After competing in *Survivor*, the duo decided to test their luck on the reality show *Amazing Race*. Also, don't forget the excitement associated with winning a million dollars! As long as Rob and Amber continue to traipse all over the country conducting interviews and competing in other reality shows, and as long as they continue to label the arousal associated with such events as love for one another, then it is unlikely that their romance will wane (i.e., don't expect Amber to don an "I Hate Rob" T-shirt anytime soon).

ANIMOSITY

Where to begin? In a nutshell, people do not always get along well on the show. What follows are a few selected highlights from various *Survivor* seasons. Would the players have behaved as outrageously in their "regular" lives? It is hard to say, but again misattribution of arousal and the response-facilitation model offer plausible explanations for the sheer amount of hostility that occurs on the show. During *Survivor: All-Stars* (the season described by Jeff Probst as "the most emotionally charged *Survivor* ever") Jenna said that Shii Ann was driving her crazy and that every time she opened her mouth, Jenna wanted to place a gun in it.

Who could forget Sue's heated speech (take your pick: season one or *Survivor: All-Stars*)? In *Survivor: All-Stars*, Sue was rightfully outraged that

Richard Hatch rubbed his genitals against her during an Immunity Challenge (in case you burned the memory from your mind, Richard Hatch loved to navigate the island nude). When host Jeff Probst questioned Sue about the event, Sue made an impassioned speech saying something along the lines of the following: "I was sexually violated to have some guy come up. . . . He went too far, he crossed the line, and he crossed the line with me. . . . I was violated, humiliated, dehumanized, and totally disrespected. Jeff, I'm spent and I'm done with this game and there is no way I can continue with my emotions pushed to the ground this much." Sue made a decision to withdraw from the game. Alicia told the camera that Sue "couldn't control her tears; she couldn't control her anger."

In season one, Sue made the now infamous "vulture speech" when she was allowed to speak her mind as to who should be the million dollar winner ("naked" Richard, or Kelly). During the reunion episode, Sue admitted that she was "pissed" at the time of the speech. Similarly, during the *Survivor: All-Stars* reunion episode, Sue said, "It takes too much emotion to play this game."

During *Survivor: Australian Outback*, an irritated Colby threw a bucket of water on Jerri, Jerri argued with Keith about fried "green" tomatoes, Kimmi and Alicia argued over slaughtering chickens, and Alicia told Kimmi, "I'm tired of you and the f***ing chickens!" Kimmi told Alicia not to wave her finger in her face; Alicia responded with "I will always wave my finger in your face!" I don't know what that means exactly, but the finger waving was a consequence of anger. Rupert (uncharacteristically) also lost his temper when Shawn lost the fishing spear (*Survivor: Pearl Islands*).

In *Survivor: Thailand*, Robb literally strangled Clay during a reward Challenge, an outburst that can be seen as even more impulsive because Robb broke the ground rules for the Challenge by attacking in the "no attack" zone (apparently it was permissible to strangle another tribesperson as long as you were in the "attack" zone). Robb's aggressive play led to several copycat instances where people behaved aggressively both in the "attack" and in the "no attack" zones. Robb's aggressive behavior was likely exacerbated because of his heightened state of arousal that resulted from trying to win a reward Challenge.

GENERAL EMOTIONS (NOT NECESSARILY ATTRACTION OR ANIMOSITY)

In *Survivor: All-Stars*, former million-dollar winner Jenna decided to withdraw from the competition to return to her mother who was dying of cancer. Obviously this was terribly sad news, but almost all of the castaways were crying when they heard about Jenna's mother. Certainly the Survivors are human and would be saddened by such news, but it is my belief that they were all more emotional than normal because they were aroused by the immunity task they each faced.

During *Survivor* it has become customary for the participants to receive a letter and/or video from home. Many of the Survivors are emotional even before watching the video or reading the letter. They cry for themselves, they cry for their tribemates—it is an emotional experience (even for the viewer). Now, thirty-nine days is a long time, but it is not that long. Would these Survivors have the same reaction if they were watching the videos in their dormitory rooms or from the comfort of home? It is possible but seems improbable. Perhaps there is something about the arousing activities on *Survivor* that makes receiving such videos and letters more touching. Even macho Boston Rob reported that he did not remember feeling ". . . this emotional about anything—ever" prior to receiving his letter and video from home. Speaking of which, who could forget Jenna's broken heart in season one when she did not receive a letter from her daughters? She was devastated (as was I).

During *Survivor: All-Stars*, Jenna took a helicopter trip with Amber and Rupert (Rupert won a reward Challenge and invited Jenna and Amber along). While flying in the helicopter, Jenna remarked, "How come I get so emotional out here?" The baseline level of arousal is likely pretty high on this show, making all the Survivors' emotions more pronounced. Again, response facilitation can speak to the intense emotions experienced on the show.

Many contestants on *Survivor* report that this was the "happiest" (Alicia in *Survivor: All-Stars* after winning a team Challenge) or "most excited I've ever been in my life" (Jerri in *Survivor: Australian Outback* when the tribe received a food basket). Obviously there is some hyperbole involved when contestants describe their emotional states;

however, their emotions probably do seem more intense on the show than in real life.

CONCLUSION

Hopefully, I have opened you up to the possibility that contestants on *Survivor* experience emotions more intensely than non-televised people because their levels of physiological arousal are almost always high on the show. I hope also that you entertained the idea that misattribution of arousal or excitation transfer are plausible explanations for Amber and Boston Rob's romantic relationship. Next time you are watching *Survivor*, reflect for a moment on whether a person would be so angry (or happy, or excited, or in some cases even so in love) if there were not an excessive amount of arousal-inducing stimuli in the environment. Understanding misattribution of arousal and the association between arousal and heightened emotions may forever change the way you view reality television.

———————

AMANDA DYKEMA-ENGBLADE, PH.D., is an assistant professor of psychology at Northeastern Illinois University in Chicago. She earned her doctorate in social psychology from Loyola University, Chicago. Her primary research interests include small group performance and decision-making. She teaches courses in statistics, research methods, social psychology, and industrial-organizational psychology.

REFERENCES

Allen, J., D. Kenrick, D. Linder, and M. McCall. "Arousal and Attraction: A Response-facilitaton Alternative to Misattribution and Negative Reinforcement Models." *Journal of Personality and Social Psychology* (1989): 261–270.

Berscheid, E. and E. Walster. "A Little Bit About Love." In *Foundations of Interpersonal Attraction*, edited by T. Hudson (pp. 355–381). New York: Academic Press, 1974.

Dutton, D. G. and A. P. Aron. "Some Evidence for Heightened Sexual Attraction Under Conditions of High Anxiety." *Journal of Personality and Social Psychology* 23 (1974): 510–517.

Myers, D. *Psychology*. 5th ed. New York: Worth Publishers, 1998.

Myers, D. *Social Psychology*. 8th ed. Boston: McGraw-Hill, 2005.

Schachter, S. and J. E. Singer. "Cognitive, Social, and Physiological Determinants of Emotional State." *Psychological Review* 69 (1962): 379–399.

Tannenbaum, P. and D. Zillman. "Emotional Arousal in the Facilitation of Aggression Through Communication." *Advances in Experimental Social Psychology* 8 (1975): 150–188.

Wade, C. and C. Tavris. *Psychology*. 8th ed. Upper Saddle River, NJ: Prentice Hall, 2006.

Walster, E. "Passionate Love." In *Theories of Attraction and Love*, edited by B. I. Murstein. New York: Springer, 1971.

White, G., S. Fishbein, and J. Rutstein. "Passionate Love and the Misattribution of Arousal." *Journal of Personality and Social Psychology* 41(1981): 56–62.

Zajonc, R. B., A. Heingartner, and E. M. Herman. "Social Enhancement and Impairment of Performance in the Cockroach." *Journal of Personality and Social Psychology* 13 (1969): 83–92.

Zillmann, D. "Excitation Transfer in Communication-mediated Aggressive Behavior." *Journal of Experimental Social Psychology* 7 (1971): 419–434.

Zillmann, D., A. H. Katcher, and B. Milavshky. "Excitation Transfer from Physical Exercise to Subsequent Aggressive Behavior." *Journal of Experimental Social Psychology* 8 (1972): 247–259.

How was Richard Hatch able to win Survivor's first season? Vivian Zayas explores aspects of Hatch's personality that allowed him to succeed. Zayas explains the complexities of how personalities and situations interact to give rise to individuals' behaviors. On that analysis, Survivor provided a highly favorable situation in which Richard Hatch's distinctive personality could lead him to victory.

Outwit, Outplay, and Outlast

What Role Did Richard Hatch's Personality Play in His Victory as the First *Survivor*?

VIVIAN ZAYAS, PH.D.

Perhaps what captivates us most about the show *Survivor* is that remarkably, despite all the outlandish situations that participants encounter (when was the last time you ate roasted rat for lunch?), the show parallels real life. So, when Colleen asks Richard Hatch and Kelly Wiglesworth in the finale of the first season, "For myself and for future players of this game, what three character traits do you think got you where you are and you think are essential and important to be where you are at this point?", the question goes beyond the game of *Survivor*. Colleen might as well have been asking what character traits or aspects of one's personality help a person succeed in life, and conversely, what aspects might contribute to one's failures. Perhaps attempting to answer Colleen's question will provide insight on the role of personality in the game *Survivor* as well as its role in real-life situations.

The rules of the game are simple: outwit, outplay, and outlast the fifteen other contestants in order to be the last lone Survivor and to walk away with 1 million dollars at the end of the season. Arguably, to survive, one needs to have the physical and mental abilities to win the Immunity Challenges that exempt one from having votes cast against oneself in

Tribal Council. Initially, the contestants work together in teams to win the Challenges. Halfway through the game, the two tribes merge and the game shifts to individual competitions, making every person fend for him- or herself. In addition to physical and mental abilities, surviving requires a high degree of social skill. Every three days, the Tribal Council meets and one member gets voted off the island. So, one needs to be skilled in social interaction in order to form social and personal bonds with individuals with whom one is simultaneously competing with and against. This is particularly important after the merge, when a Tribal Jury of voted-off members begins to form. Each week they return to watch the Tribal Council ceremony. At the end of the game, the Tribal Jury votes for one of the members of the final two to win 1 million dollars.

Here is where the puzzle lies: Richard Hatch, the winner of the first season, was not the most physically able of the contestants. In fact, out of the twelve individual Challenges, he only won one. Richard was also not the most liked. He was perceived as arrogant and overly confident, and even picked by some to be one of the first to get voted off the island. So, at least at the surface level, it is difficult to pinpoint what particular characteristics contributed to his success. This essay will apply modern-day research and theory in personality psychology to explore whether and how Richard's personality contributed to his success in the first season of the show *Survivor*.

WHAT IS PERSONALITY?

Before trying to understand what personality characteristics contributed to Richard's success, we first have to take a moment to think about what we mean by "personality." Imagine asking a good friend the question "What is personality?" The first thing you might notice is that the question makes sense. The friend doesn't look at you in a perplexed manner and say "Personality? What's that?" This is because intuitively most people believe that personality exists and also have certain beliefs about the role of personality in everyday life.

Your beliefs about personality are most likely based on your perceptions, which are subjective, at times biased and incomplete, and with some frequency lead to faulty conclusions. On the other hand, your

beliefs are based on a multitude of personal observations and, most of
the time, they are very effective in helping you understand other people's
behaviors and intentions and figuring out "What makes a person tick?"
This is where personality psychology comes into the picture. Personality
psychology is the scientific study of the individual and systematic differences between individuals. Instead of relying on subjective beliefs, intu-
itions, and assumptions, personality psychologists use the scientific
method to test hypotheses about the structure and processes of personality. Like other disciplines, personality psychologists use the tools of
science, such as research designs and methodologies, statistical tests,
and empirical data to build a theory about the psychology of the individual. What many people might be surprised to learn is that psychologists have had long and heated debates about what personality is, what
it predicts, how it interacts with one's environment, and at one time,
whether it even exists!

Despite differences in perspectives, a shared assumption among personality psychologists is that each person possesses a personality—the
unique and stable psychological characteristics of a person that describe
and explain his or her consistent patterns of feeling, thinking, and
behaving. Each individual's personality is the culmination of his or her
genetic makeup, biology, early life experiences, learning, and culture.
Therefore, no two people have the same personality. Even monozygotic
(identical) twins who share the same genetic material encounter different environmental influences and will develop distinct personalities.

THE ROLE OF SITUATIONS ON BEHAVIOR

Although one's behavior may be influenced by personal characteristics,
a person is also profoundly influenced by the particulars of his or her
environment. In fact, when the creators of *Survivor* devised the
Immunity and reward Challenges, as well as the bounty given to the vic-
tors, they capitalized on this idea. They knew, for example, that eating
live maggots would elicit strong reactions of disgust and repulsion for all
contestants, whereas eating an eight-course catered dinner over candle-
light would be highly desired.

A recurrent controversy in the study of personality has been coined the "person vs. situation" debate (Ross and Nisbett 1991). It centers on the question: To what extent is a person's behavior influenced by his or her personality versus situational factors? Although most psychologists adhere to a view that lies somewhere in the middle—acknowledging that both the characteristics of the person and the situation influence behavior—one goal of personality psychology has been to isolate the contribution of personality on an individual's behavior.

THE CONTESTANTS SHAPE THEIR SITUATIONS

A difficulty in teasing apart the effect of personality from that of the situation is that the two are intricately intertwined. People continuously shape—actively and passively, knowingly and unknowingly—the situations they encounter in the future (e.g., Buss 1987). For example, people select certain people (and not others) to be their friends and lifelong partners, they select certain professions and hobbies, and they select certain activities (and not others). Even when people aren't actively shaping their environments, their personal and physical qualities—especially those that are clearly visible to others—heavily influence how people will respond to them. Finally, on those occasions when people encounter what appears to be the same situation, they shape their situation by how they interpret and react to it. Ultimately, what is most predictive of what a person will do is based not on the "objective" situation, but on the "psychological" one (i.e., how the person interprets the situation).

Most fascinating are personality-situation linkages; the situations that a person creates for him- or herself reflect something about his or her personality. An example is that of an extremely sociable person, like Gervase Peterson, the charismatic member of the Pagong tribe. Compared to someone who was less sociable and outgoing (like Rudy Boesch, the ex-marine), Gervase encountered many more situations that involved socializing with others. For example, to relax, Gervase played cards and chatted with teammates. Because of his outward-directed energy and lighthearted demeanor, other members of his tribe also sought his company.

SURVIVOR AS THE PERFECT NATURALISTIC STUDY

Arguably, the show *Survivor* is an ideal opportunity for examining the interplay between personality and the situation in a naturally occurring setting. Sixteen people were abandoned in the middle of the South China Sea off the coast of Borneo, a desolate island. Each participant faced a seemingly similar situation: adapt to island environment, create a new civilization, meet physical and mental challenges, navigate social relationships, and attempt to be the last lone Survivor. Each was allowed to bring onto the island only one personal item. But the most important thing that they brought to the island was themselves. What personality factors made some people successful at the game and others not?

THE ALLIANCE

Any analysis of why Richard was successful in the first season of *Survivor* has to involve some discussion of the alliance he formed. Forming the alliance, and deciding whom to include and exclude in it, was a critical strategy for playing the game. By building a voting bloc, the members of the alliance simultaneously ensured that each of them would not be voted off the island and that they would decide, by coordinating their votes, who would be voted off. It was this alliance that propelled Richard into the finals. And the members of the alliance, although originally bonded by their pursuit of self-interests, developed what appeared to be genuine feelings of trust and positive regard toward one another. So, even when the alliance disbanded toward the end of the season, bonds between members lingered, giving Richard a two-vote advantage over Kelly in the final deciding vote.

The alliance that Richard formed effectively had an enormous impact on the game because it shaped the situations that every contestant on the island faced. By controlling who got voted off, the alliance minimized the effect of each individual's personal characteristics. For example, it didn't really matter if someone was liked, the most intelligent, or the most physically able. What mattered most was whom the alliance viewed as a potential threat to be eliminated.

The fact that Richard was the mastermind behind the formation of the alliance was not an accident. It was a reflection of his personality. As mentioned earlier, people shape the situations they encounter, and the situations they create for themselves both reflect and reinforce their personal characteristics. What aspects of Richard's personality contributed to the formation of the alliance and thereby led to his success on the show?

TRAIT APPROACHES

From the first episode of season one, you, like other viewers and like the contestants themselves, started forming an impression of each of the participants on the show. For example, given the physical nature of the reward and Immunity Challenges, you may have been very aware of the physical attributes, such as age, gender, race, and attractiveness, of each of the contestants. Perhaps you were not surprised when Sonja, the oldest woman on Tagi, stumbled in the first reward/Immunity Challenge—a mistake that arguably caused her team to lose the first Challenge and which resulted in her expulsion from the tribe at Tribal Council. You might have also learned other general information about each contestant, such as his or her hometown, occupation, whether he or she was married and had children, and so on. You quickly learned that Rudy Boesch was an ex-marine, that Jenna Lewis had twin daughters, that Richard Hatch was a gay corporate trainer, that Sue Hawk was a trucker from Waukesha, Wisconsin, and that Dirk Been was a devout Christian.

In these initial encounters, you started forming an impression of each contestant's personality based on the general information that you learned, but also by observing how each person behaved in those first moments on the island. Take, for instance, Ramona Gray, the twenty-something, black, female chemist who worked for a New Jersey pharmaceutical company. Because she was sick from the instant she landed on the island, you might have quickly formed an impression of her as weak, physically and mentally, and unable to carry her own weight. You also might have taken an immediate liking to Gervase, who chose playing cards as his one personal item, was always smiling, laughing, and telling jokes, and generally was easy to get along with. In contrast, Rudy immediately came across as "crotchety" and rubbed the women of his own tribe the wrong way by incessantly telling them what to do.

In a basic way, you've just formed an impression of the *Survivor* contestants using a trait approach of personality. A significant contribution of the trait approach is that it provides a taxonomy for describing people using a small set of broad traits. Traits are a general predisposition to engage in certain behaviors. One dominant framework within the field, called the Big Five (e.g., John 1990), assesses people on five traits: 1) openness to new experiences (e.g., intellectually curious, artistic, imaginative, daring); 2) conscientiousness (e.g., persistent, dependable, meticulous, achievement-oriented); 3) extraversion (e.g., outgoing, sociable, assertive, spontaneous); 4) agreeableness (e.g., cooperative, good-natured, trusting); and 5) neuroticism (e.g., emotionally reactive, tense, insecure, jealous). (A handy mnemonic for remembering these five traits is OCEAN.)

A central idea of this approach is that traits strongly influence how a person behaves across a wide range of situations and over time. For example, imagine that the contestants completed the Big Five personality inventory and that Richard had scored high (relative to other people) on the conscientiousness dimension, which taps into goal-directedness, self-reliance, and attention to detail. A trait theorist would predict that Richard would be highly conscientious in a variety of situations—e.g., during the reward/Immunity Challenges, at camp, and at Tribal Council.

WHO IS RICHARD HATCH?

Based on the first few days on the island, how would you describe Richard? Perhaps what struck you the most about Richard was that he came across as arrogant, condescending, and as a "know-it-all." Using the Big Five factors, perhaps you judged Richard as moderate on extraversion, high in conscientiousness and openness to new experiences, and somewhat low on neuroticism and agreeableness (certainly his tribe thought he was disagreeable when he lounged around the camp naked). You might have even thought, based on the interaction that occurred when the Tagi tribe initially landed on the island, that Richard was not going to fare very well on the show. Recall that he attempted to rally the group to discuss logistics, such as where to set up camp; but Rudy, the self-appointed expert on the matter given his experiences as a marine, quickly took over the conversation. At this time, Richard also attempted to convene a meeting to discuss the "process" of what the tribe was going to do, how they were going to do it, and why they were going to do it. The rest of the tribe, exhausted, hungry, and eager to set up camp, were not receptive to Richard or his corporate managerial style and they quickly dismissed his ideas. He was left sitting by himself on a tree, while the others walked away chuckling, saying, "We're done talking."

In a sense, the trait approach to personality describes people much like how you might describe someone you meet for the first time. The impressions formed are broad and general. So, knowing that Richard is high on conscientiousness does not seem to answer Colleen's question — what characteristics make a person successful on the show *Survivor*? Nor do such broad characterizations seem to account fully for the complexity of people's behavior.

GOING BEYOND TRAITS

Even though traits provide information about what a person is generally like across a wide range of situations, a lot still remains unknown. A problem with solely using traits as a means for predicting success on the show *Survivor* (or in other life domains) is that it doesn't appreciate the effect of the situation on behavior; the extent to which a trait is beneficial, adaptive, and advantageous will depend in part on the situation. Take, for example, the trait conscientiousness. Conscientiousness is typically considered a positive and highly desirable characteristic and has been shown to predict job performance in a variety of different occupations (Barrick and Mount 1993). But although it may serve a person well at work, conscientiousness, which encompasses the ability to control one's impulses for the sake of pursuing one's goals, is not always desirable, and in some instances may be unrelated or even negatively related to successful outcomes. So, what is important is not necessarily being high in conscientiousness in general, but being conscientious in the most appropriate situations (e.g., when planning who is going to run which leg of a race, but not necessarily when relaxing with teammates at camp).

A related point is that the trait approach describes how a person is in general, regardless of the situation he or she is in. In real life, however, a person's behavior varies from situation to situation (Mischel and Shoda 1995). For example, Richard was highly conscientious, persistent, and diligent in season one of *Survivor*. He never stopped thinking about ways to secure his place in the tribe and avoid getting voted off the island. But this doesn't necessarily mean that he was always conscientious. In one of the final Challenges, Rudy, Kelly, and Richard had to have one hand touching a wooden pole-like idol at all times. The one who remained standing without letting go of the idol won immunity, ensuring a berth into the final round. The winner would also single-handedly decide which of the two losing contestants would be voted off the island. Something remarkable happened in this Challenge: Richard, who had persisted in so many previous Challenges and situations and who had been doing everything in his control to win, let go of the wooden idol after only two hours. It was not an accident (like it was when Rudy made the "million dollar mistake" and unintentionally let go) — it was deliberate.

Because traits describe general behavioral tendencies and do not take into account the particulars of the situation, they are not always the best predictors of what a person will do in a particular situation. They can't, for example, explain why Richard let go of the wooden idol.

SOCIAL-COGNITIVE APPROACHES

Why did Richard let go of the wooden idol after he had been persistent in other situations? A goal of social-cognitive approaches (Mischel and Shoda 1995) to personality is to answer questions of this kind, specifically, to understand why a person behaves one way in one situation and in a seemingly contradictory way in another situation.

According to social-cognitive approaches, the fact that Richard's behavior varied across different situations reflects something about his personality that goes beyond traits. His behavior reflects, for example, how he interpreted and construed the particular Challenge, including the strategies that he saw available to him at that time and his evaluation of his abilities as well as the abilities of Rudy and Kelly. For example, Richard might have perceived Kelly as an athlete and fierce competitor, and with good reason. Kelly had won the last three Immunity Challenges, which had protected her from getting voted off the island. Winning the Challenge against Kelly would not have been a small feat for Richard. Richard's alliance with Rudy also probably figured prominently in his decision. If either Rudy or Richard won the Challenge, they both would go to the final round and Kelly would be voted off. But perhaps Richard thought that this was not the best situation. At this point in the season, Rudy was better liked than either Richard or Kelly. Richard might have calculated that the Jury would vote in favor of Rudy and that it was in his best interest to be in the final with Kelly. He might have also thought that it was in Kelly's best interest to be in the finals with Richard, and took a gamble that she would think the same.

In contrast to trait approaches, social-cognitive approaches focus on how "person variables" affect behaviors. Person variables refer simply to how a person thinks about a situation, including themselves and the people in it; for example: how one interprets the situation, expectations about outcomes in particular situations, emotional responses to particular events, one's goals, and the strategies and abilities one has available to achieve desired outcomes.

What implications do social-cognitive approaches have for understanding Richard's success on *Survivor*? First, person variables—because they essentially reflect how a person thinks about a situation—have a profound effect on what a person does in a particular situation, and account for why different people respond differently to a seemingly similar situation. Perhaps the best example of how individual differences in interpreting a situation influence what people do is how the contestants themselves differed in their interpretation of the game of *Survivor*, the rules, and how it should be played. At one point during the season, Richard said, "I arrived on this island at the same time as everyone else. We all saw the sign that said '*Survivor*—outwit, outplay, outlast.' That's what I've been trying to do since before I even got here, and the other fifteen people seemed to think they were on vacation." His interpretation of the game undoubtedly affected how he approached the game and the strategies he used, including the formation of the alliance. He arrived on the island armed with strategies as to how to play and be successful. Even though the other contestants were given the same information, they construed the game differently. As a result, they were ill-prepared to play *Survivor* as a game of strategy.

A second key point of social cognitive approaches is that person variables (e.g., strategies, expectations, abilities) are sensitive to the particular situation a person is in and therefore help explain why a given individual may behave in what appears to be contradictory ways from situation to situation. For example, the strategy Richard used in the wooden idol Challenge was strikingly different than the persistence he showed in the previous Challenge in which contestants had to stand on a wooden bar.

Finally, approaches to personality that incorporate psychologically important features of situations highlight the point that success in one situation, such as on the show *Survivor*, is not necessarily related to success in other situations or areas of one's life. Some contestants were successful in their respective professions: Ramona was a chemist and Sean was a doctor, and each had demonstrated the strategy and ability to be successful at work. Yet, when it came to *Survivor*, they were unsuccessful. Ramona did not have the physical stamina, and Sean, who chose to vote off members based on the order of their name in the alphabet, was naïve about the strategy and mental aspects required to play the game successfully. Similarly (but with opposite outcomes), Richard—who was successful at *Survivor*—ended up serving time in jail for tax evasion. Clearly, the skills and strategies he used to succeed in the show led to drastically different outcomes in his personal life.

WHAT ROLE DID PERSONALITY PLAY IN RICHARD'S SUCCESS IN THE FIRST SEASON OF *SURVIVOR*?

The idea that personal characteristics play a role in one's successes and failures in life is relatively unquestioned. But what are those characteristics, and are those the same characteristics needed to be successful in the game *Survivor*? Certainly, a person's behaviors (and associated successes and failures) are determined by a host of factors: his or her traits, the adaptiveness of his or her response to specific situations, his or her goals, and the situations, including people in them, that he or she encounters.

So what role did personality play in Richard's *Survivor* success?

Personality psychologists have long attempted to tease apart the effect of personality from the effect of the situation on a person's behavior. The problem with this approach is that the two are intricately intertwined. A key part of personality is the situations that a person creates for him- or herself. The formation of the alliance in the first season of *Survivor* was a manifestation of critical aspects of Richard's personality—i.e., his goals coming into the show, how he interpreted the game, his strategies, and his abilities. The formation of the alliance was particularly diagnostic of Richard's personality because at that time no one had played the game before him. Richard and the fifteen other contestants did not have the luxury that later contestants had of seeing successful strategies and lessons learned from previously played games. They were the first to play, and as a result, one could see how their unique personalities influenced *how* they played.

Finally, although Richard's personality made him successful in *Survivor*, it doesn't necessarily mean that these characteristics led to successful outcomes in other domains. Many aspects of personality are context-sensitive, and this explains why Richard was able to be successful on the show but not necessarily successful in his post-*Survivor* life. In the first season—in the specific context, at the specific time, with the specific individuals he competed against—Richard Hatch used the most adaptive and beneficial strategy, the formation of the alliance, to outwit, outplay, and outlast his fellow contestants. These qualities—the way he interpreted the game and the strategies he saw available to him—are central to contemporary theories of personality that go beyond traits, and account for the complexity of people's ever-changing behavior.

VIVIAN ZAYAS, PH.D., is an assistant professor in the psychology department at Cornell University. She completed her Ph.D. (2003) at the University of Washington, Seattle. Her research examines the cognitive-affective processes that regulate behaviors within close relationships and which may affect the quality of relationship functioning and an individual's mental health. Her research approaches the study of the individual

and his or her relationships from a multilevel interdisciplinary perspective that integrates the study of attachment
processes, research on executive control and self-regulation,
and methodology and theory from cognitive psychology and
cognitive neuroscience.

REFERENCES

Buss, D. M. "Selection, Evocation, and Manipulation." *Journal of Personality and Social Psychology* 53 (1987): 1214–1221.

Mischel, W. and Y. Shoda. "A Cognitive-affective System Theory of Personality: Reconceptualizing Situations, Dispositions, Dynamics, and Invariance in Personality Structure." *Psychological Review* 102 (1995): 246–268.

Ross, L. and R. E. Nisbett. *The Person and the Situation: Perspectives of Social Psychology.* New York: Mcgraw-Hill Book Company, 1991.

When we watch Survivor, what do we see? Ashley N. Hunt and Richard E. Heyman suggest that the producers of Survivor have created an analogue to "real life"—a laboratory of sorts—that yields a unique concentration of dramatic behaviors. Each season, the participants in this Survivor laboratory generate behaviors that allow viewers to observe and absorb classic psychological phenomena.

Survivor: A Series of Analogue Behavioral Observations

ASHLEY N. HUNT, M.A., AND RICHARD E. HEYMAN, PH.D.

Y ou can observe a lot just by watching," baseball great Yogi Berra once said. Fans of *Survivor* do indeed observe a lot just by watching the show. They see real people put into contrived but still realistic situations and then get to observe a fascinating array of individual and group behavior. What *Survivor* enthusiasts are observing is known within psychology as an "analogue behavioral observation" (ABO). In this chapter, we'll discuss what ABO is, the ways in which it is employed by the producers of *Survivor*, and the psychological principles that *Survivor's* ABOs have already taught viewers.

ANALOGUE BEHAVIORAL OBSERVATION

What does "analogue behavioral observation" refer to? "Analogue" is derived from the same root as "analogy"; an analogue is like something else. In this case, the analogue situation is like a real-life situation, one that is set up by the observer to see more intriguing things than would happen naturally. "Behavioral observation" means that the situation is set up to see how people act. Although we may also see what effect the situation has on the participants' thinking, feeling, or physiological reactions, the key focus is on observable action. Thus, in more scientific terms, ABO can be defined as "a situation designed by, manipulated by, or constrained by an assessor that elicits a measured behavior of interest" (Heyman and Slep 2004).

Studies of couples' communication are a prime example of ABOs in psychology, with hundreds of such studies in the published literature (Heyman 2001). In a typical study, psychologists bring a couple into the lab, give each of them a questionnaire (or interview), and find out what the biggest areas of conflict are (e.g., she would like him to spend more time with the children). The experimenter then brings them into a room (equipped with cameras and microphones) and asks them to discuss the problem and try to resolve it as they might at home. They are then left alone for ten to fifteen minutes as the video records. This process is often repeated for additional conflicts.

Why do psychologists do this? If you answered "because they have a theory that conflict is very important, and rather than sit around all day waiting for a conflict to occur, the experimenter sets it up so that there's a high probability that it will happen while the video is recording," you're right. What is the likelihood that a conflict would occur if the investigator watched any random fifteen-minute segment of the couple's at-home behavior? Not very high. In fact, one of the originators of this method, psychologist John Gottman, set up a wired apartment in Seattle and had couples stay for twenty-four hours. Unlike his other studies that tested theories about how couples handle conflict (e.g., Gottman 1994), Gottman saw very little conflict. There was so little that he and his colleagues had to come up with a different set of behaviors to study—things such as how one partner would try to get the other's attention and whether these attempts worked (Driver and Gottman 2004).

What does this have to do with *Survivor*? Well, there are plenty of situations in real life (i.e., excluding sports) where people try to outwit, outplay, and outlast each other. Corporations are one example. Getting into graduate or professional schools is another. But how boring would it be to watch people working or studying every day, going to meetings or classes, and sitting at their computers? Very boring. We use TV to escape that kind of boredom, not to watch it! It is far more interesting to put a group of people in a remote location and see what happens. That's one analogue situation, and if it proved to be dramatic enough, then perhaps all the competitions within *Survivor* would have been unnecessary. However, by shrewd design, *Survivor's* producers can set up situations that elicit extremely dramatic and memorable behavior in the players' quests to outwit, outplay, and outlast. These behaviors often exemplify well-known and well-studied psychological phenomena, such as ingroup/outgroup behavior, cognitive dissonance, social loafing, and the fundamental attribution error. For each of these mental processes, we will define the concept, highlight the findings from formal psychological studies, and then provide examples of *Survivor's* analogue situations in which you can observe these behaviors.

INGROUP/OUTGROUP

Psychologists have found that almost as soon as people are sorted into groups, their behavior and thinking becomes biased in favor of their ingroup. They demonstrate favoritism in their own behavior and in the behavior they expect from their ingroup peers. They make biased attributions, attributing success to their own purposeful behavior (but outgroup members' success to external factors) and their failures to external factors. (This is the group version of the "fundamental attribution error" discussed below.) They also make somewhat contradictory assumptions that a) members of the ingroup are more similar to themselves than are members of the outgroup and b) members of the ingroup are diverse, whereas members of the outgroup are homogenous (Taylor, Peplau, and Sears 2003).

The most famous ingroup/outgroup ABO was the Stanford Prison Experiment. Professor Philip Zimbardo built a mock prison in the basement of the psychology department. (Check out Zimbardo's Web site dedicated to explaining and exploring the study at www.prisonexp.org.) Undergraduates were randomly assigned to the role of guard or prisoner by the flip of a coin. By the second day, the guard and prisoner groups had coalesced, and the behavior observed was astonishing. The power of roles and the ingroup/outgroup status was so strong that these students started scarily acting like real guards and prisoners. Even though everything about this situation was analogue—a fake prison of three "cells" in the basement of a university psychology building, totally random assignment into groups—the behavior and thinking observed was highly generalizable to real-world situations.

Ingroup/outgroup biases have been the most pronounced psychological principles illustrated by the *Survivor* ABOs. The producers separate the contestants into tribes that are forced to live, work, and compete together for survival. In most seasons, the way in which contestants are assigned to tribes has appeared arbitrary. However, there have been several occasions during which the tribes were formed based on demographic characteristics (such as gender in *Survivor: Amazon*, gender and age in *Survivor: Panama*, or ethnicity in *Survivor: Cook Islands*). Regardless of the initial arranging factors, the original tribe assignment often creates a very strong allegiance that members are not willing to break once the tribes merge. For example, once the two tribes in *Survivor: Borneo* merged, the remaining Tagi members (Sean, Sue, Rudy, Kelly, and Richard) eliminated a Pagong member each week until they were the final five players. During *Survivor: Thailand*, five members of the Chuay Gahn tribe remained committed to the original tribal lines and took the top five positions at the end of the game. The most impressive stronghold, however, was during *Survivor: Palau*, when six members of the Koror tribe (Tom, Katie, Ian, Jennifer, Caryn, and Gregg) placed in the top six. Thus, relationships established early in the game of *Survivor* are extremely important to the outcome of the game.

Producers control and increase tribal alliance strength by limiting exposure to members of the other tribe. Tribal camps are miles away from one another and separated by dense jungles, woods, or even the ocean, thus inhibiting the amount of time players are in contact with one another to the Challenges. Additionally, the producers create team Challenges (both reward and Immunity) that encourage members *within* the team to work together toward a common goal while friction increases *between* the tribes because of the competition. For example, during an Immunity Challenge in *Survivor: All-Stars* the tribes were required to select one tribe member to call out directions while the rest of the contestants were blindfolded and had to retrieve giant scattered puzzle pieces. During this Challenge, many of the players ran into one another, dropped giant puzzle pieces on each other, and knocked each other over while transporting the pieces. This type of Challenge required trust in the "sighted" tribemate to give accurate instructions and teamwork between those who were gathering the pieces and then reconstructing the puzzle. However, this type of Challenge also created opportunities for physical contact among the three tribes, increasing the tension and rivalry among these groups. Thus, this specific Challenge fostered ingroup and outgroup allegiances.

COGNITIVE DISSONANCE

Cognitive dissonance refers to situations in which our behavior deviates from our attitudes or self-concept. If you were to do something dishonest (e.g., cheat on your partner) but think of yourself as an honest person, you would experience cognitive dissonance. Psychologists have documented that there are three ways of dealing with cognitive dissonance: a) change your behavior (e.g., stop cheating); b) justify your behavior by modifying your cognitions (e.g., "she came on to me, so I'm not at fault"); or c) justify your behavior by adding new cognitions ("it was just oral sex, so it's not real cheating").

The original behavioral observational study of cognitive dissonance (Festinger, Riecken, and Schachter 1956) watched a group of people who followed a suburban homemaker turned prophet, who foretold that the earth would be destroyed in 1956 and that they would be saved by a spaceship from a distant world. Festinger and colleagues heard about this group and thought that this would provide a remarkable opportunity to watch what happened when strongly held beliefs were disconfirmed. (The researchers were banking on the world not actually ending.) The researchers infiltrated the group and took careful notes as they watched the end of the world come (and go). Although the group members were confused and dismayed when the spaceship did not arrive and the earth kept spinning, they chose option "c" above—they concluded that their faith had forestalled the end of the world, and actually went on to proselytize more, rather than less, following the failed prophesy.

One of the clearest examples of cognitive dissonance to date on *Survivor* occurred during *Survivor: Africa* when Ethan, a physically strong competitor and sportsman, struggled with contrasting beliefs and actions. After fifteen days the contestants were forced to change their strategies as the producers shook up the game. The Samburu and Boran tribes received mail instructing each tribe to send its three "best" members to a neutral meeting point. Jeff Probst informed them that they would be heading home to the opposite camp (Boran members Kelly, Tom, and Lex were now members of Samburu; Samburu members Frank, Teresa, and Silas were now members of Boran). When Ethan, a Boran member, learned about "the switch" he became discouraged because his two strongest allies were now members of the opposing tribe, leaving him without a strong alliance. He declared, "Everything I had worked for, all the bonds I had made, my two closest friends, are now gone. I am going to have to start over." Fearing that he was a target because of his athletic abilities (he had been a professional soccer player and had coached college soccer for several years), Ethan devised a plan to target one of the newest Borans, Silas, because he was also a physical threat and not an original Boran member. Although this strategy in the game of *Survivor* is not unique, Ethan took quite a risk when he approached fellow Boran member Kim Johnson *before* the Immunity Challenge and suggested that they throw the Challenge to secure a visit to Tribal Council that night. Ethan's plan of losing intentionally would give the original Boran members a chance to vote out original Samburu members. Ethan explained his hesitation to Kim, "It's going to be tough for me to do this. I am a competitor; I have never done anything like this in my life." Ethan, a strong competitor who had been heavily involved in sports, held the belief that being a competitor required trying his hardest to win. However, he also believed that in this specific situation it might be advantageous to lose the Challenge deliberately, perhaps to put himself (and his two allies who were now targets as new members in the Samburu tribe) in a more favorable position that would have a more enduring impact. Indeed, he described the predicament as a "win-win situation" because either outcome at the Immunity Challenge advanced his position in the game; winning would mean the tribe would not have to face Tribal Council, whereas losing would allow the original Boran members to vote out a physically threatening player. Ethan's struggle between his self-concept as a competitor was in direct conflict with his planned action of throwing a competition. He believed that strong competitors should not intentionally lose. However, Ethan's plan was carried out as the Boran tribe pretended to struggle with the giant puzzle at the Immunity Challenge, thus securing a visit to Tribal Council that resulted in voting out Silas. How did Ethan reconcile the differences in his self-concept and actions? He chose option "c" from above and added the new thought that competitiveness in the game of *Survivor* included a plan for longevity and endurance and that throwing the competition served that purpose.

Although the producers of *Survivor* did not intentionally hope to illustrate cognitive dissonance specifically, by implementing "the switch" they were creating interpersonal friction which led to Ethan's internal struggle. Indeed, Probst had cautioned ". . . the game of *Survivor* is always changing, and it's about to change again," indicating that this was intended to stir up trouble at both camps. Lex articulated, "All of us have been so careful about arranging our strategies for our own security and well-being, and all of a sudden all of that has completely blown us under." Thus, the manipulation by the producers in this ABO resulted in both an interesting episode of reality television and a great example of the psychological principle of cognitive dissonance.

Another unforgettable example of cognitive dissonance occurred when Ian from *Survivor: Palau* voluntarily dropped out of the final Immunity Challenge, requesting that he be voted out. The day before, Ian struggled with possibly voting out his best friend and strong ally, Tom. Ian confessed, "I win the Challenge, Tom goes home. I don't win the Challenge, Tom's all of a sudden my best friend again," indicating that he was willing to do whatever was necessary to secure a win. After Tom won Immunity and was forced to decide whom to send home, Ian empathized that he also would have struggled with deciding whom to take to the final three. Tom became alarmed by such a statement because he had been committed to his alliance. This revelation, that Ian was not as faithful as Tom had hoped, led Tom to vote against Ian. However, Ian remained in Palau with two angry tribemates who accused him of being dishonest and untrustworthy and he defended himself, stating, "We're playing a game!"

Fearing not only losing the game but also his integrity, Ian declared,

"I didn't come out here to play the villain." Ian's conceptualization of himself did not include selfishness and dishonesty, although his behavior was interpreted as just that by Katie and Tom. These two views (that Ian thought of himself as a good person but that his actions suggested otherwise) were in direct conflict with one another. Hoping to prove himself a person with integrity and regain Tom's respect, Ian requested that Tom take Katie to the finals in his place during the final Immunity Challenge. Ian hoped that this gesture would prove that his friendship with Tom was more important than winning the game. This action (i.e., stepping down) is option "a" from above and it resolved Ian's internal struggle between wanting to be a good person and his recent behavior that demonstrated the opposite.

This was one of the most shocking episodes of *Survivor* for not only the audience, but also the host. Probst, not sure that he heard correctly, asked Ian to clarify his proposition. Clearly everyone was shocked by Ian's bold move, so how was this ABO set up to elicit such a strong example of cognitive dissonance? In the previous night's Tribal Council, Probst had asked many pointed questions about loyalty and honesty that led Ian to think about his transgressions in the game. Then, at hour eight of the Immunity Challenge, Probst pointed out that there had not yet been a single discussion of a deal between Tom and Ian, the two remaining competitors in the Challenge. Thus, Probst was instrumental in first planting the seed of loyalty and honesty in Ian's mind the night before and then initiating discussion about possible deals for the final Immunity Challenge.

SOCIAL LOAFING

Social loafing is the tendency for people to work less hard when in groups than when alone. It has been formally studied since the 1880s, when it was demonstrated that volunteers pulled harder on a rope when alone than in a group. This experiment was replicated and extended by Ingham, Levinger, Graves, and Peckham (1974), who showed that significant declines in effort occurred when the group size increases to two or three, but levels off after that. Researchers believe that the reduction of effort is due to lowered anxiety about being individually evaluated, causing individual relaxation and reduced effort (Aronson, Wilson, and Akert 1999). (Interestingly, however, social loafing holds for simple tasks only; for complicated tasks that might cause an individual to tense up, being in a group actually creates an improvement in performance.) Inevitably, the pull toward social loafing in some also leads to social compensation by others. Williams and Karau (1991) set up an ABO brainstorming task. If a participant believed that other group members wouldn't pull their own weight, he or she worked harder than when alone. For social compensation to occur, the belief that others will loaf and a belief that group performance is important must both be present.

Every season of *Survivor* has a social loafer, someone who prefers to conserve energy by avoiding work at camp or exerting minimal effort during Challenges. Morgan McDevitt, a *Survivor: Guatemala* contestant, was labeled lazy by her tribemates because she was not contributing to camp life and instead often spent her time lounging and braiding hair. Her tribemates were upset by this lack of effort because it meant everyone else had to exert more effort to finish the daily chores. Half of the Samburu tribe of *Survivor: Africa* was branded lazy because they explicitly refused to contribute to camp chores. While the four eldest members woke up early to retrieve water and build a fire (social compensation), Lindsey, Kim, Silas, and Brandon slept in and then became irritated when they woke up to the noise of the morning chores (social loafing). Lindsey explained, "They can go get the water, and we don't need to help; we can just save our strength." When Lex was forced to become a Samburu member because of the tribe "switch," he commented, "We were pissed when we got there. It looked like a bunch of lazy people had been running the camp." Many of these chore-avoiders claim that they are conserving energy for something of more importance: the Challenges. Thus, from their perspective, exerting too much effort around camp would be wasteful.

However, this explanation does not fit well with the behavior of one of the most well-known social loafers to date: Katie Gallagher of *Survivor: Palau.* Early in the season, Katie preferred to sit back and let her tribemates do most of the work at camp. Moreover, Katie continued to loaf during Challenges, often exerting more effort to look busy than actually trying to be competitive. Janu and Caryn, two women with much less strength than Katie, outperformed her; even Probst comment-ed during the Challenge that Katie was ultimately doing nothing to sup-port her team. However, when Katie began competing for individual immunity, she appeared to try harder and exerted more effort (such as in the final Immunity Challenge where she lasted over four hours bobbing on the platform in the water). Katie eventually secured a seat in the final two, but was criticized by juror after juror as being "worthless around camp," "embarrassing in Challenges," and having a strategy where she pretended to be "pathetic."

How does one elicit social loafing from others? Well, this ABO was set up in *Survivor* from the beginning stages. The very nature of having teams in the beginning half, compared to individuals, sets up this ABO. Because the tribes must be self-sufficient, someone needs to gather food, water, and tend to the fire. These tasks often become assigned to one or two individuals and contestants become "specialists," providing that skill to benefit the whole group. When there are eight players, it's easier not to do one's share because others can compensate. Also, the tribe's welfare depends upon winning Challenges as a team in the beginning half of the game, so there is less pressure to succeed as an individual and more opportunities to loaf.

FUNDAMENTAL ATTRIBUTION ERROR

People have the tendency to attribute the cause of their good behavior to their own intentional efforts or stable attributes and the cause of bad behavior to situational or unstable factors. They do the exact opposite with others—bad behavior is often chalked up to personality and good behavior to situational factors. This tendency has been dubbed the "fun-damental attribution error."

In their classic study demonstrating this phenomenon, Jones and Harris (1967) had participants in their study read essays that were either pro–Fidel Castro or anti–Fidel Castro. (This was during the days when Castro, the communist leader of Cuba, was an extremely controversial and divisive figure.) There was one condition in which the experi-menters told participants that the writer chose to write on that particu-lar topic (free choice) and another condition in which participants were told the writer was instructed to take that particular stance (no choice). Then, participants were asked what they believed the "true attitude" of the writer to be. As expected, participants rated those who had free choice and wrote pro-Castro essays as having more Castro-supporting attitudes. Surprisingly, however, the participants still rated those who wrote essays favoring Castro but had no choice about what stance to take as having higher pro-Castro attitudes, on average, than those who had written anti-Castro essays. Participants still thought that there was a relationship between essay stance and personal attitude, even though the no-choice group members had no choice on their stance! Thus, participants in this study made the fundamental attribution error by believing the behavior of others (the essayists) was reflective of stable or personality factors.

Episodes of *Survivor* are replete with examples of the fundamental attribution error (FAE). The FAE usually surfaces when contestants become upset that others are breaking alliances, lying, or "flying under the radar." For example, when Judd received a clue in a reward Challenge to help him locate a hidden Immunity Idol in *Survivor: Guatemala*, he lied to his tribemates about what the clue said and defended himself by stating, "I don't have a problem lying to the other guys at all. That's what the game is all about." However, when Gary lied in a later episode about trying to persuade one of Judd's allies to team up with him, Judd became very angry and declared, "The least person you would expect to lie is basically the biggest liar." Judd attacked Gary's character for an action that he had also taken due to the circumstances of the game; many former *Survivor* players and even Probst have claimed that it's impossible to win the game of *Survivor* without lying at some point. However, Judd was unwilling to view Gary's move as one influenced by the external situation of the game and instead attributed it to a stable factor and took a personality-based approach to criticize his character.

How could the producers and host elicit thoughts and behaviors from contestants that represent the fundamental attribution error? The structure of the game has some impact on this phenomenon, in that reward Challenges always put the winner in a more favorable situation. In this particular example, Judd won a clue that put him at an advantage to find the hidden immunity idol. Thus, by creating Challenges that result in benefiting only one player, the producers are creating situations which might lead to blaming that particular individual instead of viewing the situation as leading to their behaviors. Also, during Tribal Council Probst asks many questions that often provoke a variety of emotional responses from the players. A theme of many of his questions surrounds the issue of trust: Who is trustworthy and can one play the game of *Survivor* and win without being dishonest? Many contestants explain that it's "just a game" and that dishonesty is a result of playing the game, yet they still make dispositional inferences when push comes to shove. In this particular situation, Judd actually called Gary a liar during Tribal Council when prompted to speak by Probst. However, Gary pointed out that Judd had also lied and that his criticism was unfair because *Survivor* lends itself to lying.

CONCLUDING THOUGHTS

Philip Zimbardo, the Stanford Prison Experiment researcher, said recently that "The reason reality TV is so popular is because to observe human behavior is fascinating." *Survivor* provides an opportunity to observe some classic phenomena of human behavior and to consider how analogue behavior observation is conducted. There are a few differences to note, however, between observing human behavior the way *Survivor* viewers do versus the way researchers do. First, *Survivor* airs only a small fraction of what it shoots. Psychologists focus on data from all participants, not just the ones who offer the most extreme or interesting data. (Further, *Survivor* is edited to be entertaining, and thus even the behavior shown may not fairly represent the full context for the behaviors observed.) Second, *Survivor*'s participants are picked to make an interesting show, not to be representative. Psychologists are interested in identifying generalizable phenomena and principles that can be applied to a wide range of people. Third, psychologists, before beginning a research project, must receive approval from the Institutional Review Board, a committee that weighs the benefits and dangers of research studies and prevents researchers from inflicting unnecessary harm during a study. Most of the Challenges and obstacles that *Survivor* contestants are faced with would never be permitted in psychological studies due to the potential harm involved. Finally, psychologists begin even a naturalistic ABO study with hypotheses in mind and design the study to maintain consistency in the ABO set-up and in the variables observed and measured. Although such controls are necessary to derive scientifically sound conclusions from the observations, they are beside the point for *Survivor's* entertainment objectives. Human behavior on reality shows may be fascinating and may be illustrative of scientifically established phenomena, but entertainment ABOs lack some hallmarks of true science.

AUTHORS' NOTE

We finished writing this chapter the day that *Survivor: Cook Islands* was to air. The twenty contestants will be divided into four tribes based on race (African-Americans, Hispanics, Caucasians, and Asian-Americans). This controversial format will evidence ingroup/outgroup principles in psychology especially well. Mark Burnett, *Survivor's* producer, has described this thirteenth installment of the show as "an interesting social experiment" (Carter 6C). We're sure that, this season more than ever, we'll all observe a lot just by watching.

ASHLEY N. HUNT, M.A., is a graduate student in the clinical psychology Ph.D. program at the State University of New York at Stony Brook. Her research interests include couples' conflict and communication and the observational methodologies used to study such phenomena. Ashley hopes that her strategies and alliances will help her outwit, outplay, and outlast the challenges of graduate school.

RICHARD E. HEYMAN, PH.D., is research professor of psychology at the State University of New York at Stony Brook. His research focuses on family dysfunction, especially family violence. He has authored or co-authored more than sixty scholarly papers, book chapters, and books and has received over twenty federal research grants. His alliance with Ashley was forged two and a half years ago when she arrived at Stony Brook and her passion for *Survivor* got him to start watching the show.

REFERENCES

Aronson, E., T. D. Wilson, and R. M. Akert. *Social Psychology*. New York: Longman, 1999.

Carter, Bill. "*Survivor* to Divide Teams Along Racial Lines." *New York Times*, 24 Aug. 2006, sec. 6C.

Driver, J. L. and J. M. Gottman. "Daily Marital Interactions and Positive Affect During Marital Conflict Among Newlywed Couples." *Family Process* 43 (2004): 301–314.

Gottman, J. M. *What Predicts Divorce?* Hillsdale, NJ: Erlbaum, 1994.

Heyman, R. E. "Observation of Couple Conflicts: Clinical Assessment Applications, Stubborn Truths, and Shaky Foundations." *Psychological Assessment* 13 (2001): 5–35.

Heyman, R. E. and A. M. S. Slep. "Analogue Behavioral Observation." In *Comprehensive Handbook of Psychological Assessment. Vol. 3, Behavioral Assessment.* Edited by M. Hersen (ed.) and E. M. Heiby and S. N. Haynes (vol. eds.), (pp. 162–180). New York: Wiley, 2004.

Ingham, A. G., G. Levinger, J. Graves, and V. Peckham. "The Ringelmann Effect: Studies of Group Size and Group Performance." *Journal of Experimental Social Psychology* 10 (1974): 371–384.

Jones, E. E. and V. A. Harris. "The Attribution of Attitudes." *Journal of Experimental Social Psychology* 3 (1967): 1–24.

Taylor, S. E., L. A. Peplau, and D. O. Sears. *Social Psychology*. 5th ed. Upper Saddle River, NJ: Addison Wesley, 2003.

How do you keep a Survivor viewer in suspense? Richard J. Gerrig suggests that suspense develops when people experience uncertainty coupled with hope and fear toward alternative outcomes. Viewers' feelings of suspense become more intense as Survivor's unfolding narrative leads them to embrace particular outcomes. As such, viewers' experiences of suspense vary with their own distinct hopes and fears.

What Will the Tribe Say When It Speaks?

Suspense on *Survivor*

RICHARD J. GERRIG, PH.D.

It is August 23, 2000, right around 10 P.M. We are watching the final moments of Survivor's *first season,* Survivor: Borneo. *Jeff Probst has tallied all but one of the Jury's seven votes. The count is tied at three for Kelly Wiglesworth and three for Richard Hatch. Jeff retrieves the final vote. . . .*

If you are reading this chapter, you almost certainly know what happened next: Jeff Probst exposed the final vote and declared Richard Hatch to be the "Sole Survivor." The few seconds Jeff paused before revealing that outcome were among the most suspenseful I have experienced in my long career of TV viewing. Why did I feel such overwhelming suspense? Let's see what psychological research says about how *Survivor*, across all its seasons, has been so successful at generating suspense.

We need to start with a definition of suspense. Suspense requires, at least, a state of uncertainty. You experience suspense because you don't know whether Jeff will declare Kelly or Richard to be the winner. However, there are many circumstances in which you have uncertainty but you'd be unlikely to report that you were truly experiencing suspense.

123

For example, I've just stepped away from my computer to flip a coin. Although you are entirely uncertain about the outcome of the flip, you are probably indifferent as to whether it came up heads or tails. What might I do to get you to experience suspense?

In their broad theoretical account of emotions, Andrew Ortony and his colleagues (Ortony, Clore, and Collins 1988) suggested that suspense requires not only uncertainty, but also "a Hope emotion and a Fear emotion" (131). In a situation for which there are two outcomes, the genuine experience of suspense requires that you hope for one outcome and fear the other. (Fear, in this context, means that you anticipate that one outcome will cause you to experience negative emotions.) In situations that provide more than two outcomes, you still experience suspense when there is one outcome that is the particular focus of your hopes. With respect to my coin flip, you can see how easily I could get you to experience suspense. All I must do is to provide enough of a context to bring about hope and fear. Suppose I offered a student an A in my class if she successfully guessed whether the coin came up heads or tails? Although my dean would surely disapprove of this arrangement, I suspect the student would experience substantial suspense before I revealed that the coin had come up—have you committed yourself to an outcome?—heads.

This definition of suspense explains why the same situation gives rise to very different experiences for different people. Although two individuals may have an equal amount of uncertainty with respect to a situation, they might differ considerably in their hopes and fears. Imagine that you were not a regular *Survivor* watcher, and had tuned in only for the finale. Without the hopes and fears that accumulate over the course of a season, you might experience precious little suspense—whereas I, as a devoted fan, was on the edge of my seat waiting for the verdict. But how, exactly, do hopes and fears work to help enhance the experience of suspense?

My colleague David Rapp and I (Rapp and Gerrig 2006) carried out research to address the hope part of this question. Our study centered on a certain type of mental response that we call a *participatory response*. Participatory responses are mental expressions of people's preferences as they experience a narrative, such as "Watch out!" or "Hurry!" Consider the final episode of the most recent season of *Survivor*. To remain in the game, Cirie Fields and Danielle DiLorenzo had to start a fire. I wanted Cirie to win. (I wanted Cirie to win the whole season. With all of the talk of "playing and playing hard," Cirie was the only contestant that season who actually changed the course of the game through her wits. At least, that's how I saw matters.) As I watched Cirie and Danielle go about their tie-breaking labors, I heard a voice in my head shout "Go! Go!" every time the camera focused on Cirie. That mental roar of "Go!" is exactly what we mean by a participatory response. The roar arises because I had become sufficiently involved in the outcome. The roar reflects my preference — the outcome for which I hoped.

The experiments with David Rapp demonstrated the impact that participatory responses have on the way that people experience narratives. In the experiments, participants read fictional stories that allowed two possible outcomes. For example, in one text Charles was campaigning to become a U.S. senator. As in real political situations, this scenario presents two possibilities: Charles will win, or Charles will lose. As they read the text about Charles, participants encountered two types of information: One type of information indicated how Charles was doing in the polls (e.g., the New York Times put his efficient campaign several points ahead in its final poll). Another type of information allowed readers to develop a preference toward one or the other outcome (e.g., Charles was corrupt, taking bribes and giving favors to companies that polluted the environment). We predicted that readers' preferences would yield participatory responses along the lines of "Charles should win" or "Charles should lose."

For each of our twenty-four experimental texts, we created circumstances in which the outcome readers might expect based on life experience (e.g., candidates who are ahead in the polls generally win) was either consistent or inconsistent with the preference they would develop (e.g., corrupt politicians should not prosper). Here is a version of a full story that creates a clash between expectations and preferences:

> Charles worked hard to help the underprivileged and underrepresented have a voice in government. Charles was running for a seat on the Senate. The New York Times put his lackluster campaign several points behind in its final poll. Today was

Election Day, and people were coming out to vote. At the end
of the day, the ballots were tabulated and the outcome declared.

After participants read stories of this sort, we presented them with one
of the possible outcomes and asked them to indicate whether they
thought that was how the story would turn out. For example, they
responded "Yes, I agree this will happen next" or "No, I don't think this
will happen next" to this outcome: Charles was successful in his bid to
become senator.

Readers' responses suggested that they were influenced both by
expectations and preferences. Consider the story you just read.
Participants mostly agreed that Charles was unlikely to win. However,
the rate at which they collectively agreed was lower when the story led
them to hope otherwise: Participants shifted their choices toward the
outcomes they preferred rather than the outcomes they knew were
probable.

David Rapp and I replicated this pattern with a different measure.
Rather than having participants make overt judgments, we added the
outcome statements directly to the end of the stories. We then measured
how long it took participants to understand the sentences. As people
read a story, they generally try to create a representation of the information that fits together into a coherent whole. The question at hand is
how easy readers find it to create a coherent representation when information matches or mismatches what they expect or what they desire.

Once again, we saw the impact both of what readers knew and what
they desired. For example, participants found it easier to assimilate the
outcome "Charles was successful in his bid to become senator" when
that was the outcome they preferred, even when they knew he had been
behind in the polls. We explain these results by suggesting that readers
are rooting for the alternatives they prefer—informally, they are hearing
those voices saying "Win!" or "Lose!" As they supplement their experiences of the stories with what they want, those mental voices can bol-
ster or interfere with the process of understanding what they got.

Let's apply these results to your experience of *Survivor*. *Survivor* is all
about outcomes: reward Challenges, Immunity Challenges, and Tribal
Councils. The Challenges are often examples of perfect ambiguity—it's

impossible to know in advance which team or individual will win. For that reason, there's lots of room for hope to play a role. How often have you shouted "Come on!" at the TV screen? That's a (particularly loud) participatory response. For the Tribal Councils, you often have more of an idea who is likely to leave on a particular night. I have in mind, for example, this past season on which castaways were voted off with very few surprises. The reality of how the season unfolded allowed exactly the sort of consistencies or conflicts between what people thought was likely and what they hoped was likely that David Rapp and I captured in our experiments.

Consider day thirty-three. Most of the evidence suggested that Shane Powers was about to be voted off. For viewers who hoped that this would be the case, the episode and Tribal Council likely unfolded with very little perturbation. Those viewers were ready and willing to accept the tribe's vote. However, viewers who hoped that Shane would survive likely had a very different experience. The hope that Shane might prevail (despite the evidence to the contrary) would lend a greater degree of urgency to the way in which those viewers assessed the clues provided in the episode. You can imagine (or perhaps recall) the types of participatory responses that such viewers would emit, even as the voting unfolded: "Don't vote for Shane!" The conflict between what was expected (Shane was going to leave) and what was desired (Shane should stay) made Jeff's tallying of the votes an ordeal of suspense for these fans.

From this example, you can see that people often play a critical role in determining the extent to which they experience suspense. All the people who watched Shane get voted off saw the same episode; they saw the same series of incidents in the same order. However, if we charted what people did while they watched the show—the mental activities they carried out— we'd find very different patterns. We'd expect Shane supporters and Shane detractors to produce very different participatory responses. We'd expect those participatory responses to cause the viewers to attend to different aspects of the material available. The Shane supporters would likely seize upon any incident that was consistent with their hope that he might be spared. They could ruminate on such an incident and build a story around that incident that would eventuate in their cherished outcome. For that reason, much of the suspense leading up to Jeff's announcement—"The Tribe has spoken"—is of the viewers' own making.

I've been making the case that suspense isn't really just a feeling. Rather, it's a particular type of experience—a type of experience that presupposes a certain level of involvement on the viewer's part. This experiential approach to suspense provides a perspective on what in the philosophical literature has been called the *paradox of suspense*. This paradox is easy to state: People experience suspense with respect to outcomes about which they are actually quite certain. I tried to give you such an experience in the opening paragraph of this chapter. I hoped to put you sufficiently back into the moment just before Jeff Probst named Richard Hatch the sole survivor when you experienced some fleeting uncertainty. The existence of this type of suspense, which I will call *anomalous suspense*, requires an important amendment to our earlier definition of suspense. Suspense doesn't require that you be completely uncertain of an outcome—only that you be uncertain in the moment. But why is it possible for you to feel uncertain about a situation whose outcome you otherwise know quite well?

Scholars have offered a variety of accounts of the paradox of suspense (e.g., Brewer 1996; Carroll 1996). However, I prefer an explanation that focuses on how people's narrative experiences unfold (Gerrig 1993). In this view, what matters most is the ease with which readers or viewers become transported to narrative worlds. Several years ago, I conducted a series of experiments to support this analysis (Gerrig 1989). Consider this statement:

> George Washington was elected first president of the United States.

This is an example of the type of fact my experiments were centered on. The idea was to start with information that was unambiguously within the experimental participants' knowledge—and then go about creating suspense. Here's the story that served that function:

> George Washington was a famous figure after the Revolutionary War. Washington was a popular choice to lead

the new country. Washington, however, wanted to retire after the war. The long years as general had left him tired and frail. Washington wrote that he would be unable to accept the nomination. Attention turned to John Adams as the next most qualified candidate.

Suppose, right after reading that story, you had to agree or disagree with either the statement "George Washington was elected first president of the United States" or "George Washington was not elected first president of the United States." That brief story wouldn't exactly have you on the edge of your seat with suspense. Still, the claim is that the story is sufficient enough in transporting you to a world in which Washington was ready to retire that your ability to access the real outcome would be impaired.

To gauge the impact of this suspense narrative, we needed a baseline for performance when readers hadn't experienced suspense. Here's the version of the story that was intended to be relatively free of suspense:

George Washington was a famous figure after the Revolutionary War. Washington was a popular choice to lead the new country. Few people thought that the British could be defeated. The success of the Revolutionary War was attributed largely to Washington. His friends worked to convince him to go on serving his country. Washington agreed that he had abundant experience as a leader.

Participants who read the "no suspense" versions of the experimental stories consistently provided correct responses to the target statements (e.g., "George Washington . . .") more quickly than did their peers who read the "suspense" versions of the stories. (Note that the Washington story was one of thirty-two experimental items.)

An important goal of these experiments was to demonstrate how readily readers could get taken up by narratives. To make that point more forcefully, we created two more versions of each experimental story with an important variation. The earlier sample stories started with the simple statement "George Washington was a famous figure after the Revolutionary War." For what we called the *prior warning* versions of the story, we replaced that statement with the exact sentence that would quite shortly become the target for participants' verification: "George Washington was elected first president of the United States." Here's the suspense story with that prior warning:

> George Washington was elected first president of the United States. Washington was a popular choice to lead the new country. Washington, however, wanted to retire after the war. The long years as general had left him tired and frail. Washington wrote that he would be unable to accept the nomination. Attention turned to John Adams as the next most qualified candidate.

Given this prior warning, what do you suppose happens when participants verify the statements? Despite the very recent correct statement of fact, the gentle suspense created by this story still made it more time-consuming (with respect to the no suspense story with prior warning) for readers to state correctly where the truth lay.

These experiments demonstrate how easily people get transported by narratives. Certain types of knowledge that are highly accessible outside narrative experiences become relatively inaccessible once people's journeys have begun. You can think of the paradox of suspense as a natural outcome of that propensity to be transported. We were able to get readers to experience anomalous suspense with our modest experimental stories. If you think about the relatively immodest staging of *Survivor*'s Tribal Councils, it becomes easy to understand how repeated viewings may still allow suspense.

Of course, sometimes you'll watch a *Survivor* episode for a second time and not experience one bit of suspense. Melanie Green and her colleagues have demonstrated that people are transported to different extents by the very same texts (Green 2004; Green and Brock 2000). You probably know from your personal experience that there are some sorts of narratives that draw you right in whereas others leave you totally cold. In fact, depending on your mood and other factors, you won't find the same narrative equally transporting at all times. If you put up barriers to letting a narrative transport you, you're unlikely to experience anomalous suspense or much of anything else. (Have you ever tried to watch *Survivor* with an acquaintance who prattles on about "Reality TV," rather than giving in to the story?)

One final thought about suspense on *Survivor*. I have been focusing on the way that each individual's mental activities contribute to his or her experience of suspense. However, for me *Survivor* has almost always been a social activity. I watched the finale of the first season with four friends. We each contributed $2 to a pot that was claimed by the individual who came closest to predicting the order of the final four. That individual wasn't me. Although Richard was my personal choice, I didn't believe for a minute that he could win. As the five of us watched the final show, we voiced our participatory responses. We thereby focused our collective attention in ways that amplified the group's suspense. What a wonderful way to spend an evening with friends, working diligently to increase our shared discomfort. Such is the way of suspense! Such is the pleasure of *Survivor*!

I thank David Rapp and Benjamin Swets for persuasive comments on this chapter.

RICHARD J. GERRIG, PH.D., is a professor of psychology at Stony Brook University. He received his B.A. from Yale in 1980 and his Ph.D. from Stanford in 1984. Gerrig's primary research focuses on readers' experiences of narrative worlds. He considers both the basic cognitive psychological processes that enable readers to understand discourse and the broader consequences of readers' experiences of being transported to narrative worlds. With Philip Zimbardo, he is the author of the introductory textbook, *Psychology and Life*.

REFERENCES

Brewer, William F. "The Nature of Narrative Suspense and the Problem of Rereading." In *Suspense: Conceptualizations, Theoretical Analyses, and Empirical Explorations* (pp. 107-127), edited by Peter Vorderer, Hans J. Wulff, and Mike Friedrichsen. Mahwah, NJ: Erlbaum, 1996.

Carroll, Noël. "The Paradox of Suspense." In *Suspense: Conceptualizations, Theoretical Analyses, and Empirical Explorations* (pp. 71-91), edited by Peter Vorderer, Hans J. Wulff, and Mike Friedrichsen. Mahwah, NJ: Erlbaum, 1996.

Gerrig, Richard J. *Experiencing Narrative Worlds*. New Haven, CT: Yale University Press, 1993.

Gerrig, Richard J. "Suspense in the Absence of Uncertainty." *Journal of Memory and Language* 28 (1989): 633-648.

Green, Melanie C. "Transportation into Narrative Worlds: The Role of Prior Knowledge and Perceived Realism." *Discourse Processes* 38 (2004): 247-266.

Green, Melanie C. and Timothy C. Brock. "The Role of Transportation in the Persuasiveness of Public Narratives." *Journal of Personality and Social Psychology* 78 (2000): 853-870.

Ortony, Andrew, Gerald Clore, and Allan Collins. *The Cognitive Structure of Emotions*. Cambridge: Cambridge University Press, 1988.

Rapp, David N. and Richard J. Gerrig. "Predilections for Narrative Outcomes: The Impact of Story Contexts and Reader Preferences." *Journal of Memory and Language* 54 (2006): 54-67.

Renee Engeln-Maddox provides important insights about
Survivor's displays of women's bodies: Contradicting the real-
world truism, on Survivor it is, in fact, possible for women to
be too thin. Engeln-Maddox notes that, ultimately, no one
looks very sexy on Survivor—"They're all just too dirty." Still,
she identifies several ways in which presentation and percep-
tion of women's bodies have influenced Survivor outcomes.

An Alternate Universe

Women, Body Image, and the Paradox of Thinness on *Survivor*

RENEE ENGELN-MADDOX, PH.D.

Let's start out with some facts about the real world. In the real world, many women have *issues* with their bodies. I say this not just from the perspective of a woman, but from the perspective of a psychologist specializing in the study of women's contentious relationships with their own bodies. Serious, appearance-related dissatisfaction among women is quite common. In 1984, Rodin and colleagues coined the term *normative discontent* to describe widespread body dissatisfaction among women and girls. Other authors have referred to this phenomenon as something that, in an epidemiological sense, is now normal (Irving et al. 1998). In other words, in this culture, it would be abnormal for a woman to be satisfied with her body. If a woman tells you she is satisfied with the size and shape of her body, she's probably lying. If she's not lying, she's just odd (in a good way, of course).

One of the theories regarding why women are so often dissatisfied with their bodies suggests that the dissatisfaction stems, at least in part, from women's tendency to compare how they look with how women in the media look. When the average woman compares her appearance to the appearance of a model or actress, guess who typically comes out on the losing end? Psychologists call this process *social comparison* (Festinger 1954). The basic idea behind social comparison theory is that when you're not certain where you stand on a given attribute (such as physical attractiveness), you compare yourself to other people to figure it out. So here's the problem: the average woman in the media looks little like the average woman. In fact, for years now researchers have been pointing out the paradox: as women in Western cultures increase in size, women in Western media are shrinking (Spitzer et al. 1999). The vast majority of women in primetime sitcoms are below average weight (Fouts and Burggraf 1999, 2000). Playboy centerfolds, Miss Americas, and models are getting skinnier and skinnier while the rest of us get, well, *not* skinnier (Owen and Laurel-Seller 2000; Spitzer et al. 1999; Wiseman et al. 1992). The message from most media outlets seems to be something like this: "Thin women are beautiful, happy, and successful." But what about women on *reality* TV? What can these women tell us about women and body image? Let's find out by embarking on a series of journeys (no raft needed) between the real world and the reality TV world of *Survivor*.

In the real world: The pressure on women to be thin is intense. Women who are not thin are laughed at, discriminated against, and made to feel generally miserable (Puhl and Brownell 2001). They're even paid less than thin women. Thus, it should not shock anyone to learn that many women, and even young girls, go to extraordinary lengths to lose weight or keep from gaining weight. They starve themselves, following unhealthy, overly restrictive diets. Some develop eating disorders that can lead to organ failure and death. When you ask women how their lives would change if they looked like women in the media, they readily list the benefits they associate with that level of physical attractiveness: more friends, more (and better-looking) romantic partners, better jobs, better pay, higher self-esteem, and increases in happiness (Engeln-Maddox 2006). Many women long to emulate the waif-like appearance of fashion models. As put so bluntly in *The Devil Wears Prada*, size two is the new size four. Size six is the new size fourteen. In other words, average-sized women are moving farther away from the ideal body—even when they're not gaining weight!

On **Survivor**: Thinness is often seen as a disability on *Survivor*. During the All-Stars season, before the contestants had fire (which they desperately needed to make their water drinkable), Richard Hatch explained why he was not going to start a fire for his tribemates, even though he knew how. He said, "Look at how skinny they all are! I'm fine; they'll be dying in no time." The implication was that thinness was a weakness. In most seasons of *Survivor*, it has been clear from the beginning that the men were viewed as more valuable teammates due to their greater physical strength. After all, someone needs to carry the firewood and build a shelter. The women who were most valued were the strongest, toughest women. These were also the women typically viewed as the biggest threats (think Zoe and Tammy on *Survivor: Marquesas*). The thin women who most closely resembled cultural beauty standards (think Sarah on *Survivor: Marquesas*, Jerri on *All-Stars/Australian Outback*, or the "bowheads" on *Survivor: Vanuatu*) were generally viewed with skepticism, seen as beautiful but fragile and not necessarily useful. Physical strength was an asset for almost every Challenge—thus the thin were generally seen as weak. Looking like a supermodel is not going to help you pull heavy trunks across the bottom of the ocean, paddle a raft, or roll giant boulders in reward and Immunity Challenges. Consider Kelly from *Survivor: Africa*. After being voted off, she said, "I made it past the hard part with the boulders and whatnot; for a skinny girl that's kind of a big deal!" One instance when small size was an advantage was during the Challenge on season one when the tribes had to carry a fellow tribemate on a stretcher through the jungle. Colleen's tiny body clearly made this task easier for her tribe—however, it was still physical strength that played the most important role in the Challenge.

On *Survivor*, women typically do not celebrate losing weight, they bemoan it. Sarah from *Survivor: Marquesas* explained during a CBS *Early Show* interview that she had lost thirteen pounds, leaving her at ninety pounds. She said she was "shocked" at "seeing every rib." She even said, "It was gross." In *Survivor: Vanuatu*, Twila, not known for being friends with Eliza, still hoped at one point that Eliza would win one of the food reward Challenges, saying, "I'm just prayin' Liza wins because she looks like a little stick girl. I've been calling her Olive Oyl." Eliza agreed and explained, "I'm starving to death!" This comment was followed by several rather disturbing shots of Eliza's shoulder blades seemingly ready to jut out through her *Survivor*-tanned skin. On *Survivor* a lack of available food is associated with lethargy, and with an inability to be successful at a variety of physical and mental challenges.

In the real world: Dieting is a way of life for many women, and even young girls. The weight-loss industry in the U.S. is massive—forecast to reach $61 billion by the year 2008 (Marketdata Enterprises 2005). Many women in the real world are searching for any aid available (pills, shakes, hypnotism, surgeries, crash diets) to reduce their caloric intake. This search starts early, with a startling number of young girls and adolescents following highly restrictive diets (Stice et al. 1998). Such restrictive eating is often followed by additional dangerous behaviors such as binging and purging. Yet even the most drastic dieting efforts are unlikely to lead to permanent weight loss. The FTC and FDA recently released a report suggesting that only 5 percent of people who lose weight will maintain that weight loss long term. Nonetheless, many women view extreme caloric restriction as a way of life. Indeed, the notion that women must restrict themselves to salads and tiny portions in order to be appealing to men remains popular. Consider the recent *Burger King* commercial ("I am man") for the Texas Double Whopper. A young man leaves a date in a huff singing, "I'm way too hungry to settle for chick food." The implication, of course, is that real men can and should pig out (especially on red meat), while women are relegated to the land of salads and tofu. Eating small portions of low-calorie food is portrayed as distinctly feminine behavior. In a recent content analysis of central characters in primetime sitcoms, Fouts and Burgraff (1999) found that many female characters dieted, and those who were dieting were more likely to make disparaging remarks aimed at female characters who weren't dieting. Among women, dieting can be seen as triumph of willpower, a sign of commitment to society's body ideal for women. Dieting itself can be seen as sexy.

On Survivor: Dieting is not sexy. The women of *Survivor* are desperate to eat. By virtue of joining the cast, they have essentially signed on as guinea pigs in an experiment examining the outcomes of extreme caloric restriction—a crazy crash diet lovingly designed by Mark Burnett. They peel slimy snails off the bottom of rocks, eat bizarre sea creatures and insects, and compete, fiercely, in competitions to win additional food. While in the real world it is seen as un-ladylike to binge on food, in the world of *Survivor*, there are no such restrictions for women. The women consume rats (happily!), they binge on chicken they butchered themselves, and when they win "real" food in a Challenge, there's nothing ladylike about the way they eat.

In *Survivor: Vanuatu*, Twila was furious with the "prissy bowheads" who refused to eat maggot-infested plantains. During *Survivor: Australian Outback*, the cast members were given local currency and offered the chance to bid on various items of food auctioned off by Jeff Probst. The women were just as aggressive as the men in the bidding, and when they won, they dove right in. During her *Early Show* interview after being voted off, Mia (from *Survivor: Vanuatu*) said, "I had an appreciation for food before this show, but I'll *never* diet again."

All Survivors, perhaps especially the women, engage in ongoing moaning about their need to consume protein and sugar. No one spends an evening around the campfire dreaming of salads and tofu. The longing for food is so powerful that not a season of *Survivor* has passed without at least one scene involving cast members fantasizing about the food they would like to eat. There's a connection to make to the real world here. One popular model used to explain the etiology of bulimia, the *restraint model* (Herman and Polivy 1980), suggests that caloric deprivation (generally resulting from dieting) increases the risk for binge eating in the future. In other words, starve yourself now, binge later. This pattern is clear among the *Survivor* contestants, who frequently binge until they are ill when they win food rewards during Challenges. The images of the Survivors' abdominal distress after such binging are so common they fail to be entertaining after a while! At the reunion show for season one, when the host asked the Survivors how many had gained back weight they lost on the show, all of them raised their hands. Remember, very few dieters successfully maintain their weight loss.

In the real world: We know the Survivors are hungry and often miserable as the result of their hunger. Yet in the real world, many women envy the Survivors' ability to drop weight quickly. In the January 9, 2006, issue of *People* magazine (read predominantly by women), the cover headline "Half Their Size!" promised an issue full of advice from successful dieters. Several *Survivor* contestants were interviewed about the weight they lost during the show. While the article did include a warning regarding the dangers of following a *Survivor*-style diet, it also included praise for those contestants who were able to maintain their *Survivor*-induced weight loss. The message seemed to be something along the lines of, "It's not very healthy, but if it works, great!" In her post-vote-off *Early Show* interview, Dolly from *Survivor: Vanuatu* said (regarding her weight loss on the show), "I felt like my belly button was touching my spine. . . . It's the best diet advice I have, just take a week and you'll lose ten pounds and it's not that hard!" The public's apparent longing for a diet plan as effective as the *Survivor* plan is disturbing given evidence of the physical and psychological effects of extreme caloric restriction. In addition to a range of physical ailments that can result from extreme dieting, researchers have also demonstrated that dieting is associated with moodiness, depression, and even impaired cognitive performance. For example, a recent study (Kemps and Tiggemann 2005) demonstrated that female dieters showed impairment in central executive functioning. Think of your central executive as the manager in charge of your brain's memory and information processing. Sound important? It is. Do the *Survivor* contestants experience such impairment? Let's take a look.

On **Survivor**: The Survivors appear to suffer from a wide range of diet-ing-related ailments, both mental and physical. They have sores that don't seem to heal (remember Colleen explaining, during season one, that there were bugs living in her open sores?), unexplained swelling, and boils (remember Tom's?). They're tired, weak, and cranky. Their behavior becomes strange (or in the case of some contestants, more strange). As the days pass, they argue more, have less fun, and spend more time lying around fantasizing about a return to their normal lives. Those Survivors who stay in the game the longest complain the most of an inability to think clearly and of memory problems. They even worry they will not perform well on the less physical Challenges that require memory and concentration.

In the real world: In the real world, women are valued for their beauty. Their appearance is a constant focus of evaluation, both self-evaluation and evaluation by others. There is plenty of evidence that women and girls are frequently victims of objectification. Objectification refers to the process by which a woman's body is viewed as a thing separate from her personhood, as a source of pleasure for others. *Objectification Theory* (Fredrickson and Roberts 1997) suggests that over time, women may internalize this objectification and begin to view themselves from the perspective of an observer, from the outside. Fredrickson and Roberts explain that for women, physical attractiveness can serve as a type of currency. Women know that their sex appeal can sometimes be used to get them what they want. This knowledge encourages them to focus even more on their physical appearance, which results in further objectification. Are the women of *Survivor* objectified? Is beauty a form of currency on *Survivor*? Let's do some investigating.

On Survivor: One of the interesting facets of *Survivor* is that to some extent, nobody looks sexy after a week or so—they're all just too dirty. Beyond the dirt, though, female Survivors are drawn further away from cultural beauty ideals than male contestants. For a man, growing a beard and being sweaty can be sexy. However, most in this culture don't find it sexy when women grow hair on their legs and underarms. Furthermore, the women of *Survivor* are left without the beauty aids that so many women rely on in the real world—no makeup, no hairdryers, no styling products. Do they miss these luxuries? You bet. On *Survivor: All-Stars*, when one tribe won bath products during a reward Challenge, a male tribemate pointed out during an interview that the toiletries "lifted the women's spirits." Later in the same season, when Rupert won a Challenge and chose Jenna and Amber to go on a trip to a resort with him, the women were extremely enthusiastic about the opportunity to put on makeup and be "pretty" and "girly."

While strength and endurance are of primary importance for most of the Challenges on *Survivor*, female contestants have used their bodies in other ways while playing the game. When Amber was announced as the winner of *Survivor: All-Stars*, she admitted, "I was going to flirt with everybody out there to get me to the end." In *Survivor: Vanuatu*, Julie (famous for naked sunbathing) is compared to Ginger on *Gilligan's Island*. Sarge said of her, "Oh hell yes, Julie's using her sex appeal, her young age, and her body to try to get to the men, there's no doubt about it." He concluded, "If you've got it, sunbathe it!" Julie told an interviewer, "Hey, if the boys want to keep me around strictly for *visual stimulation*, well then, hey, I got it in the bag then, right?" (Not so much, Julie—the tanning of the bare bottom could only take you so far.)

On *Survivor: Marquesas*, Sarah's body and how it would influence the game was a subject of much discussion from the very first episode. According to Vecepia, "Sarah has a very cute body, she paid a lot for it, and if you have it, of course, flaunt it. . . . I do not think that Sarah is using her body to get through this game, but I do think if she connects with the right individual, then that will definitely help her get through it." Lindsey (*Survivor: Africa*) used her sex appeal to become a contestant—her audition tape featured her naked (with the exception of body paint) riding a bike. In *Survivor: Amazon*, during one of those "stand on this small thing for as long as you can while Jeff offers you food to get you to quit" Challenges, Jenna and Heidi offered to take off their clothes for chocolate, peanut butter, and soda. Jeff Probst was able to magically procure the requested items, and gratuitous nudity ensued. In the real world, body dissatisfaction drives women to shun high-calorie food and avoid being naked in front of others. In the world of *Survivor*, hunger drives women to strip down publicly (on national TV, in fact) in exchange for high-calorie food.

Do the men of *Survivor* objectify the women of *Survivor*? Sure they do, and often with help from the host. In *Survivor: Vanuatu*, when the tribes were still split by gender, Jeff Probst asked the men, "Anyone you wouldn't mind being on a tribe with?" ("Being in a tribe with" is clearly a not-so-subtle way of identifying women with whom they might like to engage in "other activities.") One of the men responded, "Yeah, there was a couple girls who had really nice tails." In one brief conversation, the entire tribe of women was reduced to nothing more than a collection of body parts to be appraised by the men.

Boston Rob (*Survivor: Marquesas* and *All-Stars*) in particular seemed to excel at just this sort of behavior. In the very first episode of All-Stars, Rob listed off the different roles he thought his tribemates would play. While he assigned others roles according to what they did (e.g., the "mom" role), Rob simply assigned Jerri the "hot chick" role. On All-Stars he said, "Amber and I have an alliance for obvious reasons, she's beautiful." During the Marquesas reunion episode, after Rosie O'Donnell made a crack about Sarah's presumably surgically enhanced breasts, Rob quipped, "I was also glad Sarah brought her breasts." When under threat during their time on Marquesas, Rob and Sean disparaged the physical appearance of tribemates Tammy and Zoe, calling them "men" (presumably because they were strong and muscular). During the All-Stars reunion, Rob C. (*Survivor: Amazon*) was actually asked by the host, "How important *are* hot women to a good season of *Survivor*?" Rob C.'s answer was unclear. I guess the jury is still out on that one.

Where does this analysis leave us real-world dwellers? Feeling oddly hungry for protein? Wondering how our bodies would hold up in a swimming/diving/climbing contest? The challenge of *Survivor* is not to be the thinnest or the sexiest. Instead, the spoils of victory go to those who outsmart and out-endure. In the mirrorless world of *Survivor*, the quest for physical beauty takes a back seat to other pursuits. Okay, so the other pursuits mostly involve deceiving others and participating in contrived Challenges—but there's still something to be said about the freedom of life without mirrors. Here in the real world women are still objectified, overweight women are still stigmatized, and the longing for thinness runs deep and wide. A world where women are not defined by the size and shape of their bodies sounds lovely. However, even Mark Burnett's powers are somewhat limited, so it appears we shall have to create such a world ourselves.

Renee Engeln-Maddox, Ph.D., is a faculty member in the department of psychology at Northwestern University (Evanston, IL). She earned an M.A. in clinical psychology from Miami University (Oxford, OH), and a doctorate in social psychology from Loyola University, Chicago. Her research interests include portrayals of women in the media, body image disturbance, and media literacy.

REFERENCES

Engeln-Maddox, R. "Buying the Beauty Standard or Dreaming of a New Life? Expectations Associated with Media Ideals." *Psychology of Women Quarterly* 30 (2006): 258–266.

Festinger, L. "A Theory of Social Comparison Processes." *Human Relations* 7 (1954): 117–140.

Fouts, G. and K. Burggraf. "Television Situation Comedies: Female Body Images and Verbal Reinforcements." *Sex Roles* 40, no. 5–6 (1999): 473–481.

Fouts, G. and K. Burggraf. "Television Situation Comedies: Female Weight, Male Negative Comments, and Audience Reactions." *Sex Roles* 42, no. 9–10 (2000): 925–932.

Fredrickson, B. L. and T. Roberts. "Objectification Theory: Toward Understanding Women's Lived Experiences and Mental Health Risks." *Psychology of Women Quarterly* 21 (1997): 173–206.

Herman, C. P. and J. Polivy. "Restrained Eating." In *Obesity*, edited by A. Sunkard (1980): 208–225.

Irving, L. M., J. DuPen, and S. Berel. "A Media Literacy Program for High School Females." *Eating Disorders: The Journal of Treatment and Prevention* 6, no. 2 (1998): 119–131.

Kemps, E. and M. Tiggemann. "Working Memory Performance and Preoccupying Thoughts in Female Dieters: Evidence for a Selective Central Executive Component." *British Journal of Clinical Psychology* 44 (2005): 357–366.

Marketdata Enterprises. 2005. The U.S. Weight Loss & Diet Control Market. 8th ed.

Owen, P. R. and E. Laurel-Seller. "Weight and Shape Ideals: Thin Is Dangerously In." *Journal of Applied Social Psychology* 30, no. 5 (2005): 979–990.

Puhl, R. and K. D. Brownell. "Bias, Discrimination, and Obesity." *Obesity Research* 9 (2001): 788–805.

Rodin, J., L. Silberstein, and R. Striegel-Moore. "Women and Weight: A Normative Discontent." *Nebraska Symposium on Motivation* 32 (1984): 267–307.

Spitzer, B. L., K. A. Henderson, and M. T. Zivian. "Gender Differences in Population Versus Media Body Sizes: A Comparison over Four Decades." *Sex Roles* 40, no. 7–8 (1999): 545–565.

Stice, E., J. Killen, C. Hayward, and C. Barr Taylor. "Age of Onset for Binge

Eating and Purging during Late Adolescence: A 4-year Survival Study." *Journal of Abnormal Psychology* 107, no. 4 (1998): 671–675.

Wiseman, C.V., J. J. Gray, J. E. Mosimann, and A. H. Ahrens. "Cultural Expectations of Thinness in Women: An Update." *International Journal of Eating Disorders* 11, no. 1 (1992): 85–89.

Each season of Survivor *has had outcasts—contestants who suffer social isolation by virtue of shifting tribes or shifting alliances. More recent seasons of* Survivor *have introduced Exile Island to enforce social isolation through physical separation. Benjamin Le and Gary Lewandowski, Jr., identify the psychological consequences—both positive and negative—of social isolation and, at an extreme, deliberate ostracism.*

Castaways, Outcasts, and Cyberball

Social Isolation, Interpersonal Rejection, and Ostracism on Exile Island

BENJAMIN LE, PH.D., AND GARY LEWANDOWSKI, JR., PH.D.

One of the stars of *Survivor: Panama*, which aired in the spring of 2006, was forty-six-year-old Terry Deitz. Terry, a graduate of the U.S. Naval Academy, former lieutenant commander in the Naval Reserves, and commercial airline pilot, became a fan favorite, ultimately taking home third place in the game. Part of Terry's appeal as a player was undoubtedly due to his unsurpassed performance in Challenges, winning five individual Immunity Challenges in a row. In addition, Terry experienced the newest *Survivor* twist more than any other player, being banished to Exile Island four times during the contest. But what makes Terry a particularly important player in the *Panama* season was his role in two different group alliances. In the first, he and his fellow male La Mina tribemates (Austin, Nick, and Dan) openly acknowledged that they intended to vote out their only remaining female teammate, a social worker from Chicago named Sally Schumann, mainly because of the "male alliance" that was held.

Following a merge with the Casaya tribe, the tables were turned on Terry, when, ironically, his only remaining La Mina teammate was Sally, following the departures of Dan, Nick, and Austin. When Terry won individual immunity, Sally was voted out, leaving Terry socially isolated, much as he and his male alliance had previously done to Sally. The former Casaya tribe members outnumbered Terry six to one and openly schemed to send Terry home. Although he was clearly marginalized by his new tribemates, Terry persevered and outperformed them in Immunity Challenges, surviving to be one of the final three contestants.

INDIVIDUALS AND GROUPS

Survivor is a game about individuals and groups. Individuals are placed into groups (tribes), with these individuals' tribes competing against one another in a series of Challenges. Then, after tribes have merged into a single group, individuals compete against the members of their own tribes. At the heart of these interactions is group membership, because being an asset to the tribe may be a key to being a successful player in the game, and being a member of a larger tribe furthers one's chances of winning. Likewise, being an outcast from your group puts you at risk of being eliminated from the game. Much of the game of *Survivor*, including the voting process—and, more importantly, the social maneuvering prior to the vote—is designed to identify the outcast in the group.

In addition to creating social isolation, which is a common feature of all *Survivor* seasons, *Panama* included a new aspect of the game in the form of geographic isolation that accompanied banishment to a deserted island. The twist of being banished in such a manner was first introduced in *Survivor: Palau*, when Janu was exiled for one day and ultimately quit the game; but in Panama, this was taken to an extreme. Players sent to the island spent several days living alone, completely cut off from daily camp life and the ever-changing social dynamic. Although there were benefits to being exiled, such as the hidden immunity idol and absence—and, therefore, safety—from Tribal Council, with the addition of Exile Island, this season of *Survivor* greatly increased the potential psychological isolation and loneliness that players would experience.

The goal of this chapter is not to examine the group dynamics that go into deciding whom to send home from the island or the deception and negotiation that lead up to this decision. In some ways, the focus here is not on the group at all. Instead, this chapter seeks to explore the experience of being an outcast from the group. What does it feel like to be on the Tribal Council chopping block? How do players with targets on their backs cope with their tenuous group status? What is the experience of social and geographic isolation? In many ways, this is the story of Terry Deitz's psychological experience of being an outcast on *Survivor: Panama*.

THE NEED TO BELONG

Social psychologists Roy Baumeister and Mark Leary (1995) outline a framework for understanding the fundamental human motivation to form and maintain social relationships, as evidenced by a half-century of theory and research on the topic. Dubbed "the need to belong," they argue that this motivation is at the foundation of many aspects of interpersonal behaviors, and that social relationships are among the most pressing of all human goals. Many seemingly diverse behaviors, such as those related to achievement, social influence, helping others, and romantic liaisons, fall under the overarching umbrella of a motivation to build and nurture social relationships. Furthermore, it is hypothesized that the need to belong to groups has a strong foundation in evolutionary adaptiveness. There is strength in numbers, and those meeting their social needs (i.e., successfully being part of a group) were more likely to survive, meet reproductive partners, and raise successful offspring. In addition, the belongingness motivation may be at the core of maintaining a social fabric within a culture and promote norms of communal harmony. In a sense, cooperative living has benefits over a solitary existence, and those individuals living in groups fared better than those who were alone. Thus, the drive to form and maintain group affiliations became universally ingrained within our cultures and the human psyche.

It is clear that people have a strong predisposition toward social interaction and group existence; the flip side is that violations of this preference should be experienced extremely negatively. As an extreme example, a link between social isolation and suicide has been demonstrated (Trout 1980). In short, we should not enjoy the experience of being isolated from the groups in which we are; in fact, it produces some of the most negative feelings that people have. This is primarily why banishment to Exile Island is such an undesirable outcome; given the choice, people would rather spend time with others than spend time physically isolated. Likewise, even when we are physically close to others, the experience of social isolation should be equally unpleasant.

OSTRACISM IN *SURVIVOR: PANAMA*

After the La Mina and Casaya tribes merged, Terry and his former La Mina teammates (Nick, Austin, and Sally) found themselves outnumbered by two. The Casaya members put Terry at the top of their list for elimination—but after he won several individual Immunity Challenges, they systematically eliminated his former mates, leaving him at a six-to-one disadvantage. In the episode ten reward Challenge, in which players were forced to voice their opinions about each other, he was immediately eliminated by his tribemates and was once again sent to Exile Island. Terry could obviously read the writing on the wall: Casaya's plan was to get rid of him next, unless he continued to save himself by winning immunity. Terry found himself marginalized—isolated in the group; he was ostracized, with no allies or support.

Ostracism is defined as being socially isolated, rejected, or excluded from a group and has been studied extensively by social psychologist Dr. Kip Williams of Purdue University. In addition to violating the fundamental belongingness need, ostracism is especially destructive because it is at odds with other important human needs (Warburton and Williams 2005). In particular, the need to maintain self-esteem is threatened because one is not viewed as worthwhile or necessary to the group. Likewise, it threatens one's sense of meaning—the importance of being significant in the world. Finally, personal control is lost because there may not be anything that one can do to rejoin the group. It is the group's decision to end or continue the social isolation. Drawing a parallel to a dating relationship, it's like the group broke up with you and doesn't want you back, and there's nothing you can do about it. So, it's likely that Terry felt insignificant and bad because the group found him to be expendable—although it is probably the case that he was also flattered because they perceived him as a strong player and a threat—and was frustrated by the fact that he had no control regarding his reintegration into the group. The only thing that he could do was keep winning

Challenges so that he could stay in the game. However, the decision to allow him back into the group (or not) was totally out of his hands.

It is clear that *Survivor*, and particularly *Panama*, are especially well suited for an examination of social rejection and ostracism. However, experimental psychologists rely on laboratory studies rather than television shows to demonstrate the importance of the topics they study and to learn about the psychological process at the heart of human experiences, such as rejection and ostracism. Television and psychology studies are not completely unconnected, though. For example, Mark Leary (2005) cites *Survivor* as one of his influences in designing lab studies on social rejection. But, generally speaking, one goal that most experimental psychologists share is to design research studies to test their hypotheses.

OSTRACISM IN THE LAB

Williams and colleagues have conducted many research studies to investigate the effects of ostracism. One important feature of these studies is the creation of a state of ostracism for participants in the lab. To create a strong experimental design, typically a group of participants (i.e., the experimental group) is made to feel ostracized, and these individuals are compared to participants who are not ostracized (i.e., the control group). But how do researchers make participants feel rejected and excluded in their studies? Although there are many techniques that have been employed in lab studies, one particularly effective method is inspired by the grade school play yard. As any ten-year-old will confirm, it is particularly painful when other kids don't want to play with you.

In this ostracism manipulation (Williams and Sommer 1997), participants work on a questionnaire task in the lab, alongside two other "participants" who are doing the same task. However, unknown to the participant, these other two people are actually "confederates" who are working for the experimenter. They have been told how to act and are in cahoots with the researchers. Following the completion of the questionnaire task, the three individuals (one participant, two confederates) have five minutes until the next phase of the study. One of the confederates looks through a box of toys that is in the lab and finds a rubber ball. He or she starts bouncing the ball and then passes it on to the other confederate and the participant. In short, they play catch with each other, with all three people included.

In the ostracism condition, the participant is included in the game of catch for one minute, and then, without saying anything or looking at the participant, the two confederates begin to throw the ball only to each other, totally ignoring the participant. This continues for four minutes until the experimenter returns and instructs them to begin the next phase of the study. The ostracism condition is contrasted with two other conditions: one in which the participant is included in the game of catch for the full five minutes ("inclusion condition"), and another—the control condition—where participants sit quietly for five minutes without playing with the ball at all.

Kip Williams and colleagues (Williams, Cheung, and Choi 2000; Williams and Jarvis 2006) have also employed an electronic version of this manipulation, which they have termed "cyberball." Cyberball is a true online version of their "playing catch" task, with the participant sitting at a computer terminal that is supposedly connected to two other individuals in the study. The screen replicates the lab version of the task with three icons displayed: one for the participant and one for each of the other two players. Again, the players begin to throw the cyberball to one another, including the participant. Upon receiving the ball, the participant picks another player to whom to throw it. And again, in the ostracism condition, after a while the other players systematically begin to ignore the participant and do not throw him or her the ball, resulting in the negative experience of being excluded. (It should be noted that at the end of any of these studies employing an ostracism or social rejection condition, efforts are made to elevate participants' well-being, thus negating the temporary effects of the manipulation.)

TERRY KEEPS WINNING

One reason for Terry's popularity with viewers was his performance under pressure, winning the first five individual Immunity Challenges. In addition, being outnumbered and an underdog, and having to win to save himself, made him a fan favorite. But is it possible that being an outcast helped his performance? On physical tasks requiring endurance and a tolerance for pain, it is possible. For example, Terry won the Immunity Challenge in episode eleven, in which players had to hang on a rope and were forced to hold increasing amounts of weight. This Challenge pushed the castaways—with their hands and arms burning from supporting their weight over the duration of the Challenge—to their physical limits. Terry's win in this Challenge is consistent with research indicating that participants who have had their feelings hurt or anticipate being lonesome—for example, by being ostracized—have higher thresholds for and are less sensitive to pain (DeWall and Baumeister 2006; Macdonald, Kingsbury, and Shaw 2005). Being marginalized might have given Terry extra motivation to succeed. Furthermore, the act of ostracizing another person has negative consequences on the performance of those doing the excluding. It has been shown that after ostracizing another person, one's own physical endurance is diminished (Ciarocco, Sommer, and Baumeister 2001) because doing so takes energy and psychological resources. So, in an ironic twist for the members of Casaya, the fact that they wanted Terry gone might have actually fueled his winning streak. By shunning him, their performance suffered while he performed better and stuck around longer!

Interestingly, hurt caused by social exclusion is remarkably similar to physical pain (MacDonald and Leary 2005). In fact, neuroimaging studies show that the same brain regions are associated with both physical and social pain caused by ostracism (Eisenberger, Lieberman, and Williams 2003). It is likely that both types of pain share a neural pathway, given that they both evolved to promote one's well-being. In other words, feeling physical or social anguish acts as a motivator to remove oneself from a harmful situation. Both are signals of danger, and both require a response to rectify the situation.

TERRY LOSES HIS EDGE AND HIS COOL

Terry's winning streak was helped by the fact that the Challenges were largely physical in nature; he was lucky that there were several physical Challenges in a row. However, his luck began to run out as the tasks became more intellectual, relying on problem solving and memory skills.

Being socially excluded does not improve performance on all types of tasks. While it seems to reduce pain sensitivity, it has also been shown to negatively impact cognitive functioning (i.e., information processing), especially on difficult tasks (Baumeister and DeWall 2005; Baumeister, Twenge, and Nuss 2002). In addition, being outcast can lead to a reduction in self-regulation (i.e., the inhibition of impulsive behavior and unwanted outbursts). Furthermore, social exclusion can lead to aggression by those who have been isolated. This is very clear when one looks at the profile of those who perpetrate school shootings. Typically, the shooters are social outcasts (such as those at Columbine) who have been marginalized by their peers.

Lab studies on social exclusion and ostracism clearly show that being an outcast can lead to aggression. However, because of ethical boundaries, psychologists cannot typically elicit overt aggression (e.g., physical responses against others) in their experiments. It just doesn't seem right to encourage research participants to go postal! So how does one study the link between social rejection and aggression, if causing true aggression is unacceptable? Psychologists have come up with clever and creative solutions to this issue in designing their studies. First, they employ ostracism or social exclusion manipulations, similar to those previously discussed. They then set up situations where they can measure behaviors that represent aggressive responses, without allowing physical aggression to take place. For example, Jean Twenge and colleagues (Twenge, Baumeister, Tice, and Stucke 2001) allowed participants—some of whom were previously socially excluded—to administer blasts of white noise through headphones to others against whom they were playing a game. (Although there was not really anyone else at the receiving end of the blasts, participants believed there was.) As predicted by the experimenters, there was a large difference between the experimental and control groups. Participants who had been previously rejected administered both louder and longer blasts of noise than those who were never excluded. Interestingly, this result was found not only when the partner in the game (i.e., the target of the aggression) was believed to be someone who had previously rejected the participant, but also if it was an innocent third party. In short, social rejection can lead one to retaliate against the perpetrator of the rejection and also against a neutral, uninvolved party.

Likewise, Wayne Warburton and colleagues (Warburton, Williams, and Cairns 2006) employed an ingenious measure of aggression in their research on ostracism. Using the "ball toss" manipulation of ostracism, they then assessed aggressiveness through a "hot sauce allocation" task. That's right—participants got to decide how much hot sauce their partners in the study, who had previously stated a dislike for spicy foods, would have to consume. Warburton and colleagues found that participants who had been previously ostracized by their partners allocated nearly *four times* as much hot sauce to them (about twenty-seven grams, approximately the size of three packets of hot sauce at Taco Bell®).

Although they were short on hot sauce at *Panama*, similar behaviors can be seen in *Survivor*. Upon returning from the Tribal Council that set the final four as Terry, Aras, Danielle, and Cerie, Terry lashed out and yelled at Cerie for leaving her torch in the middle of a pathway—further alienating him from the group. Clearly, he was beginning to succumb to the mounting pressure caused by his social exclusion, and his frustration was starting to spill over. Then, in the subsequent reward Challenge (which required players to move past each other, clipped to ropes, while remembering counts of objects to help them unlock a combination) Terry lost his cool, getting into a shoving match with Aras. In addition, he failed to understand fully the rules of the game, which led to the end of his winning streak. Terry reacted with negative behavior directed at his tribemates, including becoming verbally and physically aggressive against them, and his cognitive functioning started to suffer. He then lost his first Immunity Challenge on a puzzle task (where participants solve puzzles and reveal coordinates for subsequent puzzle pieces—another intellectual assignment). Luckily for him, the threat of his immunity idol, which he discovered on his first trip to Exile Island, still propelled him into the round of the final three.

BUT IT'S JUST A GAME . . .

If *Survivor* is just a game, shouldn't the players be numb to the tactics and group alliances that form? They know full well going into it that the game is all about strategy and that voting tribemates off the island is to be expected; so why should it have such a psychological impact? When voting out a tribemate, players often look into the camera as they write someone's name down, proclaiming that "It's not personal, but it's your time to go." Very rarely are castaways told that "We're getting rid of you because we don't like you." If everyone knows that this is how the game is played, and being voted off (or threatened to be voted off) doesn't mean that everyone hates you, why should the ostracism and exclusion in *Survivor* impact a player's performance at all? Interestingly, this has been studied in psychology labs, as well.

Recall cyberball, the computerized manipulation of ostracism employed in Kip Williams's lab. In this research, participants who believed that the other players in the game didn't want to throw them the ball showed the negative effects of being outcast. Remarkably, their pattern of results were replicated even when participants were told that they were playing with a computer, not other people, and that the computerized sequence of throws was scripted beforehand and not due to choice (Zadro, Williams, and Richardson 2004). In other words, players are told that it's a computer that is not throwing them the ball and that the computer is programmed to ignore them, rather than doing it intentionally. In short, this is akin to *Survivor*, where "It's not personal; it's just part of the game." Even when they know it's "not personal" these participants feel just as bad as those who think they are being intentionally ostracized by human players. It's the mere fact that one is socially rejected, and not necessarily the reason behind the rejection, that causes the negative consequences.

In addition, what is so remarkable about the manipulations employed in psychology labs is the magnitude of the effects created with seemingly benign tasks, such as being ignored by others throwing a (cyber)ball back and forth for a few minutes. If this type of temporary and mild rejection can have such an impact on participants, what is the experience of people who are chronically exposed to much more acute and important forms of social isolation?

BEYOND THE ISLAND

It's clear that social exclusion and ostracism play an important role in *Survivor*. The game is set up to accentuate existing human behavioral tendencies and group phenomena, and *Survivor* provides the context that highlights the undoubted importance of understanding social rejection and isolation. Just as Terry's experiences and subsequent feelings and behaviors were in large part due to his position within his group, most people will experience ostracism and rejection from social groups at some point in their lives. Perhaps even worse, every person has the potential to ostracize others in the social groups that they form on a daily basis. An understanding of the group behavior in *Survivor*, coupled with a grasp of psychology, can tell us a lot about the real world effects of ostracism and exclusion. It certainly can help us to comprehend the risk factors that predict suicide or school shootings, and if we acknowledge the power of rejection we can identify ways of reducing the negative effects of social isolation.

ACKNOWLEDGMENTS

We'd like to thank Mike Halenar and Amelia Mutso at Haverford for their help in preparing this chapter. In addition, we're thankful that Jen and Colleen haven't voted us off our respective islands.

BENJAMIN LE, PH.D., is a native Californian and currently an assistant professor of psychology at Haverford College, after having completed his undergraduate degree at Grinnell College and Ph.D. in social psychology at Purdue University. His research is on commitment, emotions, and social networks in close relationships. Le has not yet applied to be on *Survivor*, for fear of being rejected.

GARY LEWANDOWSKI, JR., PH.D., originally from Fairless Hills, PA (a suburb of Philadelphia), received his bachelor's degree from Millersville University of Pennsylvania. He received his master's and Ph.D. from the State University of New York at Stony Brook in Long Island, NY. He is currently an assistant professor of psychology at Monmouth University (the alma mater of former *Survivor* contestants Katie Gallagher and Stephenie LaGrossa) in West Long Branch, NJ. His research focuses on romantic relationships including interpersonal attraction, relationship maintenance, and break-ups.

REFERENCES

Baumeister, R. F. and C. N. DeWall. "The Inner Dimension of Social Exclusion: Intelligent Thought and Self-Regulation Among Rejected Persons." In *The Social Outcast: Ostracism, Social Exclusion, Rejection, and Bullying*, edited by K. D. Williams, J. P. Forgas, and W. von Hippel. New York: Psychology Press, 2005.

Baumeister, R. F. and M. R. Leary. "The Need to Belong: Desire for Interpersonal Attachments as a Fundamental Human Motivation." *Psychological Bulletin* 117 (1995): 497–529.

Baumeister, R. F., J. M. Twenge, and C. Nuss. "Effects of Social Exclusion on Cognitive Processes: Anticipated Aloneness Reduces Intelligent Thought." *Journal of Personality and Social Psychology* 83 (2002): 817–827.

Ciarocco, N. J., K. L. Sommer, and R. F. Baumeister. "Ostracism and Ego Depletion: The Strains of Silence." *Personality and Social Psychology Bulletin* 27 (2001): 1156–1163.

DeWall, C. N. and R. F. Baumeister. "Alone but Feeling No Pain: Effects of Social Exclusion on Physical Pain Tolerance and Pain Threshold, Affective Forecasting, and Interpersonal Empathy." *Journal of Personality and Social Psychology* 91 (2006): 1–15.

Eisenberger, N. I., M. D. Lieberman, and K. D. Williams. "Does Rejection Hurt? An fMRI Study of Social Exclusion." *Science* 302 (2003): 290–292.

Leary, M. R. "Varieties of Interpersonal Rejection." In *The Social Outcast: Ostracism, Social Exclusion, Rejection, and Bullying*, edited by K. D. Williams, J. P. Forgas, and W. von Hippel. New York: Psychology Press, 2005.

MacDonald, G. and M. R. Leary. "Why Does Social Exclusion Hurt? The Relationship Between Social and Physical Pain." *Psychological Bulletin* 131 (2005): 202–223.

MacDonald, G., R. Kingsbury, and S. Shaw. "Adding Insult to Injury: Social Pain Theory and Response to Social Exclusion." In *The Social Outcast: Ostracism, Social Exclusion, Rejection, and Bullying*, edited by K. D. Williams, J. P. Forgas, and W. von Hippel. New York: Psychology Press, 2005.

Trout, D. L. "The Role of Social Isolation in Suicide." *Suicide and Life-Threatening Behavior* 10 (1980): 10–23.

Twenge, J. M., R. F. Baumeister, D. M. Tice, and T. S. Stucke. "If You Can't Join

Them, Beat Them: Effects of Social Exclusion on Aggressive Behavior." *Journal of Personality and Social Psychology* 81 (2001): 1058–1069.

Warburton, W. A. and K. D. Williams. "Ostracism: When Competing Motivations Collide." In *Social Motivation: Conscious and Unconscious Processes*, edited by J. P. Forgas, K. D. Williams, and S. M. Laham. New York: Cambridge University Press, 2005.

Warburton, W. A., K. D.Williams, and D. R. Cairns. "When Ostracism Leads to Aggression: The Moderating Effects of Control Deprivation." *Journal of Experimental Social Psychology* 42 (2006): 213–220.

Williams, K. D., and B. Jarvis. "Cyberball: A Program for Use in Research on Ostracism and Interpersonal Acceptance." *Behavior Research Methods, Instruments, and Computers* 38 (2006): 174–180.

Williams, K. D. and K. L. Sommer. "Social Ostracism by Coworkers: Does Rejection Lead to Loafing or Compensation?" *Personality and Social Psychology Bulletin* 23 (1997): 693–706.

Williams, K. D., C. K. T. Cheung, and W. Choi. "Cyberostracism: Effects of Being Ignored Over the Internet." *Journal of Personality and Social Psychology* 79 (2000): 748–762.

Zadro, L., K. D. Williams, and R. Richardson. "How Low Can You Go? Ostracism by a Computer Lowers Belonging, Control, Self-Esteem, and Meaningful Existence." *Journal of Experimental Social Psychology* 40 (2004) 560–567.

Robert Batsell suggests that research on the limits of human behavior provides important clues for the optimal design of reality TV programs. By reviewing this research literature, Batsell is able to identify components of Survivor *and other successful reality shows that assure their success. Based on these observations, Batsell proposes Quadruple-D: a program that maximizes deception, deprivation, disgust, and danger. Happy (prospective) viewing!*

Quadruple-D

Deception, Deprivation, Disgust, and Danger
in the Reality Show of the Future!

ROBERT BATSELL, PH.D.

TO: NETWORK PROGRAMMING DEVELOPMENT, REALITY
TELEVISION DIVISION
DATE: Winter, 2007

Psychology is commonly defined as the systematic study of the behavior and mental processes of living organisms (e.g., Westen 1999). There are a number of questions that this definition brings to mind, but one of the most compelling to great thinkers is, "What are the limits of human behavior?" Consider the person or persons marooned on a deserted island. After a high-school literature class, one might surmise that a *Lord of the Flies* scenario would emerge, with the eventual disintegration of social norms (Golding 1959). Or, if a person is abandoned alone, we might picture a descent into self-cannibalistic behavior (as in Stephen King's short story "Survivor Type," 1985). There are a few firsthand accounts of individuals who have been lost at sea (e.g., *Adrift*, Callahan 1986), but it is hard to interpret these accounts because we do not have complete reports from those who did not survive. Psychologists were making steady progress on understanding the limits of human behavior through the 1960s, as exemplified by the following three research enterprises into deprivation, hypnosis, and obedience.

DEPRIVATION

Research into deprivation can reveal what is really important to people and what they need to remain mentally and physically healthy. Obviously, food is necessary to human survival, and one would not expect a person to live long without *any* food; but how would people react when deprived of their normal food intake? The most comprehensive experiment of this nature occurred at the University of Minnesota during World War II under the supervision of Ancel Keys, who was the originator of the K ration and an early advocate of controlling cholesterol (Tucker 2006). The study's purpose was to understand rehabilitation from starvation to help malnourished Europeans in the food-depleted time after the war. Keys studied thirty-six male conscientious objectors for a six-month period during which they received half of their normal caloric intakes, and then a three-month rehabilitation phase with increased rations. On average, the volunteers lost a quarter of their body weight, and their fitness levels decreased by 72 percent. Volunteers reported an increase in fatigue and decreases in attention, comprehension, and ambition. The volunteers soon became obsessed with food to the exclusion of other drives, such as sex. Indeed, some participants hoarded cookbooks and lustily read recipes; others had dreams of food and nightmares of cannibalism. In 1979, Keys reminisced about the study: "I doubt another of its kind will ever be done" (Hoffman 2006).

A different type of deprivation experiment emerged in the early 1950s. Fueled by rumors that sensory deprivation (SD) was one of the techniques used by our political rivals at the time (the Chinese and the Russians) to facilitate "brainwashing," a host of researchers conducted experiments on the effects of SD. The initial experimental work in this area was conducted at McGill University (Suedfeld 1969); soon researchers from the military and other prestigious institutions, such as Princeton University, Duke University, the University of Michigan, and the National Institute of Mental Health, began SD experiments. The methodology of these experiments ranged widely. In some studies, sub-

jects were confined to a bed with opaque goggles and mittens; others utilized immersion in water with a breathing tube; still others placed subjects in a dark, soundproof room. To produce visual deprivation, subjects were blindfolded, placed in a boring environment, or subjected to
complete darkness. Auditory deprivation was achieved through either a
soundproof room or a masking white noise. In some cases, movement
was also restricted through a soundproof, coffin-like apparatus. The subjects in the SD studies reported complex hallucinations, a decline in
intellectual abilities, an increased willingness to believe propaganda, and
strong desires to quit the experiment.

Isolation Tolerance is the amount of time a participant can endure SD.
The data are clear that a short period of SD (less than twenty-four hours)
is not particularly disturbing, but periods up to seven days can affect the
subjects. For example, eighteen of eighteen subjects completed a one-
day SD study, but only twenty-one of forty subjects completed a seven-
day SD study (Myers 1969). There were pronounced individual differences in participants' tolerances of SD. One reason is that when individuals are removed from variety in external stimulation, they tend to focus
their thoughts inward. Yet, without many external cues to direct their
thinking, they engage in dream-like or fantasy thinking. One notable
limitation of this work is that it generally used young volunteers from
the military or academic institutions in which their overall mental
health could be ascertained; the analysis of those with weaker constitu-
tions remains undetermined.

HYPNOSIS

A different means to test the inquiry "How far will people go?" is to
assume that people actively inhibit their inappropriate and antisocial
behaviors. If released from these inhibitions, a person might engage in
the full range of behaviors available to him or her. One possible way to
release these inhibitions is hypnosis. Orne and Evans (1965) tested the
limits of hypnotized individuals and whether they would engage in
apparently dangerous behavior. To test this hypothesis, they designed a
series of tasks, including three potentially dangerous ones. The dangerous tasks included: 1) *venomous snake*, in which the subject reached into

a chamber to grasp a live, poisonous snake; 2) *coin in acid*, in which the subject retrieved a coin from a beaker of bubbling nitric acid; and 3) *throwing acid*, in which the subject pitched the acid into the face of the experimenter's assistant. (In reality, none of these tasks was ultimately dangerous, as the subject's reach into the snake chamber was prevented by an unseen glass panel, a soapy solution was present to neutralize the nitric acid, and the nitric acid solution was exchanged for a safe solution before the face-scorching instruction was given. But the participants did not know this.)

When the researchers asked faculty colleagues to participate in these activities, none could be persuaded to perform any of the three acts, lending credence to the idea that these tasks were indeed dangerous. Yet, the response from the experimental subjects was quite different; Orne and Evans reported that five of the six hypnotized subjects performed all three dangerous tasks. Although this result would appear to support the idea that hypnotized people will do anything while unhypnotized people will not, the results of two control groups suggest otherwise. A group of six subjects was asked to act like they were hypnotized in order to "fool" the experimenter; all six completed the three dangerous tasks. A group of "normal" participants, who were only asked to follow instructions, showed a similar pattern of responding, with half trying to grasp the venomous snake and five of six retrieving the coin and tossing the acid. The results of the control groups undermine the idea that it is the act of being hypnotized that compels subjects to carry out dangerous acts—because normal individuals can be equally compelled to do these same acts. Why would subjects complete these apparently dangerous tasks? Post-experiment interviews with the subjects confirmed that many concluded that reasonable experimenters would not ask them to do anything truly dangerous, and so they followed instructions without question—which leads us to our next topic.

OBEDIENCE

A third way to observe limitations of human behavior is to place subjects in a situation that forces them to do something they would not normally do. As mentioned in previous chapters, the most famous example of this is the Milgram obedience experiments conducted in the 1960s. Subjects and confederates were "randomly" assigned to roles where the subject became the Teacher, and the confederate became the Learner. In one variation, the experimenter took the Learner to an adjacent room where the Learner was attached to a shock generator and given the instructions that whenever an error was made, a powerful (but not dangerous) shock would be administered. The Teacher was then escorted to the lab and shown the machine that he or she would use to deliver shocks to the Learner. The Teacher was given the instruction to read word pairs to the Learner (e.g., blue-boy) and then later prompt the Learner with the word "blue"; the Learner should then correctly choose "boy" from a list of four alternatives. If the Learner answered incorrectly or provided no answer, the Teacher would punish the Learner with a shock, and the correct answer would be provided. Moreover, the punishment would gradually increase with each incorrect answer from a slight fifteen volts to a severe 450 volts!

In reality, the Learner did not receive any shocks, but merely played a recording of screams. The true purpose was to determine the effect of the authority figure telling the Teacher to deliver dangerous shocks to an innocent person; Milgram was interested in this question to understand why normal individuals engaged in atrocious behaviors in Nazi Germany. Earlier, Milgram had surveyed a number of scientists and asked them to predict how many subjects would follow orders and use every shock setting. These experts predicted less than one-tenth of one percent of the Teachers would administer the 450-volt shock; in actuality, 65 percent of the Teachers obeyed the experimenter and delivered the most painful shocks. Thus, this experiment and others confirmed that people will often engage in antisocial behavior if they are told to do so by an authority figure. One unanticipated consequence of this work was the mental distress experienced by the Teachers: they sweated and fidgeted during the experiment, frequently asking if the study could be discontinued—yet, most Teachers obediently delivered another shock on command.

Tragically, these clever experiments couldn't be conducted today. The reason for this is that the American Psychological Association (APA) adopted a code of ethics for research with humans in 1973, which was most recently updated in 2002 (Goodwin 2005). Current research must first be submitted to an Institutional Review Board (IRB) that determines if the risks of participation are equal to the risks encountered in every-day life, and whether the benefits of conducting the research outweigh the psychological and physiological costs to the participants. Some other notable aspects of these ethical guidelines are:

1. *Informed Consent*: Participants must be informed of any potential risks (such as electric shocks) they may experience while partici-pating in the study.
2. *Confidentiality*: The data should never be presented in a manner where the responses of any given individual can be identified.
3. *Freedom to Leave at Any Time*: Participants should be able to quit the experiment at any time and not suffer any consequences for doing so.

Sadly, this "noble" code of ethics limits research in at least two ways. First, experimenters are constrained by ethical standards and the over-sight of an IRB, so they have to eliminate all potential physiological and psychological dangers in their studies. Second, because the participants are aware that they are in a study, and they are informed of any possible harm that may befall them, they enter a unique situation where their true responses are surely compromised.

Why is this change such a loss? Because the studies that are now approved are so watered-down, the results tell us little about the limits of human behavior. Consider this example in which psychologists examined the limits of human behavior by gauging how far participants will go in completing disgusting tasks: Rozin, Haidt, McCauley, Dunlop, and Ashmore (1999) conducted research in which their participants were requested to perform up to twenty-five behaviors, many of which would be considered disgusting. Some of the tasks (and the percentage of people who did it to completion) included eating dog food (7 per-cent), bringing a mealworm to the lips (9 percent), eating a grasshopper (12 percent), drinking water from a clean bedpan (28 percent), and eat-ing cremated ashes (1 percent). In addition to these tasks, participants also watched three different disturbing video clips (infant facial surgery, eating live monkey brain, and butchering cattle in a slaughterhouse). Again, participants were allowed to stop viewing the videos at any point of their choosing. After completing these activities, participants agreed the experiment was interesting, enjoyable, and recommendable. Interesting? Enjoyable? Recommendable? These are not words used by people who have reached their limits. By the turn of this century, it was clear that psychological research had become nothing more than the study of innocuous behaviors—and personally, I feared the questions regarding the limits of human behavior would never be answered.

EMERGENCE OF THE ALTERNATIVE

Luckily for those of us who are seekers of the truth, reality television emerged as an alternative to conventional research, and leading the charge was *Survivor*. One must recall how the original *Survivor* captured the American television viewing audience in the summer of 2000. Prior to this time, reality television had had little impact on American's television viewing habits, as the major broadcasters spent most of their money on scripted programs. Furthermore, *Survivor*'s premise was different from any other type of show: a group of sixteen "regular" people would be abandoned in a harsh and dangerous environment, deprived of any resources or the basic necessities of life, and forced to survive.

Survivor's format provided a perfect way to experiment and update some of the research I described earlier. For example, deprivation is a key factor on the show. Contestants have been placed on an island with little to no food, no potable water, no shelter, and no social support from family or friends. We have seen intelligent contestants who recognized the necessities of life and immediately spent the first crucial hours building shelter, making fire, and trying to procure food and water; on the other hand, we have also seen idiots wasting time to share background stories and act like they were on vacation. And it wasn't long before we saw the effects of removing people from the typical American diet, as thin women began to show their ribs, and the pants were even falling off Richard Hatch. Later, we often saw the "food fantasy" episodes, when contestants sat around lusting after their favorite foods and longingly describing what they planned to eat once home. By this point, food had become a powerful reinforcer that could motivate taboo behaviors. A classic example of the effects of food deprivation occurred in *Survivor: Amazon* when Jenna and Heidi bared their breasts for chocolate and peanut butter—now that was great television!

Disgust has also played a key role in *Survivor*. Often, the producers have employed regional foods that would be considered disgusting to the American diet as a reward or Immunity Challenge obstacle. For example, the Immunity Challenge in the second episode involved eating live bugs. This is a classic approach-avoidance conflict in which the contestant really wants the immunity but must overcome a task that he or she would normally avoid (bug eating) to earn it.

At other times, the conflict is between food deprivation and disgust. After seven days of food deprivation, the Pagong tribe from season one considered surf and turf—minnows and rats. Later seasons showed more adventurous and experienced survivors, like Rafe, eating ants to fight hunger (*Survivor: Guatemala*).

Danger is also an element of *Survivor*. The contestants are constantly putting themselves at greater risks than they would in everyday situations. Numerous contestants have experienced injuries that have ranged from somewhat mild (a jellyfish sting that required urine treatment in *Survivor: Marquesas*) to game-ending (Michael from *Survivor: Australian Outback*, who was burned severely when he fell in the fire).

Regrettably, deception has been underutilized by the producers of *Survivor*. One can sense that they almost pride themselves on having situations that appear respectable. Still, from season to season, the producers have changed the rules of the game without informing the contestants, and the players make strategic moves anticipating that the game will transpire as it has in the past. In this sense, the contestants have been deceived, and this has produced some of the show's best and worst moments. In the former category falls the look of surprise on Shii Ann's soon-to-be-evicted face once she realized that her double-dealing had been exposed because she assumed that the tribes coming together meant a merge had occurred during *Survivor: Thailand*. On the negative side, the producers earned the fans' ire when they allowed eliminated contestants Burton and Lillian back into the game during *Survivor: Pearl Islands*. Although *Survivor* has given us insights into human behavior that we haven't been able to obtain through psychological research, the producers have gotten soft.

Since the initial season of *Survivor*, the producers have made the acquisition of food and water harder and harder, but at some point they acquiesce and let an impoverished tribe "earn" food or water. Ironically, the ability to survive is now a detriment as individuals with real survival skills and strengths are quickly eliminated as threats (e.g., Hunter from *Survivor: Marquesas*). Indeed, over the years, *Survivor* has evolved into a social psychology experiment in which people make alliances, lie to other people, and try to advance through each Tribal Council to win the title of "Sole Survivor." Although this social survival can be quite fascinating, especially in the hands of a true strategic player (see *Survivor* strategy columns at www.RealityNewsOnline.com), *Survivor* has strayed from its premise as a scenario in which we could learn the limits of human behavior. Thankfully, other television producers have recognized that the American television audience enjoys watching people suffer, and subsequent shows have stepped up to advance our understanding of deprivation, disgust, and deception.

The producers of other reality shows understand the potential of deprivation and have used it as a means to produce conflict. For example, the central component of *Big Brother* is the isolation of contestants in a house without access to television, books, computers, or their families. Recently, Fox's *Solitary*, in which nine contestants were placed in solitary confinement and tested by the computer Val, took deprivation even further. In each episode, the contestants were subjected to "psychological games"—such as lying on a bed of nails, food deprivation, undergoing sleep deprivation, tests of equilibrium, and other manipulations—that tested their patience. Wow! The producers of *Solitary* are starting to get it right and realize the true potential of reality television. They are subjecting the contestants to psychological manipulations, recording their responses, broadcasting it across the country, and doing more than just scratching the surface of deprivation.

More than any other show, *Fear Factor* has exploited disgust. Indeed, I recommend that *Fear Factor* be renamed *Disgust Factor* because the second of three Challenges often requires the contestants to eat disgusting objects, such as stink beetles, bile, Madagascar hissing cockroaches, worms, cow eyeballs, and—in a memorable holiday episode—reindeer penis. The best moments of this show are watching the contestants fight to avoid elimination and overcome their disgust responses by choking back their gag reflexes and suffering through a nausea-inducing meal for our benefit. But even the producers of *Fear Factor* must go further. By now, the contestants know that many of the chosen foods are consumed outside of American culture, or—just like the subjects in the hypnosis experiment of Orne and Evans (1965)—they tacitly assume that they wouldn't be asked to eat something that would really kill them. So, even though *Fear Factor* has shown us that people will devour insects and entrails for money, I know these depths can be plumbed further.

Deception has been the core concept of other reality television programs. One of the first reality television shows to be built around deceit was *Joe Millionaire*. In this program, a group of attractive women shared a chateau with supposed-millionaire Evan. The program's conflict arose during the final episode when Evan picked his suitor Zora, and she was told he wasn't a millionaire after all, but, heaven forbid, a blue-collar worker! Would she still love him now that she knew he was poor? Even a general psychology student who was familiar with cognitive dissonance knew there was no way Zora would say "no." After convincing herself that she was interested in Evan for his "personality" and not his money, how could she then reject him because he didn't have money and show the viewing audience how shallow she was?

If *Joe Millionaire* was one of the first to use deception to place contestants in positions to humiliate themselves in front of America, *My Big Fat Obnoxious Fiancé* took deceitfulness to a whole new level. In this show, two mismatched contestants, an attractive blonde female and a slobbish male, were told they could win a big money prize if they could convince their families that they had fallen in love and were getting married within a week. The brilliance of this program was that the family members were not the only ones being deceived: the slobbish male fiancé was not really a contestant, but an actor who was hired by the producers to be as obnoxious as possible to cause the female contestant immense amounts of stress. Each episode showed the actor becoming more and more boorish and the female contestant becoming more frazzled and alienating her family more by the minute. As the fake wedding approached, we saw the female contestant continue her pursuit of the money at the expense of her family relationships.

There is no way a psychologist would or could have done this experiment. The female contestant and her family would have had to be informed of the possible consequences of participating, and their responses would have been kept confidential. Where is the fun in that? Luckily, the TV network has clever lawyers who crafted a liability waiver that allowed the TV network to publicly humiliate this family on national television for their profit and our enjoyment. Once I saw that the TV network could subject this family to public ridicule without any consequences, I knew it was time for *QUADRUPLE-D*!

THE PROPOSAL

At this point, a few things should be clear: First, most competition-type reality television programs share the same format. In these shows, the contestants are motivated by large sums of money, the possibilities of love, the bragging rights of winning a game, or their fifteen minutes of fame. But in all of these shows, the contestants have to endure certain conditions or challenges that are designed to produce conflict, and the shows that are most successful are those that produce the largest amounts of conflict. Moreover, conflict can occur between different contestants (inter-individual) or it can be within a given contestant (intra-individual). The key to inter-individual conflict is to select individuals who will fight and argue because of their personalities or to produce inter-individual conflict by pitting them in competition with each other. Intra-individual conflict is produced when individuals must overcome some challenge or condition to win, and we get to watch them struggling with their inner psychological turmoil. Second, the concepts of deception, deprivation, disgust, and danger can be used to generate both inter-individual and intra-individual conflict and, thereby, produce reality television shows that will attract sizable audiences. The following proposal describes the framework of the program *QUADRUPLE-D* that should earn a good market share for your network, while also allowing us to learn the limits of human behavior.

Certain measures will be given during the contestant screening process to ensure sensitivity to our manipulations. First, to maximize the disgust quotient, potential applicants will complete the Disgust Sensitivity Questionnaire (DSQ: Haidt, McCauley, and Rozin 1994), which is a thirty-two-item scale that can reveal those participants who would be most likely to experience disgust and overreact—because nothing kills the drama faster than a contestant with an impaired olfactory system or reduced disgust sensitivity who can consume all of the disgusting items without gagging or complaining. Thus, no contestant should be selected for the program unless he or she has a high score on the DSQ. Second, although there is no scale that will predict who will be most susceptible to SD, Myers noted "deprivation-intolerant subjects tend to be youngish, television-watching, non-reading smokers" (305). We should have no problem finding this group! Third, the producers should remember the hilarity during *Survivor: Panama* when Shane was trying to endure caffeine and nicotine withdrawal while competing; imagine the good television that could be produced by a couple of methadone addicts! Fourth, twelve contestants sounds like a good number, with an equal number of males and females; I trust that the producers will select the contestants based on the body shape they hope will attract the desired demographic.

The setting for *QUADRUPLE-D* is crucial to ensure that the elements of deprivation, deception, disgust, and danger can be employed to the fullest. The key is to have the contestants in a confined environment where they can interact with a computer, and the possibility of danger is palpable. I propose an underground morgue of a decommissioned military facility; this setting is plausible because other reality shows have been set in underground or creepy settings, such as an abandoned prison. The contestants can even be told that the show is similar to *Survivor*: they will compete in Challenges, eliminate contestants every couple of days, and win a big cash prize.

The underground setting will have two rooms. The Living Quarters will contain plush accommodations with comfortable bunks, a dining table that can accommodate twelve adults, a sufficient number of easy chairs, and clean, full-sized restrooms. Of course, the contestants will only be staying in the Living Quarters for two days, because the Morgue will actually be the contestant's main living quarters for the majority of the program. The Living Quarters will be separated from the Morgue by a vault-like door.

The Morgue should be a sterile and bland circular room with dull, white walls to promote SD. The ceiling should be too high to reach and have an extensive sprinkler system. It will also contain very bright lights, appropriate for surgery, that are covered with an unbreakable polymer. In the center of the room should be a stainless-steel operating table that is affixed to the metal grid floor (the reason for this will soon be apparent). The walls of the Morgue will contain eight coffin enclosures; these should be operable, but with a retractable mechanism so that they will close unless a person continues to hold them open. Some of these caskets should be scented with a decaying flesh odor and ash-like material to convince the contestants that this facility was once a working morgue. Of course, hidden infrared cameras and microphones will be embedded in the ceiling, walls, and in each casket.

The only other features of the Morgue will be a closed-circuit television monitor, keyboard, and dumbwaiter. During the initial days of the study, the contestants will be able to view the host and receive written instructions on the closed-circuit television, communicate with the host and the computer via the keyboard, and receive food and rewards through the dumbwaiter. For example, the contestants would be called to the Morgue and told via the screen that if they correctly solve the Challenge, the computer will dispense a tasty dinner reward, but if they are incorrect, their dinner reward will be undesirable. Moreover, for each consecutive wrong answer, the quality of the meal will decrease. To facilitate learning, during the first two days the contestants will be given at least one easy puzzle, which will earn a meal of lobster, steak, and champagne; but they will also be given one unsolvable problem that will earn spoiled milk and moldy cheese.

One limitation of previous research and reality television shows is that the contestants assume that no reasonable researcher or television producer would actually expose them to dangers that were not pre-tested or reversible. *QUADRUPLE-D* will change that! On Day Three, the contestants will be called to the Morgue for a Challenge, and as always, the door separating the Morgue from the Living Quarters will be sealed. The contestants will be listening to the Challenge instructions on the closed-circuit television when they observe the above-ground facility being attacked by terrorists. This should involve some good special effects that involve the TV producers and host being shot and killed, and various explosions. It is crucial during this time that the transmission on the closed-circuit television be lost for periods of time, the door separating the Morgue and the Living Quarters permanently sealed, and the lights extinguished to plunge the contestants into darkness. The upshot is that the contestants should be convinced that the individuals who have been responsible for their safety are no longer alive, and they are in real danger. Now the fun really begins!

During the following days, the contestants can be subjected to a variety of different treatments—the only limits are our imaginations. I propose they be subjected to complete darkness for as long as necessary to observe the effects of complete SD. At other times, the lights can stay on so that the heat and light are relentless; this should promote the level of skin baring that is a prerequisite for reality television audiences. Also, because the "terrorist attack" damaged the infrastructure of the underground facility, the contestants can now be subjected to unpredictable dousings of cold water from the overhead sprinkler system, ear-piercing noises, noxious odors of death and decay, low levels of radiation to induce nausea, and occasional shocks delivered through the floor. Eventually, if the contestants do not become too helpless, the steady dose of cold-water dousing and painful shocks should prompt them to realize that the only escape in the Morgue is a coffin, and we should see their inner conflicts as they want to avoid the shock and water but fear living in a coffin. Of course, they will have to decide how twelve people fit into eight coffins!

Obviously, the contestants will not have any water or food in the Morgue. Water can be delivered randomly via the overhead sprinkler system, but there will be no cups to collect it. I recommend a single, stained bedpan be placed in one of the coffins. We will see if the participants are as comfortable drinking from a bedpan if they think it was used! Luckily for them, the computer will still work erratically enough to allow them to complete increasingly difficult puzzles for increasingly disgusting food items. On some trials, it will be entertaining to provide a puzzle that the contestants can eventually solve to earn a desired food reward, which we can lace with pharmaceuticals. Imagine the confused couplings produced by a cocktail of hallucinogens, laxatives, and Viagra. Alternatively, imagine the stress and strain as contestants work at an esoteric Challenge because the last meal they received was maggoty meat. How hard would they work if the computer indicated that their next reward for a wrong answer were a single piece of five-day-old fish? Or their own pet? At this point, the show can continue for as long as we wish. The contestants can be maintained on enough food and water to keep them alive and, once and for all, we can determine the true limits of human behavior.

You may be wondering which contestant is the winner of *QUADRU-PLE-D*. Who cares?! The television audience, your network, and my research are the real winners.

AUTHOR'S NOTE

Obviously, the show proposed in this paper is a work of satire. Bob Batsell has served on a number of research review boards for both human participants and animal subjects, he upholds these ethical standards, and he has the utmost respect for the cited research that adheres to these standards. The purpose of this essay is to illustrate the potential abuse and ethical wasteland possible in the escalation of reality TV show ideas. Nonetheless, if any producer steals the ideas from the *Quadruple-D* proposal, Batsell fully expects royalties.

ROBERT BATSELL, PH.D., is originally from Brownsville, Texas. He earned bachelor's degrees in biology and psychology from Southern Methodist University, and his Ph.D. in experimental psychology from Texas Christian University. Currently he is the Kurt D. Kaufman Associate Professor and Chair of Psychology at Kalamazoo College. He is a biopsychologist whose teaching interests include general psychology, experimental psychology, psychology of learning, and biopsychology. His research focuses on the learning mechanisms that underlie food aversions in humans and nonhumans. He spends way too much of his time watching *Survivor* along with his nine-year-old son Evan. He is indebted to Karen Doyle, Dan Jacobson, Suzanne MacDonald, and Andy Mozina for their feedback on this manuscript.

REFERENCES

American Psychological Association. *Ethical Principles in the Conduct of Research with Human Participants.* Washington, DC: American Psychological Association, 1973.

American Psychological Association. "Ethical Principles of Psychologists and Code of Conduct." *American Psychologist* 57 (2002): 1060–1073.

Callahan, S. *Adrift: Seventy-six Days Lost at Sea.* New York: Ballantine Books, 1986.

Golding, W. *Lord of the Flies.* New York: Capricorn Books, 1959.

Goodwin, C. J. *Research in Psychology: Methods and Design.* 4th ed. Hoboken, NJ: John Wiley & Sons, Inc., 2005.

Haidt, J., C. McCauley, and P. Rozin. "Individual Differences in Sensitivity to Disgust: A Scale Sampling Seven Domains of Disgust Elicitors." *Personality and Individual Differences* 16 (1994): 701–713.

Hoffman, W. "Meet Monsieur Cholesterol." MBBNet: Minnesota Biomedical & Bioscience Network. 2006. <mbbnet.umn.edu/hoff/hoff_ak.html>

King, S. "Survivor Type." In *Skeleton Crew* (361–378). New York: G.P. Putnam's Sons, 1985.

Milgram, S. *Obedience to Authority.* New York: Harper & Row, 1974.

Myers, T. I. "Tolerance for Sensory and Perceptual Deprivation." In *Sensory Deprivation: Fifteen Years of Research*, edited by J. P. Zubek (289–331). New York: Appleton-Century-Croft, 1969.

Orne, M. T. and F. J. Evans. "Social Control in the Psychological Experiment: Antisocial Behavior and Hypnosis." *Journal of Personality and Social Psychology* 1 (1965): 189–200.

Reality News Online (2006). Retrieved at www.realitynewsonline.com.

Rozin, P., J. Haidt, C. McCauley, L. Dunlop, and M. Ashmore. "Individual Differences in Disgust Sensitivity: Comparisons and Evaluations of Paper-and-Pencil versus Behavioral Measures." *Journal of Research in Personality* 33 (1999): 330–351.

Suedfeld, P. "Introduction and Historical Background." *In Sensory Deprivation: Fifteen Years of Research*, edited by J. P. Zubek (3–15). New York: Appleton-Century-Croft, 1969.

Tucker, T. *The Great Starvation Experiment: The Heroic Men Who Starved So That Millions Could Live*. New York: Free Press, 2006.

Westen, D. *Psychology: Mind, Brain, & Culture*. 3rd ed. New York: John Wiley & Sons, Inc., 1999.

If Charles Darwin were still among us, he might be surprised to learn how "survival of the fittest" applies to Survivor. Brad Wolgast and Mario J. Lanza analyze data from twelve seasons to support the proposition that "In Survivor, small, non-threatening women are far more dangerous than brawny men." Wolgast and Lanza proceed to identify the skills that make women more fit to survive on Survivor.

"What? How Did *SHE* Win?"

Or, I Will *Always* Wave My Estrogen in Your Face

BRAD WOLGAST, PH.D., AND MARIO J. LANZA

Back in 2000, when you first heard about a show called *Survivor*, your first reaction was probably similar to that of the average American. Odds are, the first thing that popped into your head was something along the lines of, "Contestants live on an island for as long as they can, and the last one left standing wins? You mean people are actually going to die on national TV? Cool!"

Although it might seem strange to today's audiences, *Survivor* was originally presented to the public as a "survival of the fittest" game of natural selection. All we knew about the show was that people were going to be tossed onto a deserted island, they were expected to live there until they couldn't hack it anymore, and the last remaining player would be crowned the "Sole Survivor." Then he or she would be rewarded with riches and fame. That was all we knew! As unsophisticated *Survivor* viewers, we had never heard of such a thing as a "voting strategy." We were completely unaware that you were supposed to have four people in an "alliance" (whatever that was). We had absolutely no idea that an otherwise intelligent neurosurgeon would think it was a good idea to vote people off alphabetically. We were blissfully unaware of all of this, and were fascinated to see how this game show was actually going to play out.

All we knew back in 2000 was that *Survivor* was going to be survival of the fittest. It was going to be a Darwinian contest of natural selection, and it was going to play out on prime-time TV. The best-suited outdoorsman was going to win, the cream was going to rise to the top, and in the end, the last person standing would inevitably be the best. It would be the purest case of natural selection ever seen on network TV.

Well, as of this writing, there have now been twelve seasons of *Survivor*. And by this point, it's safe to say that the above descriptions now sound hopelessly naïve. This show was supposed to be survival of the fittest? The cream was supposed to rise to the top? The most natural outdoorsman was going to win every time? What the heck were we talking about? After all, didn't Jenna Morasca win the Amazon season, despite the fact that she was a twenty-one-year-old swimsuit model who washed her underwear in the drinking water? Didn't Sandra Diaz-Twine win in *Pearl Islands*, despite the fact that she couldn't run, jump, swim, or find food to save her life? How on earth do we explain Tina Wesson's win in *Survivor: Australian Outback*? After all, she couldn't have weighed more than ninety-five pounds by the end. Not to mention the fact that she was so finicky she would only eat two things, rice or fish, and only if cooked to her exact specifications. Yet this woman ended up winning *Survivor*? Tina Wesson won a contest of survival of the fittest? A woman who gagged when the rice was too pasty?

The examples listed above are meant to be extreme, but it's perfectly evident that all three of them had several key factors in common. In fact it should be obvious to everybody at first glance that Jenna, Sandra, and Tina were all:

a) Women

b) Not particularly outdoorsy

c) Completely unlikely to win a game based on natural selection

and

d) *Survivor* champions

The gender of Tina, Sandra, and Jenna is particularly noteworthy here. After all, it does provide good evidence of the evolved dispositions (Eagly and Wood 1999) that feminist psychologists have been describing for years. This theory helps explain why women (and less physical men) have won *Survivor* far more often than aggressive alpha males, and aren't likely to stop anytime in the foreseeable future. It also explains why *Survivor* is a game that females play better than males. It's all due to the way that American women approach life, at least in comparison to men. Don't worry; we'll explain this in greater detail later. Suffice it to say that women have dominated this game for a long, long time.

If a small, unlikely, non-outdoorsy woman had won *Survivor* one time, we might have dismissed it as a fluke. Maybe all the other players drowned ("Ostened") that season while trying to go for a swim. Who knows? If it had happened once, we could have brushed it off. But the problem is that it *hasn't* happened once. It hasn't happened even *close* to once. In fact, statistically speaking, the "small, unathletic, unthreatening female" is the *single most successful demographic* in *Survivor* history.

Don't believe it? Just check out the list (Table 1) of successful female *Survivor* players on page 180. Look at how far they got in their respective seasons. Keep in mind that *none* of these players would have fared well if stranded on an island all alone. Most of them would have been dead of starvation within a week.

Looking at the list on page 180 should dispel the notion that *Survivor* has *anything* to do with natural selection. Because there are twenty-four successful players there who would argue that physical strength, the ability to catch food, and the ability to build a shelter are completely irrelevant to success in the game of *Survivor*. When you have twenty-four solid examples of unthreatening women winning, or coming oh-so-close to winning, the game of *Survivor* in just twelve seasons, it can no longer be considered just a random coincidence. And the surprising conclusion we inevitably come to is this:

> **In Survivor, small, non-threatening women are far more dangerous than brawny men.**

This is not to say that women are inherently better at the game than men; there is no way you could prove that one way or another. But the game *has* evolved in a way that women fare much better than men overall, and the facts are right there on the table for anyone who wants to

TABLE 1: Non-Threatening and Unlikely Female Players Who Won (or Came Close to Winning) *Survivor*

Unlikely Female	Description of Unlikely *Survivor* Qualities	Final Place, Season
1. Tina Wesson	100-pound nurse who gagged on rice if it was too sticky	Winner, *Australia*
2. Vecepia Towery	Super-religious office manager whose views were called hypocritical	Winner, *Marquesas*
3. Jenna Morasca	Washed her underwear in the drinking water	Winner, *Amazon*
4. Sandra Diaz-Twine	A terrible liability in the challenges; also had the mouth (and vocabulary) of a sailor	Winner, *Pearl Islands*
5. Amber Brkich	Quiet and non-aggressive young woman whom nobody considered to be a "real All-Star"	Winner, *All-Stars*
6. Danni Boatwright	Rail thin, ultra-moralistic small-town girl from Kansas	Winner, *Guatemala*
7. Kim Johnson	Collapsed in several early challenges	2nd place, *Africa*
8. Neleh Dennis	Mormon college student who wouldn't lie, cheat, steal, or swear; known for saying "Oh my heck!"	2nd place, *Marquesas*
9. Katie Gallagher	Unathletic young woman known for publicly mocking the majority of her teammates	2nd place, *Palau*
10. Danielle DiLorenzo	Abrasive young athlete who made multiple enemies by the end of the game	2nd place, *Exile Island*
11. Jan Gentry	Fifty-three-year-old woman best known for holding a funeral for a dead baby bat	3nd place, *Thailand*
12. Jenna Lewis	Known throughout Borneo and All-Stars as "the woman who would never shut her mouth"	3rd place, *All-Stars*
13. Scout Cloud Lee	Partially handicapped woman with an artificial hip; could barely walk	3rd place, *Vanuatu*
14. Elisabeth Filarski	Sweet-as-pie young woman who was morally opposed to ever turning against a friend	4th place, *Australia*
15. Darrah Johnson	Young mortician/wannabe model; Due to thick Southern accent, other players assumed she was stupid	4th place, *Pearl Islands*
16. Eliza Orlins	Motor-mouthed college student who got under everyone's skin by the end of day one	4th place, *Vanuatu*
17. Jenn Lyon	As Jeff Probst described her, "a hot nanny from L.A."	4th place, *Palau*
18. Lydia Morales	Unathletic fishmonger who barely made it through the first challenge	4th place, *Guatemala*
19. Cirie Fields	Overweight, self-described "couch potato" who had never been camping before in her life; also scared of leaves	4th place, *Exile Island*
20. Heidi Strobel	Best known for getting naked in exchange for chocolate and peanut butter	5th place, *Amazon*
21. Julie Berry	Best known for dating Jeff Probst	5th place, *Vanuatu*
22. Caryn Groedel	Abrasive attorney from Chicago whom nobody seemed to like	5th place, *Palau*
23. Colleen Haskell	Shy and meek college student who made fun of *Survivor* because the concept was silly	6th place, *Borneo*
24. Amber Brkich	A meek, shy secretary who at that point was the youngest player in the history of the show	6th place, *Australia*

(NOTE: We are leaving Lillian Morris [2nd place, *Pearl Islands*] off this list because technically she had already been voted out in episode three. Due to the "Outcast Twist" that season, she was allowed to return to the game.)

see. A simple look at the evidence tells us that, in nearly every *Survivor* season, the under-the-radar or non-threatening female in the cast will probably make the final four. That's just the way that *Survivor* works. All you have to do is look at the names on the above list and see that it happens season after season after season. After seeing the evidence pile right up in front of you, there is really only one way you can summarize it: A physically weak, benign-appearing, out-of-her-element female is the single most dangerous person in this game.

TABLE 2: Women Comprise the Majority of Final Four Contestants

Season	Women in the Final Four	Cumulative Final Four Percentage Women	Cumulative Final Four Percentage Women: Seasons 7–12 Only
1. *Borneo*	2	2 of 4 = 50%	
2. *Australia*	2	4 of 8 = 50%	
3. *Africa*	1	5 of 12 = 42%	
4. *Marquesas*	3	8 of 16 = 50%	
5. *Thailand*	2	10 of 20 = 50%	
6. *Amazon*	1	11 of 24 = 46%	
7. *Pearl Islands*	3	14 of 28 = 50%	3 of 4 = 75%
8. *All-Stars*	2	16 of 32 = 50%	5 of 8 = 62%
9. *Vanuatu*	3	19 of 36 = 53%	8 of 12 = 67%
10. *Palau*	2	21 of 40 = 52%	10 of 16 = 62%
11. *Guatemala*	3	24 of 44 = 54%	13 of 20 = 65%
12. *Exile Island*	2	26 of 48 = 54%	15 of 24 = 62%

Even though *Survivor* was originally pitched as "survival of the fittest," we have actually seen more women surviving into the last stages of the game than we have men, as you can see from Table 2. When the final four groups from the first twelve seasons are compiled, we find that twenty-six of forty-eight players in the final four have been women, or about 54 percent. This disparity is even *more* pronounced in the more recent seasons of the show, when the players have been smarter, wiser, and more strategic. In seasons seven through twelve, women have made up over 62 percent (fifteen of twenty-four) of the final four.

We can further drive the point home by looking at all the post-merge players (not just the final four). In Table 3, the final eight players of each season are pared down to the point when the game most favored the men, and then to the point when the game most favored the women. This is not a statistical test taught in graduate school; what we're doing instead is stacking the odds favorably for both groups, in an attempt to determine which gender emerges with more players at the true end-stages of the game.

TABLES 3 AND 5 METHOD

To create Table 3 and Table 5 we took a few steps. First, we trimmed down the final eight players of each season to the point where the gender ratio most favored men, and then to the point where it most favored women. This was done to determine which gender has truly made the best showing. To decide where to draw the line within the final eight each season, both ratio and total numbers were considered. We were looking for the best ratio for each gender, but also for the largest number of the target gender and the smallest number of the other gender. We also decided not to go beyond the final four, since Table 1 covers this.

The *Guatemala* season provides an excellent example of what we are trying to do. The final eight players in *Guatemala* included four men and four women. However, three of those men were eliminated first, while only Rafe lasted until the final three. So the best ratio for the men in Guatemala is 1:1, at the point in the game where only eight players remained (4:4). So the "final eight" ratio was selected for the men, because it was their best showing in the endgame, at least in terms of ratio. For the *women* of *Survivor: Guatemala*, however, we chose the final four, because that's when they held a 3:1 ratio advantage.

Using this strategy of attempting to find the best showing for each gender, we arrive at the statistic that forty-eight of seventy "endgame" players were women, or about 61 percent (see Table 3). When the most favorable final eight ratio is determined for men, we find that only thirty-four of sixty-two final players were men, or about 55 percent.

In other words, when the statistics are stacked in favor of men, they can account for little more than half of the endgame players overall. But conversely, when we do the same thing for the women, we find that they can account for more than *60 percent* of the final players. That's where we come to the conclusion that, in the words of Kathy Vavrick-O'Brien (*Survivor: Marquesas*), "chicks rule."

TABLE 3: Men versus Women: "Most Favorable" Analysis by Both Genders of Final Eight

Season	Men's Most Favorable Ratio (M:W)	Men vs. Women Cumulative = Best Percentage for Men	Women's Most Favorable Ratio (W:M)	Women vs. Men Cumulative = Best Percentage for Women
1. *Borneo*	2 : 2	2 vs. 2 = 50% Men	3 : 3	3 vs. 3 = 50% Women
2. *Australia*	3 : 2	5 vs. 4 = 56% Men	3 : 3	6 vs. 6 = 50% Women
3. *Africa*	3 : 1	8 vs. 5 = 62% Men	3 : 3	9 vs. 9 = 50% Women
4. *Marquesas*	3 : 3	11 vs. 8 = 58% Men	3 : 1	12 vs. 10 = 55% Women
5. *Thailand*	4 : 2	15 vs. 10 = 60% Men	2 : 2	14 vs. 12 = 54% Women
6. *Amazon*	3 : 1	18 vs. 11 = 62% Men	3 : 3	17 vs. 15 = 53% Women
7. *Pearl Islands*	2 : 3	20 vs. 14 = 59% Men	5 : 2	22 vs. 17 = 56% Women
8. *All-Stars*	3 : 2	23 vs. 16 = 59% Men	5 : 3	27 vs. 20 = 57% Women
9. *Vanuatu*	1 : 3	24 vs. 19 = 56% Men	6 : 1	33 vs. 21 = 61% Women
10. *Palau*	3 : 3	27 vs. 22 = 55% Men	3 : 2	36 vs. 23 = 61% Women
11. *Guatemala*	4 : 4	31 vs. 26 = 54% Men	4 : 1	40 vs. 24 = 63% Women
12. *Exile Island*	3 : 2	34 vs. 28 = 55% Men	3 : 3	43 vs. 27 = 61% Women

So was *Survivor* always like this? Did the game always develop in a manner where the alpha males would be taken out early and the deceptively harmless females would slip through the cracks until it was too late? No, in fact, it did not. The first season of *Survivor* (*Borneo*, 2000) was *far* more like the original concept the producers had in mind when they first conceived the show. Borneo featured the alpha males (Richard, Joel) leading their tribes into battle episode after episode after episode. It also featured the weaker, less athletic players (Stacey, Sonja) being weeded out early so they would not harm the tribe during physical Challenges. All of these actions were perfectly in line with the original show concept of "survival of the fittest," and it explains why Borneo looks positively primitive when compared to later seasons of the show. You see, Borneo was the only season in which being an alpha male was a *good* thing. Because starting in the second season (*Australian Outback*), the players figured out that success in *Survivor* was achieved by keeping the spotlight away from *you*, and on somebody *else*. And that is where the women really started to shine.

Australian Outback was the first *Survivor* season in which the players truly "got" it. All sixteen players had seen the *Borneo* season on television, they all knew how the game was going to play out, and that meant it was open season on alpha males such as Michael Skupin and Kel Gleason from the very start. This targeting of "physical threats" may not have been as blatant as it was in later seasons (such as the way Maraamu treated Hunter in *Survivor: Marquesas*), but it was still shocking to see Kel Gleason, a young army officer in his athletic prime, being voted out in the second episode of *Survivor: Australian Outback*. In the first season, to oust an athletic young male so early would have been virtually unthinkable.

TABLE 4: The Sad Fate of the *Survivor* Alpha Male

Alpha Male (Season)	Description	Fate
Joel Klug (*Borneo*)	Handsome, athletic young health club operator	Women ganged up to take him out in episode six
Michael Skupin (*Australia*)	Super fit and athletic; camping enthusiast	Was openly mocked and derided by his tribe, right before he left the game due to injury in episode six
Carl Bilancione (*Africa*)	Wealthy, athletic leader-type from Florida	Voted out by younger members of the tribe in episode three
Hunter Ellis (*Marquesas*)	Muscular, ex-military pilot	Voted out by other wannabe alphas in episode three
Gabriel Cade (*Marquesas*)	Athletic, well-liked love-child; raised on a commune	Voted out by more hardcore players in episode five
Ken Stafford (*Thailand*)	New York City policeman	Tried to lay low, but got nailed by the less athletic players right after the merge
Roger Sexton (*Amazon*)	Bossy and sexist construction worker	Weaker players were ready to blindside him in episode one. He was eventually blindsided in episode seven
Lea "Sarge" Masters (*Vanuatu*)	Intimidating drill sergeant	Voted out unanimously by the women very soon after the merge
James Miller (*Palau*)	Formerly in the Navy; also a steel worker	Voted out by younger teammates right before the merge
Judd Sergeant (*Guatemala*)	Loud and intimidating doorman from NYC	Blindsided by his own allies in episode twelve
Gary Hogeboom (*Guatemala*)	Former NFL quarterback	Voted out by more organized players in episode eleven
Shane Powers (*Exile Island*)	Intimidating and micro-managing control freak	Blindsided by his more grounded allies in episode eleven
Terry Deitz (*Exile Island*)	Ex-Navy fighter pilot	Almost made it! He was hunted almost the entire game until he finally lost immunity at the final three

Since *Survivor: Australian Outback*, we have had season after season of *Survivor* in which the alpha males are running for their lives from the very first day. They constantly look over their shoulders for that blind-side vote, they do their best to blend back into the scenery and appear like everyone else, and for the most part none of this seems to work. New York City firefighter Tom Westman may have pulled off an "alpha male" victory during *Survivor: Palau*, but most people would agree that was an anomaly. Because other than Tom, *Survivor* alpha males have been an endangered species for more than half a decade.

In seasons seven through twelve, women especially dominated the endgame. In fact, they did it *much* more handily than the (otherwise successful) women from the first six seasons. Because when we pare the final eight players from the later seasons (seven through twelve) down to the most favorable ratio for women and for men, this is when we start to see some truly unbalanced gender comparisons. This is where we see that women truly *are* the dominant gender in *Survivor* history.

Table 5 shows women dominating seasons seven through twelve when both genders are given the best possible ratio among all the final eight possibilities. As you'll see, women have made up more than two-thirds (68 percent) of the final eight players in these last six seasons, while men have been able to account for less than half (48 percent).

TABLE 5: Men Versus Women. Most Favorable Analysis by Both Genders of Final Eight in the Most Recent Six Seasons

Season	Men's Most Favorable Ratio (M:W)	Cumulative Best Ratio Men: Seasons 7–12	Women's Most Favorable Ratio (W:M)	Cumulative Best Ratio Women: Seasons 7–12
7. *Pearl Islands*	2 : 3	2 vs. 3 = 40%	5 : 2	5 vs. 2 = 71%
8. *All-Stars*	3 : 2	5 vs. 5 = 50%	5 : 3	10 vs. 5 = 66%
9. *Vanuatu*	1 : 3	6 vs. 8 = 43%	6 : 1	16 vs. 6 = 73%
10. *Palau*	3 : 3	9 vs. 11 = 45%	3 : 2	19 vs. 8 = 70%
11. *Guatemala*	4 : 4	13 vs. 15 = 46%	4 : 1	23 vs. 9 = 72%
12. *Exile Island*	3 : 2	16 vs. 17 = 48%	3 : 3	26 vs. 12 = 68%

Not only is *Survivor: Palau*'s Tom Westman the only alpha male to win *Survivor* in the past four years, he is also one of the very few alphas even to make the final *two*! Most alpha males are weeded out long before that, so you have to conclude that Tom's victory in Palau was basically a fluke.

It just does not fit the pattern of the rest of the seasons. Before Tom, the previous alpha male winner was *Survivor: Thailand*'s icy-cold used car salesman Brian Heidik (season five). In fact, Brian's victory in Thailand was (probably not coincidentally) followed by three under-the-radar female winners in a row, suggesting that there's nothing like a sexist male winner to mobilize the women into rallying together for a while. In other words, Brian might be better known as "the last alpha male ever to be given a chance."

The funniest (and most ironic) part of the alpha males' *Survivor* demise is the fact that, even today, people still consider them to be the biggest threats in the game. Despite the fact that only one alpha male (Tom) has won *Survivor* in the past four years, players *consistently* target the alpha males very early on in the game, always referring to them as "the biggest threat." But honestly, in a game like *Survivor* how could a player this visible *ever* be the biggest threat? Especially when the late-game Challenges are rarely even physical! No, the person you have to watch out for on *Survivor* isn't the big, bad dominant male. The one you have to watch out for is the one you are not paying attention to. She's that quiet one sitting over there in the corner. Remember her?

This leads us into the basic question asked by this chapter: Why are women so much more successful at *Survivor* than men, and why are women never viewed as "the threats" when by all rights they really should be? Is there a chance that alpha males will ever again be a threat to win? Will we ever come to a point where the weaker players (females included) will actually let these poor saps have a chance?

WHY WOMEN SUCCEED

The reason that women succeed so often in *Survivor* has much to do with the way the game itself has changed ("evolved") since that initial season in Borneo. Because, interestingly, the evolutionary ("natural selection") model that the producers expected never really came to fruition. The game turned *far* more social than they anticipated, the concepts of alliances and banding together changed *everything*, and this really undermined everything that the producers planned when they put together this type of game. The producers expected natural selection, but what they got was the exact opposite. What they got was the weak banding together to take out the strong.

As we said before, what has developed with *Survivor* gives a great deal of credence to feminist theory and helps to explain why alpha males regularly leave the game so early. Eagly and Wood's (1999) introduction of *social role theory* is a good place to start, because it attempts to explain the differences between the way men and women view their surrounding environment. According to social role theory, men and women have traditionally been placed into different roles, based on the needs and pressures of their culture. These gender roles (social or physical) may not be inherently equal, but they both have strengths and weaknesses built into them. In a case like *Survivor*, it is the *social* roles that will inevitably be the most important. After all, no one has actually ever died on *Survivor*. In other words, surviving the elements is not the primary objective in this game (no matter what the producers would have us believe). So the best player in *Survivor* won't be the most physically adept. The best player in *Survivor* will be the most socially adept. It will be the person who demonstrates the most influence on his or her environment, particularly on the other players he or she is competing against.

For example, if a player is capable of deflecting power and attention, he or she can maintain a comfortable connection with the other players at all times. This person does not have to be the most charismatic, the most capable, or even the most likable. He or she simply has to be able to deflect power. The ability to do this can make a person *very* powerful in a social competition like *Survivor*. For evidence, just look at some of the under-the-radar winners of *Survivor* throughout the years, and you will see that this deflection of power (or "avoiding the vote") is one of the most common features these winners share. Sandra Diaz-Twine, Danni Boatwright, Tina Wesson, Vecepia Towery—these were all *Survivor* champions, and all of them were *exceptionally* good at "avoiding the vote." Heck, Vecepia and Sandra could probably teach a master's level course in avoiding the vote. That was their bread and butter, their nearly flawless strategy, and they were doing it practically from the very first minute of the game.

CULTURE MADE ME DO IT

So why is it that this strategy works so well for women? Social role theory tells us that women and men are both products of their environment. They act and behave the way they do because of their particular culture. This is where we see the true gender differences begin to rear their head in *Survivor*. Because, after all, American culture historically rewards men who aspire to, compete for, and maintain power. Men are taught to seek power and prestige at an early age, and this is precisely the way they play the game of *Survivor*. On the flip side, American culture historically rewards women who shun power and focus instead on the communal aspects of day-to-day living. These interpersonal skills are precisely the traits that make a player good at a game like *Survivor*.

Do women purposefully come into *Survivor* with the intention of playing a social game instead of a physical one? Do they specifically try to avoid holding a lot of power, simply because they know it will lead to their dismissal? Not according to the *social role* and *social construction* theories. According to those two theories, women (and men) play the way that they do because their roles have been internalized and negotiated long before they got to the island. In other words, *Survivor* is little more than a representation of the roles we have adopted through our culture.

Oh yes, except there *is* one difference between American culture and *Survivor* culture. One very significant difference. In American culture, women have historically received lower wages (and lower prestige) as a result of playing their traditional roles. But in *Survivor*, women are rewarded for doing the exact same thing. In *Survivor*, women are given a free pass to sit quietly, observe the other players, and subtly influence the vote. That's a distinct advantage they hold over the (normally more aggressive and threatening) *Survivor* men.

SEX MADE ME DO IT

Another reason that women dominate *Survivor* is the fact that, for the most part, they just play the game *differently* than men. After all, most women are not able to physically dominate a game in which they are competing against players much bigger and physically stronger than themselves. Thus, women are forced to play a more adaptive game. And they learn how to react to changes that happen around them. This is all perfectly natural, according to the theory of Eagly and Wood. As explained in this theory, women have historically adapted to domestic roles in American society. With these roles come female-dominated occupations, which traditionally tend to support "interpersonally facilitative and friendly behaviors that can be termed communal" (413). In other words, women have been playing the "team-building" game for a long, long time before they ever set foot on *Survivor* terrain.

It is with this sort of background that women begin the game of *Survivor*. It is for this reason that women inevitably use some sort of socially reactive strategy. Women tend to make teammate and friendship bonds that many men are unwilling or unable to make. As a result, women end up with far more options in terms of a path to success. After all, American women have been culturally and socially trained to be flexible. They have been forced to be able to change strategies on the fly. This ability to adapt is what helps them dominate in the complicated world of *Survivor*. Because, as we've seen on the show, the more complicated the seasons (and twists) get, the better the women tend to do. It's all because they approach the game differently than the men.

Why do women and men approach *Survivor* differently? Well, according to Eagly and Steffen (1984), it is because of the way men and women have been taught to approach their lives. Women have traditionally held the role of "nurturer" in American society. While women tend to grow up with advanced interpersonal skills, including the ability to interpret nonverbal communication, men, historically, have not been required to excel in these skills. Traditional male roles in America have stressed the importance of acquiring and holding employment, as well as being competitive, assertive, and independent. All of these have traditionally been male culture traits, and all of them have focused on obtaining what psychologists call a "product," such as a paycheck, or a promotion. Males tend to focus their efforts on acquiring such a product, while females tend to go just the opposite route. Females will often focus their efforts on developing a social network, or maintaining a nurturing environment (e.g., for purposes of child-rearing). In other words, females don't focus on the product. Females tend to focus on the process. Females are more concerned with the process of getting there, as opposed to the cheese at the end of the maze. This is completely backward from the power-hungry, anything-to-win mindset of the traditional American male.

This is not to say that men are incapable of being nurturing. Nor does it say that women can't make aggressive power plays. Many can, and do, both in the real world and in the world of *Survivor*. However, playing the role of the opposite sex does not usually bode well for men *or* for women. According to Rhoda Unger (1988), culture has taught both women *and* men to uphold the norms they have been taught—otherwise there will be no way to maintain the social order. This is backed up by social construction theory, which maintains that there are social consequences for those who dare to break from traditional roles.

Not sure about this? Just look at how Gabriel Cade was treated in *Survivor: Marquesas* when he admitted, "I am not here to play the game. I am here to see if eight people from all around the country can come together and live and be happy." This was a strikingly non-masculine, non-power-seeking focus. It came from a kid who was raised in a non-traditional, non-aggressive commune environment. Gabriel's utopian comments weren't received very well by his power-hungry tribemates, and he was voted out the very next day. Social construction theory would tell us that Gabriel broke from playing the "male" role and the rest of the players couldn't handle it; therefore Gabriel quickly paid the inevitable price.

On the flip side there was Tina Scheer, the lumberjill from *Survivor: Panama*. Tina was an overly assertive dominant female, who came from a profession dominated by males. Tina was placed onto an all-female tribe in *Panama*, and she quickly threatened everybody with her un-female-like aggressiveness. Tina came in the first day and she started a fire. Then she went out and caught some fish. Then she volunteered to lead the tribe in the first Challenge. Do you know what she got for her efforts? She became the very first player voted out of the game. The rest of the females just had no idea how to relate to her.

PRODUCT VERSUS PROCESS

As stated before, American males generally approach things like work and games with the sole intention of obtaining a "product." This is the way that men tend to think, and it is indeed a linear way of approaching a goal. You start from point A, you get to point B, and you get C as a reward. This is the way that most males approach the game of *Survivor*, as their inevitable goal is that product (the million-dollar check) that is waiting for them at the end. Because they are such linear thinkers, men will often attempt to portray themselves as indispensable to the rest of the tribe. Males often want to be the leaders. Males often want to be the providers. They especially want to prove themselves as being too strong for the tribe to do without. This is textbook alpha-male thinking, and it goes a long way toward explaining why men often try to dominate the game from day one. Because to a person with a linear mind, the surest way to *Survivor* success is to prove that your tribe just cannot live here without you. The fact that you are irreplaceable will inevitably lead you all the way to that million-dollar product.

Women, on the other hand, tend to be much more aware of the social dynamics in their tribe. They aren't trying to dominate anything. This is because American women approach *Survivor* in a "processing" style. They aren't here specifically to win. They are here more for the journey. Oh sure, most females aren't going to *complain* if they're handed a million-dollar check at the end, but there really is more to the game than that for most of them. This is why a stealthy female player will usually know what the rest of the players are thinking. She'll usually know who gets along with whom. She'll usually know where everybody stands on a given issue. Is this the most dominant and entertaining way to play the game? Certainly not. But it may be the most successful. Because what happens is that women end up with a strategy that is stealthier, less intensive, and far more prone to result in victory in the end.

As an added bonus, "processing" women do not have to exert as much energy in *Survivor* as the much more aggressive men do. Because, after all, while the linear men are building shelters, winning Challenges, hunting for food, and putting great big targets on their backs, what are their female opponents doing? That's right, the more stealthy women are back at camp, making social bonds, at a fraction of the level of physical exertion. What happens is that women have more energy left as they get to the end of the game. During the last week or so of *Survivor*, women will have greater endurance, since they will have expended far fewer calories along the way, and they will likely have far less trouble in "surviving" the thirty-nine-day grueling experience. After all, did you ever wonder why women win the endurance Challenge at the end of the game much more often (64 percent) than the men? Did you ever think it might have something to do with the fact that the men were just flatout exhausted?

TABLE 6: Winners of the Final Three Endurance Challenge (Seasons 1–12)

Season	Final Three Endurance Challenge Winner	Gender
Borneo	Kelly	Female
Australia	Final Three Challenge was trivia questions, not endurance	N/A
Africa	Kim J.	Female
Marquesas	Neleh	Female
Thailand	Brian	Male
Amazon	Jenna M.	Female
Pearl Islands	Lillian	Female
All-Stars	Rob M.	Male
Vanuatu	Chris	Male
Palau	Tom	Male
Guatemala	Danni	Female
Exile Island	Danielle	Female

SUMMARY

Why are women better *Survivor* players than men? Well for starters, it is because *Survivor* success relies on social networks and social politics, and these skills are much more ingrained into the American female. *Survivor* may not have *started* as a game of social politics; it may have been born in 2000 as a physical contest of natural selection. But that does not take into account the fact that the game changed as it went along, and eventually evolved into the socially reactive contest that we know and love today.

The game has evolved so much, in fact, that the most common type of *Survivor* winner is indeed the under-the-radar, unassuming, nonthreatening female. In their theory, Eagly and Wood state that traditional gender roles require females to show subordinate behavior. In other words, if they want to fit into American society, females must be "compliant to social influence, less overtly aggressive, more cooperative and conciliatory" (412). This, in fact, is also the perfect description of the successful under-the-radar *Survivor* playing style.

From Tina Wesson to Vecepia Towery, this *is* the player you need to be looking out for. From Jenna Morasca to Sandra Diaz-Twine, this *is* the player that is going to be the most dangerous. From Amber Brkich to Danni Boatwright, this *is* the single most successful demographic in *Survivor* history. Because if you have not noticed by now, half of the *Survivor* winners of all time (six out of twelve) have been seemingly innocuous, non-threatening females.

So is an under-the-radar female a good *Survivor* player? You're darn right she is. She may be derided on message boards as being "lucky" or "a fluke," and *Survivor* fans may bemoan her as "the worst winner of all time." But that does not take away from the fact that she avoided the drama, she kept her options open along the way, she stayed far away from the vote when she needed to, and she somehow convinced a jury to vote for her in the end. If *that* is not the mark of a successful *Survivor* player, I don't know what is. Who cares if she didn't know how to light a campfire, or if she can't run a mile? Who cares if she didn't speak the entire season, or if she would be dead of malnutrition if stranded on her own? All you have to know is that she beat you in the game of *Survivor*. Maybe someday you'll figure out how she did it.

When people talk about *Survivor*, they often refer to it as a "survival of the fittest." The ironic thing is that they are actually *right*. The only problem is that "fittest" is not referring to the Darwinian model in a game like *Survivor*. It is actually referring to the exact opposite. The "fittest" *Survivor* player is often the person you are not afraid of in the slightest. And if you don't realize that, she's going to slip by you nearly every single time.

In summary, the feminist model of evolved dispositions gives a clear explanation as to why women can and do succeed in *Survivor*. Women pay attention to the process of the game. They are attentive to leaders, the underdogs, and the alliances. Women will be the first ones to tell you that the "dominant leader" type usually has very little power at all. No, the true power in *Survivor* lies with those who understand the dynamics that evolve throughout the smaller moments of the game. Women get this, and women understand. Women adapt. Mainly because women more or less don't have much of a choice.

So why have under-the-radar females won *Survivor* more often than any other demographic in the history of the show? Mainly because

Survivor has evolved into a female game. The game is set up for a female to excel, it's set up for an alpha male to crash and burn, and it has been that way for a long time. The show really *is* the "survival of the fittest," and it always has been. The only problem is that "fittest," at least in the case of *Survivor*, has an entirely *different* definition than the one we've all been led to believe. . . .

AUTHORS' NOTE

Since we wrote this chapter, of course alpha males had to go and win *Survivor: Cook Islands* and *Survivor: Fiji* (seasons thirteen and fourteen), essentially making us look like a pair of idiots. But we still stand by our thesis. After all, of *course* an alpha male is going to wind up with the hidden immunity idol every season. They're the only ones who get sent to Exile Island, so what do you expect? Why not give them a hunting rifle and a hotel bed, too? So we don't believe Yul's or Earl's victories negate anything we said in this chapter. If anything, we feel like the new additions of a hidden immunity idol and Exile Island have deliberately stacked the game in favor of alpha males. So yes, we stand by this chapter, and no, we're not sore losers. We just don't happen to think the last few seasons can really be considered the same *Survivor* anymore.

BRAD WOLGAST, PH.D., is a staff psychologist and the coordinator of the post-doctoral fellowship in psychology at the Counseling and Psychological Services at the University of Pennsylvania, which is actually just an elaborate ruse to have a captive audience to bore with his latest thoughts about *Survivor*. Brad was born into a good family; something just happened along the way that turned him into a *Survivor* junkie. He would like to thank Dr. Kate Richmond and Dr. Vinai Norsukunkkit for their superior assistance with this project. And he would have gotten away with it, if it weren't for that meddling Mario Lanza.

MARIO J. LANZA is a well-known writer and humorist, whose "*Survivor* Strategy" column was one of the most widely read on the Internet between the years 2001 and 2004. He was recently called "one of the foremost *Survivor* experts in the world" by *Survivor: Amazon* contestant Rob Cesternino. Mario does not hold a Ph.D. from Stanford University. And he did not study applied psychology at the University of Washington. And it would be wrong to call him a cognitive neuroscientist at Cornell University. Mario claims that he has a B.S. in psychology from Santa Clara University but, really, that's about as far as it went. When he's not writing about *Survivor*, Mario enjoys baseball, horror movies, writing sketch comedy, stripping for chocolate and peanut butter, and not pursuing advanced degrees. You can read his other *Survivor* writings at http://members.aol.com/AllStarHawaii.

REFERENCES

Eagly, A. H. and V. J. Steffen. "Gender Stereotypes Stem from the Distribution of Women and Men into Social Roles." *Journal of Personality and Social Psychology* 46 (1984): 735–754.

Eagly, A. H. and W. Wood. "The Origins of Sex Differences in Human Behavior: Evolved Dispositions Versus Social Roles." *American Psychologist* 54, no. 6 (1999): 408–423.

Unger, R. K. "Psychological, Feminist, and Personal Epistemology: Transcending Contradiction." In *Feminist Thought and the Structure of Knowledge*, edited by Mary McCanney Gergen (124–141). New York: New York University Press, 1988.

Each week, Jeff Probst reminds Survivor *contestants that they are making decisions that could earn them or cost them a million dollars. To characterize contestants' thought processes, P. A. Hancock contrasts rational and naturalistic models of decision-making. This contrast allows Hancock to provide a detailed analysis of Richard Hatch's famous decision to cede his final Immunity Challenge to Kelly and Rudy.*

Cold Calculation
or Intuitive Instinct
Solving the Secrets of Sustained Survival

P. A. HANCOCK, PH.D.

OVERVIEW

It is getting down to crunch time in the first-ever season of *Survivor*. Richard, Rudy, and Kelly now stand alone with their hands firmly fixed to a post in the penultimate Challenge. It is called the "hands-on immunity." The winner is certain to go to the round of the final two. It is a three-way duel of endurance. Who will survive?

One million dollars is on the line and many millions of viewers are on the edge of their seats. Suddenly, Richard removes his hand from the post; has he gone mad? Is he voluntarily giving up his chance of winning the million dollars after scheming so hard for so long and having gotten so close?

No, Richard is a cunning player, perhaps the most cunning. He has assessed the value of winning this particular Immunity Challenge and has realized that victory at this stage will mean almost certain loss at the next and most crucial, final stage. It is true that he is putting his *Survivor* "life" on the line right now, but it is a bold gamble for the million dollars. And, as we now know, his gamble paid off in a big way.

This chapter examines how cognitive decision-making strategies change during the various phases of the game. In particular, I am going to look in detail at Richard's specific choice at that time and try to explain the psychological basis of his extraordinary decision at that penultimate stage of the game. Of course, Richard's action depended on the character of the remaining contestants and the nature of the final Challenge itself. However, there are important commonalities across all of the seasons at this "down to three" point in the game that make *Survivor* so intriguing as a psychological conundrum and, consequently, the cause of such compulsive viewing.

IT'S THE DECISIONS YOU MAKE

Landing on a remote island, you are dropped into a "tribe" of people whom you did not select, knowing explicitly that they each stand between you and a million dollars. Early on, it's about tribe strength. The better your tribe does, the greater your personal chances of surviving. This early situation requires some degree of cooperation—although you wouldn't know it from the actions of some players! Reward Challenges provide much-needed sustenance; they help you to maintain vital physical and mental fitness.

However, Tribal Council is where the most significant events of the game occur. It is here that you will meet your fate at the hands of your fellow contestants. Council is a form of a predator-prey relationship known as "devil take the hindmost." At all stages of the game, you are not required to win—but you must avoid losing at all costs. The game remains in this form until the start of Jury selection time. All participants voted off now become members of the Jury. They are still very much part of the contest, even though they cannot personally win. At this juncture, it matters not just which tribal members are voted off; it matters what they think of you and your role in the process that disposed of them.

As we have seen throughout the respective *Survivor* seasons, revenge proves to be a very strong motive for many of these decisions. Technically, someone wins in the final decision. However, given that you and your last opponent have successfully eliminated all other members of the Jury from their chance of winning a life-changing bonanza of cash, it very much reverts to a case of again making sure that you do not lose. You must try to ensure that Jury members hate the other final contestant more than they hate you. Who can forget Sue's vitriolic speech about choosing between the "rat" and the "snake"? The Jury's choice often devolves to selecting the lesser of two evils. It is against this background of multiple levels of decision-making that we must consider Richard's choice in the last Immunity Challenge of the first season of *Survivor*.

FROM PILLAR TO POST

I'd like to refresh your memory with a brief picture in words of that fateful contest. *Survivor* was then a sensation because of the format of its Challenges, its cast of rapidly emerging personalities, and its breakthrough as the pioneer of "reality" television. The cast of competitors (and the host, Jeff) were now household names and watercooler heroes. But who was going to win the million dollars? In the previous episode, Sue was voted off. Her antipathy toward Kelly was evident. Certainly, among the three contestants left, Rudy was the popular hero. The down-to-earth, honest old fellow could have been anyone's grandfather. The very epitome of American pragmatism and independence, Rudy was exactly the sort of regular guy almost everyone would have loved to see win. In short, anyone up against Rudy in the final two most probably was going to lose. As Richard stood there on the sunny beach, his problem was how to stop Rudy from reaching that critical stage without appearing to be his traitorous executioner—after all, Rudy and Richard had an alliance, right? Someone had to be seen as the bad guy, and Kelly was the only other person left in the game.

The final Immunity Challenge was well-selected. No energetic running about, no mental conundrums; this was not going to be anything more than a test of sheer, bloody-minded endurance. It promised great tension but was troublesome as a television spectacle because it is very hard to convey the effort involved in the hours of the stand-off as each contestant baked in the tropical sun. Surely the idea was to win this vital Challenge. It would appear that, by winning, one would then be in control of the game and apparently in a position to dictate the outcome. But at this very moment, when everything seemed to be on the line, about two and one-half hours into the Challenge, Richard voluntarily—and very publicly—took his hand off the post. It eliminated him from contention and put his very *Survivor* existence in peril. *Why?* It seemed such a strange and inexplicable thing to do. But there was method behind Richard's madness—so let's look at psychological explanations for his decision.

Looking at this event from a decision-making perspective, the first thing to do is to examine the potential outcomes for Richard in the form of what psychologists call a hierarchical decision tree. This is shown in the diagram below. This technique allows us to consider all of the possible outcomes and also to bear in mind the utility of each of these individual results as they relate to winning the final vote. As we go through each of these options in detail, it becomes clear that Richard's best chance of winning the money does *not* come from winning this final Immunity Challenge. Indeed, if he does win, he either faces the popular Rudy in the final or, alternatively, becomes the bad guy who gets Rudy kicked off at this juncture. (It is of course possible to generate similar decision trees from both Rudy's and Kelly's perspective, although these are not shown here.)

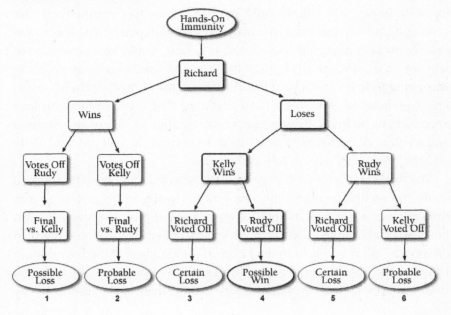

If Richard is voted off, of course, he suffers a certain loss, as shown in options 3 and 5, ranged along the base of the outcome hierarchy. The other four outcomes are almost symmetrical. Richard, in the final versus Rudy, as shown in options 2 and 6, each results in a probable loss. The difference is that in option 2, Richard is seen as the "bad guy" and, of course, Kelly will be on the Jury. The final versus Kelly, options 1 and 4, give a possible loss for option 1, because Richard is again the "bad guy" in getting rid of Rudy, and now Rudy is on the Jury. Therefore, option 4 gives Richard the best opportunity for a win. In this case, Kelly proves to be the "bad guy." In getting her to do his dirty work for him, Richard eventually pockets the million dollars (although later he does not prove equally facile in his dealings with the IRS!).

One of the questions we can ask ourselves is whether Richard actually ran through all of these options in his mind, or whether he made a much more sudden and intuitive choice. While it is only Richard who can truly answer this, the question itself highlights two very radical ways—which are now battling it out in the realms of academic psychology—of understanding human decision-making.

On one hand, the traditional approach to decision-making has been founded on a conception called the *rational model*, in which each of the options are considered, and a probability of success is associated with each option. A measured decision is then made upon these respective options to maximize utility or the prospect of a successful outcome (as we have done with the decision tree hierarchy). Some of the early gains in understanding how humans actually made decisions were in showing how people deviated from what should have been their most rational choices based upon the mathematical calculation of probabilities. For example, the Nobel Prize–winning scientist Daniel Kahneman and his colleague Amos Tversky showed that, in general, people are excessively averse to loss and overly optimistic with respect to gain (Kahneman, Slovic, and Tversky 1982). These studies were very informative, but they led to a degree of frustration when it became clear that pure logic failed to predict people's actual decisions in the real world. One of the reasons for this seeming irrationality is that the real world rarely gives you all of the options and the associated probabilities like laboratory-based problems typically do. But, after all, this uncertainty is why we tune in to *Survivor* in the first place! If it were all perfectly predictable, we would not watch.

Along with keeping all of the options from you, the real world does not give you unlimited time to make a decision, either. Indeed, many real-world decisions have to be made literally in seconds, right on the spur of the moment (which is one central theme in Malcolm Gladwell's recent book *Blink*). Many decisions also have to be made under extremes of stress, where time itself can become distorted (Hancock and Gardner 2007; Hancock and Weaver 2005). As a result of these concerns, a newer approach to decision-making, which, because of its emphasis on real-world issues, has been termed naturalistic decision-making (Klein 1995). Here, the emphasis is on the pattern of cues to which the decision-maker is sensitive when attempting to make an informed, expert choice. What is it about a specific putt that Tiger Woods sees that we mere mortals do not? Why is Peyton Manning able to identify the defense and the appropriate receiver in the scant seconds that he has available, while the rest of us (after running for our lives) would be brutally sacked each time? In a military context, what is it that makes the hairs on the back of a grizzled combat veteran's neck stand up and tell him that this is a very bad situation, while the rookie blindly blunders forward, only to find that death and mayhem await him? Gladwell explains the mechanisms of these sorts of decisions made by experts in an instant, seemingly without conscious thought. Experts "see the pattern" and so appear to know what to do immediately and intuitively—thus giving them a powerful advantage in these time-limited and stressful decision-making circumstances.

In actuality, these two approaches to decision-making are not necessarily in total conflict at all. In different situations, each has its own crucial role to play. They are simply reflections of a concept that in psychology dates back to Freud: the conscious versus the unconscious mind. In this case, the conscious mind is represented as a coldly efficient calculating machine, busy weighing up costs and rewards and making sterile, mathematical decisions based purely on probability. In contrast, the intuitive decision-making mind (the unconscious) is seen as basing its response on a hunch, a feeling, a familiarity that reminds it of some previous occasion. It is viewed as being much more affected by emotion.

The truth is that all decision-making most probably represents a blend of these two perspectives, with initial pattern matching as an intuitive step, which is then monitored and moderated by conscious and deliberate mental simulation that represents a predominantly rational analysis (Klein and Crandall 1995).

DICK'S DILEMMA

Making a decision for your own advantage is beneficial, but that is your private, personal assessment of the situation that you keep to yourself. Just as important, however (and, in the case of the final Immunity Challenge, perhaps even more important), is what the other two people think of your decision and the motives behind it. Now we go beyond decision-making into the realm of deception, and in this capacity Richard proved to be very adept. Having made his decision, he now had to convince the others about his motives; he could not just leave it for them to ponder as to why he did what he did. After all, they might have figured it out! Let us hear from him in his own words, uttered at the time of his action. It is a million-dollar speech:

> RICHARD: I think it's time for a speech. I'm thinking I'm probably never going to outlast you, Kelly. I'm gonna hope that either one of you just recognizes what I've done to get here, and I wish you both luck. [Removes his hand from immunity post.]
>
> This game is about a lot of different things, and one of those things is mental strategy. And I thought to myself, it's doubtful that I would outlast Kelly because she just stands there until the cows come home, period. And it doesn't mean I'm giving up a million dollars necessarily.
>
> JEFF: How come?
>
> RICHARD: It means that whoever is immune has to pick between the other two people as to who goes to the Jury.

Each of them could 50/50 pick me. I really can't tell. Even
if I am somebody that she'd be better up against, I don't
know that she would do that. And even if Rudy has been
loyal the entire time, I don't know that he would continue
to be so. I think that it's all a game of odds, and who knows
what somebody is going to actually do?

The two remaining contestants were now left to ponder Richard's statement as the heat and fatigue of the Challenge went on and they stood
there glued to the immunity post for another hour and a half. With
respect to Kelly, Richard tried flattery, and it worked in his favor. Kelly
saw him as a wimp and, after winning the Challenge, opined that
Richard was "tired and wanted to let go." Almost inevitably, she took
him to the final two, where, again, you do not have to be popular on an
absolute scale; you only have to be more popular than the person sitting
next to you. Given the degree of obnoxious behavior that Richard had
exhibited during some episodes of the *Survivor* experience, it is hard to
see how he eventually won, but Kelly's action had apparently tipped the
balance. With Rudy, Richard appealed to loyalty and the sorts of values
Rudy exhibited throughout the series. Subsequent events suggest that
Rudy was not fooled by Richard. He became painfully aware that in acci-
dentally taking his hand off that post and allowing Kelly the victory, he
had made a million-dollar mistake. As he rightly noted, it was indeed a
"dumb move," and one for which he paid the price at the next Tribal
Council when Kelly voted him off.

PAYING YOUR DUES

There is an old saw that says, "You can fool some of the people all of the
time," and on the island it is indeed true that Richard did fool some of
the people all of the time they were there. It goes on: "you can fool all
of the people some of the time," and again, in respect to the tribes to
which he belonged, Richard was successful in this. However, the kicker
is that "you cannot fool all of the people all of the time." When Richard
left the *Survivor* Challenge, he seems to have forgotten this. Indeed, it is
one of the very great ironies of life that it was the very capacity for deci-

sion-making and deception, which proved so pivotal in enabling Richard to win the million dollars, that also (according to U.S. District Judge Ernest Torres) earned him a number of extra months in the penitentiary on the tax evasion charge for which he was convicted.

This is an important lesson because *Survivor* isolates individuals in a small group to which they have no fundamental allegiance. When the show is over, it's over. However, in society in general, it may well be the individual whom you deceive today who subsequently has a pivotal role to play in making decisions about you tomorrow. In essence, the game is a lifelong one.

At one time, America represented the great opportunity for deceivers. They could accomplish their "stings" and move on; for indeed, there was a "sucker born every minute." When the East Coast was saturated, the Midwest and the West still beckoned. Even Butch Cassidy and the Sundance Kid didn't exhaust all options, going to Bolivia when they became too infamous for America. But the modern electronic world is effectively a much smaller place. Thieves and scam artists now have to be much more aware of technology. Biometric identification will make the job of the serial deceiver much more problematic. Indeed, some have apparently discovered that it is now much easier to make the law than to break the law. But that is another story altogether!

ACKNOWLEDGMENTS

I am very grateful to Gary Klein and Karol Ross, who were each kind enough to review the present work. Their comments were most instructive and helpful in revising the text.

P. A. HANCOCK, PH.D., does research on the decision-making of individuals under extreme stress. He is a professor at the Department of Psychology and Institute for Simulation and Training at the University of Central Florida in Orlando, FL, where he is just trying to survive.

REFERENCES

Gladwell, Malcolm. *Blink: The Power of Thinking Without Thinking*. New York: Little, Brown, & Company, 2005.

Hancock, Peter A. and Michelle K. Gardner. "Time and Time Again, Muggles Watch Wizards Clock." In *The Psychology of Harry Potter: An Unauthorized Examination of the Boy Who Lived*, edited by Neil Mulholland, Ph.D. Dallas: BenBella Books, 2007. (In press)

Hancock, Peter. A. and Jeanne L. Weaver. "On Time Distortions Under Stress." *Theoretical Issues in Ergonomic Science* 6, no. 2 (2005): 193–211.

Kahneman, D., P. Slovic, and A. Tversky (Eds.). *Judgment Under Uncertainty: Heuristics and Biases*. New York: Cambridge University Press, 1982.

Kahneman, D. and A. Tversky. "On the Reality of Cognitive Illusions." *Psychological Review* 103 (1996): 582–591.

Klein, Gary. *Sources of Power*. Cambridge, MA: MIT Press, 1998.

Klein, Gary and B. W. Crandall. "The Role of Mental Simulation in Naturalistic Decision-Making." In *Local Applications of the Ecological Approach to Human-Machine Systems*, edited by Peter A. Hancock, J. Flach, J. Caird, and K. Vicente. Mahwah, NJ: Erlbaum, 1995.

Tversky, A. and D. Kahnamen. "Rational Choice and the Framing of Decisions." *Journal of Business* 59 (1986): S251.

Many of us have fantasies of becoming Survivor contestants. Stephanie deLusé wishes to ensure that if we play, we'll play to win. She describes the important psychological processes of social comparison and attribution. From her reviews of these processes, deLusé develops ten concrete recommendations that will help the fortunate readers of this volume to become the next Sole Survivor.

How to Win Friends and Influence Votes

Tips and Tactics for Winning *Survivor*

STEPHANIE R. DELUSÉ, PH.D.

For there is nothing either good or bad, but thinking makes it so.
—ACT II, SCENE 2 OF SHAKESPEARE'S *HAMLET*

Admit it: as you watch *Survivor* you've often wondered how you would do, haven't you? You've sat there in the comfort of your home and thought, "I could do that!" or "For heaven's sake, what a silly move, I'd have handled that better!" Well, let me tell you, fellow *Survivor* fan, that I certainly have. Perhaps you have prepared an audition tape and sent it in. I did. Deep inside, like me, you believe you could outwit, outplay, and outlast your way to being Sole Survivor. But could you? If you were selected, what would you do?

It's sad to admit, dear reader, but I was not accepted onto the show. I'm over the hurt and now spend as much time thinking about the interesting group dynamic twists the *Survivor* puppet masters could do than how I could personally survive on an island. No, I didn't let the rejection embitter me and now I leave it to you to claim one of the few seats on the special ride that is *Survivor*. Since I won't get to use them myself, let me share with you some psychological insights that may help you win when you do get your ticket to ride (and aid in interpreting some sub-tleties should you decide to stay on the couch instead). Don't worry—while you're welcome to share the prize money with me, I'd be satisfied with your simply and graciously mentioning my name when you win.

There are so many insights to share but, space being limited, we'll talk about two areas of psychological principles—social comparison and attribution—that will help you go farther in, if not win, the social game of *Survivor*. We'll distill those down into specific tips to win the game. You'll note that most tips can be used positively or negatively. Positively, they can protect you and those you care about in the game with neutral to positive intent or impact. Negatively, they can be used as tactics to play dirty—to manipulate or subvert others as it suits your plans and your conscience.

THE IMPORTANCE OF SOCIAL COMPARISON

Often in *Survivor*, you'll have some He-Man (not always but, yes, it is usually a man) tell the camera how he plans on winning his way to the million by feeding the troops or by leading the motley crew of contest-ants to domestic harmony and victory over their opponents. All too often, these self-proclaimed heroes go home or fall in pecking order because their confidence is read as cockiness or, more often, their skill and abilities threaten the others. Why, you might wonder, would a team of people want to get rid of or stop appreciating the person who organ-ized them to build a shelter or win a victory? Why would they think they could get by without the fish he provides?

Social comparison, that's why. Social comparison, in psychology-speak, is evaluating one's self (abilities, opinions, beauty, utility, etc.) by comparing to others as opposed to an objective benchmark. This is a part of human nature. But it is whom we choose as a referent—the per-son or group to which we compare—that is the interesting part. You can either compare up to groups or people who are "better" than you or compare down to those over whom you feel you have some sort of advantage. It may not surprise you to learn that depressed people tend to compare up. They may see everyone as better than them, having more skills, attractiveness, friends, possessions, etc. Comparing up, however, can also be a positive thing when your referent is, say, a role model or someone you aspire to be like. In that case, it can spur you to action and growth instead of depression or feeling "less than." Comparing down, on the other hand, almost always makes us feel better as it reminds us of how lucky or fortunate we are to have something (over those who don't) or when we want to see how far we've come. These comparisons we humans so frequently make—whether we are conscious of it or not—can influence voting decisions.

In the case of *Survivor*, social comparison is at work in different ways as it may influence both 1) immediate pecking order, and 2) perceptions of deservedness of winning. Pecking order ties us back to the aforementioned perils of leadership. *Survivor* contestants are generally capable, non-depressed people. Capable people don't like to feel like chopped liver, so if a superstar player is always rising to the top (catching all the fish, winning all the immunities), social comparison makes the rest of them feel uncomfortable, if not threatened, leading to a desire to rid themselves of the leader. Many will diminish the good things the leader does or convince themselves—often erroneously—that they can do whatever the leader does equally well, to downplay the leader's contribution. They'll forget about loyalty and watch for opportunities to oust the leader by looking for another in the ranks who may want to mutiny, or by waiting for the leader to lose an individual Immunity Challenge to vote him or her off. A leader who manages to stick around will still wind up lower in the pecking order. In contrast, loafers—people who do nothing or next to nothing—are at risk because people will compare down and see themselves as more useful than the freeloaders, putting wind in their sails to argue for themselves as being higher in the pecking order and to get rid of those torpor-filled layabouts. The only time this starts to shift is toward the end of the game. If the go-getters and doers have, for whatever reason, kept a slacker in their midst until the final five or so, sometimes that person will suddenly be the preferred person to keep around because of, again, social comparison. At this point many assume that, all else being equal, having a slacker with you in the final two will result in the Jury rewarding the harder worker with the million dollars because the slacker will be lower in the pecking order. Brian (*Survivor: Thailand*) did this by taking good ol' boy Clay to the final two with him.

Clay had ridden on Brian's coattails most of the season and Brian pointed out how little effort Clay made to help in camp compared to himself. Even though Brian had betrayed several people along the way, his having worked harder than Clay helped him win the million in the final comparison.

Related to pecking order is deservedness. Deservedness is different in that it has less to do with how the contestants perform on the island and more to do with what each person comes to *Survivor* with from his or her personal life and background. Social comparison suggests that players will feel those who are neutral to needy deserve the money more than those who have, or are assumed to have, a lot of money or have had some nifty professional career. This is a moving target, of course, as how one personally compares will, until group processes take over, be initially based on one's own income. That said, birds of a feather recognize each other and there can quickly be some unspoken understanding that "*we* are all similar—just working stiffs with everyday problems—while *that* person has had a good life already and is just in this for the adventure. He (or she) doesn't need it." If you happen to be *that* person, this is not good. But even though we can't *really* tell how financially secure others are just based on what they do (medical problems, divorce, poor money choices in the past, etc., can decimate a "good" income), people go by this cognitive shortcut and decide who is more deserving based on precious little data. Remember how Gary Hogeboom a.k.a Hawkins (*Survivor: Guatemala*) decided not to tell people he used to be an NFL football hero? In the terms discussed here, his choice made sense to reduce how threatening a competitor he'd be seen as, comparatively speaking, and to not undermine his deservedness. He could be financially solid now in his landscape business or he could be on the brink of homelessness—but that he used to be something special could cause people to compare up to him, then feel less good about themselves in contrast, and cope with it by deeming Gary less deserving.

Likewise with astronaut Dan (*Survivor: Panama*), who only strategically shared his unique career history. At first he only told fighter-pilot Terry, swearing him to secrecy, to bond with him based upon the fact they both had exciting and intellectually advanced/challenging backgrounds in common. Sometime later he shared it with the remaining others when he started feeling he might be next to go, hoping the respect he might garner would save him. Sadly, it didn't. Pecking order based on contribution at camp and, in his case, the most recent Challenge did him in. On the flip side, people will share their hard-luck stories of ill health, single parenthood, or other struggles to curry comparative favor and appear more deserving of the money than others. Surprisingly, this doesn't happen as often as one might think, at least not on the edited bits we see on the show. I believe this is for two reasons: the first is pride, and the second is that fostering effective downward comparisons in others is challenging to manipulate. People don't want to seem too needy or it weakens them, making them seem something of a pathetic, rather than sympathetic, figure. So as a general rule, dear future contestant, if you are going to strum this chord, do it artfully, lightly, and strategically, rather than, say, making a heavy emotional confession or breaking down in front of the whole group, or it may backfire. Likewise, there can be people or situations that can get complicated in terms of leveraging comparisons. For example, the deaf Christy (*Survivor: Amazon*) and Chad, the cancer-survivor with one artificial leg (*Survivor: Vanuatu*), come to mind. On the one hand, many would downward compare to them (seeing themselves as "better" or more capable of winning) but also upward compare — realizing that the contestants with disabilities are elevated by comparison for overcoming their obstacles and still contributing and succeeding, which makes them a threat in terms of generating sympathy or admiration for both pecking order and deservedness.

SOCIAL COMPARISON TIPS AND TACTICS

So what does more consciously knowing a bit about social comparison mean to the *Survivor* contestant? You may not like this, but it means to cultivate *strategic mediocrity*. Perhaps you'd prefer to think of it as "finding the middle way" that is an important part of many spiritual traditions, particularly Buddhism. Let's put this into some specific tips and tactics so you remember them when you get to the beautiful, bug-ridden island.

1. *Don't be the overt leader.*
No matter how much you may want to be or are capable of being the

leader, don't step into the role overtly. Be the emergent leader on a case-specific basis. Pull strings and nudge decisions on a subtler level. Due to social comparison, the overt leaders often get picked off by disgruntled or threatened others. The emergent leaders, however, just come to the rescue to lead in a moment of crisis, when everyone else is in disarray or arguing and/or the overt leader has made a mistake. The emergent leader then shines, helping to bring resolution, just long enough to be appreciated but not long enough to be threatening. Thus he or she garners the benefits of "leadership" without the costs. Ozzy (*Survivor: Cook Islands*, second place) emerged as a leader on several occasions. In one instance, the tribe was spending too much time and energy talking about how to get coconuts instead of doing or even trying anything. He cut to the chase and climbed up the tree, voila!, to get the coconuts. The deed was done and there was a collective sigh of relief and positive comments to or about Ozzy. This is a low-risk example, but I trust you take the point: emergent leaders are more action-oriented than talk-oriented (words can come back to bite you), and they engage in what I call *stealth leadership* where they make themselves useful—but only carefully so in the overall pursuit of strategic mediocrity and winning the prize.

In terms of using this tip against others as more of a tactic, allow (or even privately encourage) someone else to take the lead—someone who you think would be either bad or good to the point of self-destruction. Then, strategically with selected others, subtly comment on this person's words or actions to increase the perception that this leader has to go. I say "subtly" so that the seed is planted but it isn't so overt as to come back and bite you in some embarrassing direct quote to your fellow players or filmed footage in the reunion show. For instance, Sekou (*Survivor: Cook Islands*) considered himself the leader and immediately set about bossing others around, but didn't have enough skills to compensate for his over-direction of others. The others let him go on "leading" with his scattered approach and his taking frequent breaks while others were doing what he ordered them to do. But, despite his having an ally, it's no surprise his teammates decided they were better off without his "leadership," and he was the first to be voted off from that tribe.

2. Win bread, but don't be the main breadwinner . . .

. . . or the fish-catcher, as is more often the case in *Survivor*. If you have the skill, catch enough to earn your keep and be of value to the group, but not enough to engender jealousy. Consider teaching willing others how to fish so that you may be seen as magnanimous and not hoarding of the power of bringing in the scarce resources. If you aren't a breadwinner, always publicly show gratitude for the breadwinner's efforts—but in an effort to undermine him or her, mention in passing to strategic others that the breadwinner has a little bit of an attitude, that he or she is too proud, or remind them that the breadwinner has some other annoying habits that don't compensate for the food he or she provides. Especially if it is getting closer to the end of the thirty-nine days, let it slip how, with the end in sight, that person's support is no longer critical to survival.

3. Don't work too much or too little.

While some will appreciate the person who works all the time, it isn't worth the risk. Work enough, maybe even a tad more than enough, but also take adequate strategic breaks to hang with the lethargic or lazy. If you have taken care to be seen, or acknowledged, by other workers to be doing more than sufficient work, it is relatively safe to announce that you are taking a brief break. The other hard workers will forgive you, and the slackers will think you're a little more like them (and as you sit there with them you'll build relationships). This way, you'll curry favor in both camps (the givers and the takers) without alienating either. Ah, but I can't help showing my bias, being a worker bee myself—if you, dear friend, want to win and happen to be one of the torpor-filled layabouts, get up off your fanny and do a bit more or at least help those that are doing! Don't let others see you as a laggard or you'll lose pecking order status.

To use this tip as more of a negative tactic, subtly draw attention—usually in one-on-one conversations—to the failings of others in a "Gee, I sure wish we'd had another hand with the wood collecting today. . . . I guess Jane just didn't feel up to helping" kind of way. But don't let others do this to you or yours. If someone starts to say things about you or someone with whom you have an alliance, be sure to intercept or deflect the thought with "You're right, Jane wasn't feeling up to it today and yet remember how yesterday she helped so much with . . ." and finish appropriately. Consider the case of Billy (*Survivor: Cook Islands*) who was a textbook example of a layabout as he so often slumbered and neglected to pull his weight around camp that his teammates intentionally lost an Immunity Challenge for the opportunity to get rid of him. Now in this case, it was Ozzy who suggested to the team that they throw the Challenge. Throwing a Challenge is a risky move, much riskier than simply scurrying up a tree for coconuts. And to be the one to suggest it is even riskier, but this ties back to the idea of stealth leadership—offering another example of how Ozzy watched and waited for the right moment in group mood to emerge with an idea or action that helped make clear what others were feeling or wanting done but were afraid to say or act about themselves. Once the seed was planted, subtly or not, Ozzy stealthily faded back a bit and didn't push too hard, lest he make himself the target.

4. *Play some or most of your cards close to your chest.*
As mentioned about Gary (the former football star) or Dan (the former astronaut), watch what you divulge about yourself and when. Don't overtly lie upon direct questioning (lest you get caught!), but don't tell everything about your personal life or work history. I know, it can get boring on the island and you may be tempted to ramble on about your life as an open book, but the more skilled players will listen more than they talk. They'll show interest in others and ask questions of them (to gain insights possibly to use later) but not over-volunteer key information about themselves. And, as a related aside, remember to enjoy peaceful silences. Realizing we only get to see a snippet of edited footage each week of the season, it would appear that those whose mouths drone on endlessly (think Cao Boi, *Survivor: Cook Islands*) are often seen as annoying and are at risk of being voted off to keep the peace.

As a tactic, draw others out about their voting plans but don't divulge your own plans too readily. Talking too much or too often about voting allows for dangerous forms of comparison and speculation about alliances. Don't volunteer whom you're voting off to just anyone unless you really need to. And, if you ever wind up in the middle (two groups wanting you to vote their way), don't seem too on-the-fence or you'll be seen, compared to those who haven't waffled, as either wishy-washy or unable to be influenced or counted on. The uncertainty will get you gone as it did, for instance, with Christy (*Survivor: Amazon*) and Dolly (*Survivor: Vanuatu*). If you can't agree, or don't want to lie that you agree just to protect yourself (as *Survivor: Vanuatu* winner Chris did), simply nod like you mean it as you listen and say "I see your point," and let them assume you agree. Hopefully you can leave it at that. If pressed to offer assurances that you will vote someone off, try a phrase like "that sounds like a plan" that implies consent but doesn't truly offer it. If push comes to shove, you may need to lie (if you are open to it) and give a firm answer to get them off your back and secure yourself as *not* being the swing vote. Then use your free time until the betrayal is revealed to think about how you can explain that, say, something important came up that changed your mind yet there was no time to talk about it again, you knew they'd understand it was for the good of the group (or alliance), and that you'd never lied before and don't intend to lie again (this kind of spin will be discussed in more depth in a later tip).

5. Counsel your family on the kind of family home video to make.

Think positively! You'll make it far enough to see the heart-wrenching video sent from home. So plan ahead and avoid the kind of video Brian (winner, *Survivor: Thailand*) was sent; as I recall, it showed his beautiful wife strolling past the big pool or grand piano in the large house and featured the fancy sports car he missed driving. Beautiful wife aside, this clearly allowed people to compare up to his already-existent wealth and feel discouraged about their own lot in life. Such videos allow people to see the one who "has it all" as less deserving of the prize. Instead, have a video with family showing your soft, human side (maybe with the family pet), talking about how much they miss you, and portraying something quirky and endearing about you or your family. That builds the good feelings other contestants will have about you. But, you may be thinking, Brian *won* season five. Yes, he did, but he won because he was a truly masterful player (even though, no, he didn't see an advance draft of this chapter), and he built relationships with people that he used to his advantage and then discarded. Still, Brian's video nearly cost him his win as people commented on how much he already had—enough so that Brian even commented (in a sidebar after the videos were viewed) that his video might have led the others to think he didn't "need" the money. So don't take a chance on it.

Naturally, as a negative tactic you'd use other people's videos against them. If you do, be sure to do it with tact so as not to seem unnecessarily critical or conniving. As before, it is usually best to do this with one or two key people at a time as opposed to publicly to the whole group—for if it is not skillfully done it could engender a defensive response, and you only want to risk that in small doses. Indeed, don't cause scenes that allow someone else to gain social plaudits, taking such from you by putting out a social fire you started.

THE WISDOM OF A SOCIAL COMPARISON APPROACH

To emphasize the wisdom of using your new hyper-awareness for social comparison, and to underscore the value in cultivating strategic mediocrity in general, simply look at the *Survivor* winning history. With the exception of fireman Tom (*Survivor: Palau*), I'd argue that none of the winners were consistently overt leaders or the hardest workers. And none of them had fancy-pants careers. In contrast, several terrific potential leaders or skilled outdoorspeople were voted off "too" early, such as Hunter (*Survivor: Marquesas*) and lumberjill Tina (*Survivor: Panama*). Tina, for instance, was clearly an outdoor-skilled boon to her group, doing everything from starting and maintaining the fire to catching fish with her bare hands. But the more people-skilled Cirie orchestrated Tina's exit by encouraging people to socially compare to Tina, emphasizing the threat she represented with her myriad skills, and suggesting that they'd never be able to beat her in a Challenge (despite the fact that personal-level Challenges were weeks away). Goodbye, Tina, we hardly knew you. Social skills trumped genuine outdoor survival skills, and it was Cirie who made it to the final four despite being deemed the weakest link with her initial outdoor ineptitude, including a fear of leaves.

So you might be thinking, "I'm just going to be me! I'm going to do my best and I hate this idea of being mediocre." Listen, if you're good enough to be another Tom, go ahead and go for being the overt leader—

he pulled it off. If you aren't, give it your honest all on each Challenge, but around the camp find the middle way and you'll be there longer. Yes, if you have to err on one side or the other do more rather than less as the lazier folks are at risk until, if they are lucky, the very end; but if you are strategically mediocre around camp—shining only when a hero is needed—you'll garner more influence through people liking you and perceiving similarity with you. Whether you should be or not, you'll be more trusted and appreciated by more people so you can influence their votes and win them in the end.

THE IMPORTANCE OF ATTRIBUTION

We all attribute. We do it all the time. Attributing, in this case, is psychology-speak for how we explain other people's behavior. Of course other people are making attributions about us at the same time, too, and it is important to understand how that may affect situations on *Survivor*. The kinds of attributions people make about their fellow contestants can make or break relationships and could cost the game.

As we go through the day we attempt to understand not just ourselves, but also what others do. We make judgments in hopes of finding a pattern or consistency in what someone does or how something happens. A big piece of this has to do with where we place cause or, put differently, where we place blame or control. Another piece is whether that cause seems typical (normal) or atypical (unusual). Let me explain by starting with how we attribute about our own behaviors, and then we'll talk about how it works in pairs of people or groups.

When we attribute inside ourselves about happenings in our life, or our own behaviors or the results thereof, we locate a causal explanation along three different dimensions. Without even consciously thinking of it our brain calculates, "This action or event's cause or impact is . . .":

1. *global* (this changes everything; it's a house of cards about to fall down) vs. *specific* (this impacts only this situation or a narrow set of situations);
2. *internal* (it's me that caused this) vs. *external* (there are other factors outside myself involved here); and

3. *stable* (this always happens; it's going to be this way forever; it's permanent, or very hard to change) vs. *unstable* (this is unusual; this too shall pass; this is temporary or mutable).

To the degree and frequency that individuals interpret their worlds by making global, internal, and stable attributions for negative life events, they will be less happy and may be depressed or predisposed to depression (arguments of causal direction notwithstanding). Non-depressed people tend more often to interpret events in ways that maintain or elevate their own self-concept or self-esteem. Even if it is wrong, it helps them not get stuck in an unhappy place. When you're on *Survivor*, you'll want to be very careful about whether you are making global or specific, stable or unstable, and internal or external attributions about yourself and others—and how others are attributing about you. Because we often make mistakes. . . .

BEWARE OF THE FUNDAMENTAL ATTRIBUTION ERROR WHEN DEALING WITH OTHERS

PLAYER 1: "Dude, you're a liar!"
PLAYER 2: "Oh yeah? Well, you're sneaky!"
INSIDE PLAYER 1'S MIND: "I'm no liar; I'm simply playing the game."
INSIDE PLAYER 2'S MIND: "I'm not sneaky; I'm simply strategic."

This hypothetical exchange represents how people point fingers and make judgments but don't necessarily see that their actions are actually similar. They judge themselves by a different standard, and excuse their own behavior while vilifying another who quite often did a variant of the same thing. While these exact words may not have been uttered on *Survivor*, almost any fan knows the sentiment is expressed often enough. Often back at camp (when someone who thought they were in an alliance was blindsided by how the vote went down, or at the post-vote confessional) contestants will lament that they couldn't trust anyone even though they themselves were not trustworthy (or perhaps they were on the fence so often no one could believe where they stood).

This is an example of what social psychologists call "the fundamental attribution error." As we go through the world trying to understand and explain other people's behavior, we usually attribute what someone does to either internal causes (personality, mood, disposition) or to external causes (situational, physical, or social circumstances). So an attribution is how we make sense of what someone said or did; it's where we assign credit for their actions. The error comes in when we realize that some of the "logical" ways we do this aren't that logical at all. The fundamental attribution error we often make in judging *others* is to underestimate the effect of external causes and overestimate the effect of internal causes. In contrast, when explaining our own behavior we typically do just the opposite: we blame the circumstances we are in or something external to us. So if you trip on the sidewalk, I call you a klutz (I make an internal attribution about you that is somewhat stable in nature). In contrast, if I trip on the sidewalk I claim it's because of the uneven or slippery surface (I make an external attribution about myself that is temporary in nature).

Experiments have demonstrated that we make this attributional thinking error very often, so much so that it became considered and named "fundamental." It is so consistent that even when we are explicitly told that someone's behavior is fake, forced, or situationally driven, we tend to disregard that information. For instance, even if we know for a fact that someone has been told to act very friendly or was paid to be nice, we disregard the situational aspect (he was under orders to be friendly) and believe instead that the person is indeed friendly (when he may really be rotten or hate your guts). For ourselves, on the other hand, we may snap at someone and never take responsibility for the fact that we may often be a bit edgy and, instead, immediately write it off to any available external factor (the fact that it's hot, we just battled traffic, we need a cup of coffee, or we skipped a meal).

Why do we do this? Why is the fundamental attribution error so, well, fundamental? Besides being adaptive in helping us keep our self-esteem intact, it happens to be a quite natural perceptual cognitive shortcut that is related to whose eyes you are looking through. As you inhabit your body and look out your own eyes, what you see around you are the environmental/situational factors. You are, in essence, an *observer* of your environment . . . you see the crack in the sidewalk and the slippery surface, you feel the weight of the heavy bag you are carrying, you know you are hot, thirsty, and tired, and you are painfully aware that the heel of your shoe is wobbly. You don't see yourself as the *actor* in the situation but are focused on what you are observing in the situation you are dealing with, so it is easy to blame the situational, external factors. When you are looking at someone else, however, that person is the focus—they are clearly the *actor* on the stage. The person is in the foreground of your visual field and your mind, while the background or external factors fall away. So it is easy to blame the person's characteristics. That same person, looking out of his or her own eyes at the situation, sees something different than you do. Research experiments have demonstrated, for example, that you can even impact who an observer will consider in control of a conversation simply by how you place them in the room and whom they primarily see.

ATTRIBUTIONS: TIPS AND TACTICS

How will knowing a bit about attribution and the fundamental attribution error help you win *Survivor*? Simply recognizing that there are three basic dimensions along which we explain behavior and how easily we make mistakes is potentially powerful. Much of it comes down to the accuracy of the explanations you make about yourself and others. Think for a moment, for instance, about how many times you have had a fight with a family member or friend because you had wildly different interpretations of the same event. It is easy to assume that what we see or "know" is true because we trust our senses and perception when, in fact, if we take the time to explore it, the other person's perception was quite different. Often we quickly polarize our thoughts and dig our heels into our position when it would be more productive to take a moment to engage in "perspective-taking" and put ourself in that other person's shoes, see momentarily through their eyes. This increases one's empathy for how or why they did what they did. It is always wise—in *Survivor* as well as life outside the game—to seek first to understand, *then* react.

So, say you do spend a moment stepping out of yourself to understand other people's perspectives and choices; by no means does this mean you have to agree with or endorse what they did, but at least you understand it and may be better prepared to understand, explain, or predict their behavior in the future and possibly prevent further hassles. As touchy-feely as this may sound to some, it's just good advice. You'll hear people on *Survivor* say "I'm not here to make friends. I'm here to win a million bucks." But making friends, or at least being perceived as fair and possibly friendly, is the way to the million bucks á la previously mentioned winners Brian and Chris as well as winner Tina (*Survivor: Australian Outback*). You'll also hear people say, "I'm not going to let my values go; I'd rather have this potentially lifelong friend than win the million dollars." Situations are powerful and yet, despite the power of the competitive game and tantalizing prize, not everyone will play by the same rules and one's personality sometimes stands strong even against a very powerful situation. Whichever camp you fall in—money motivated or values motivated—use these attribution-related tips to help you succeed:

1. *Manage your own moods via wise use of attributions.*
I know this is tough when you may not be eating enough or drinking enough water. I know it is a challenge to handle the bugs, the weather, the constant people, and the incessant scheming. Still, to the degree that you can, re-frame things to keep your mood lifted. Keep a close eye on your own thinking about your own behavior; be aware of if you are making internal or external, global or specific, and stable or unstable attributions. How you explain your ups and downs to yourself and others (as we'll get to shortly) could mean the difference in whether you stay or go. Are you having a bad day because you think you are tired (a temporary attribution, for tonight your fatigue may let you sleep better) or because you think you are irretrievably exhausted (a stable/permanent explanation)? Did you do poorly on that Challenge because you think you really have bad aim (a specific shortcoming) or because you think you're a "loser" who can't contribute anything to any Challenge ever (a global attribution)? And so on. Don't descend into the pit of a pessimistic explanatory style or, if you do, don't stay there for long. If you need to beat yourself up or cry, wait until you are alone or maybe talking to the camera in one of those private sidebars. Remember the *Hamlet* quotation this chapter started with: "For there is nothing either good or bad, but thinking makes it so." It's true. Something can be objectively icky—such as a

huge rainstorm or losing a Challenge—but don't let emotions take over or blow something out of proportion.

An example of this comes from Stephannie (*Survivor: Cook Islands*) who unwisely publicly declared herself as the weakest link and deserving to be voted off after her tribe lost an Immunity Challenge. She may as well have painted a target on her back with this global, internal, stable attribution ("I'm the weakest link"). She'd have been much better off to spin the loss as a shared defeat and stress how hard she worked and that her poor performance was unusual (specific and temporary) and could have been suffered by any of the others who had to deal with such stress and materials (external). They were about to vote her off based on her *statement*, not her performance, but her demise was delayed when the tribe opted to get rid of another cocky leader (J. P.) first. With that gift of time she could have recovered her standing, but she sealed her fate when, after the next failed Immunity Challenge, she once again made a remark that was interpreted as self-defeating, and thus team-defeating by extension. It was a silly throwaway remark about how maybe mashed potatoes would taste good that night if she went home but, taken together with her earlier remark, it put her torch out. So watch how you talk about yourself and the attributions you lead others to make about you. Remember that there is a fine line between being modest, humble, and accepting some little bit of responsibility for an outcome, and full-on self-destructive statements.

2. *Strategically manage the moods of others.*
Do so such that you support your friends and tear down your enemies. If someone you'd like to see gone mentions his own fatigue in subtle passing or open whining, build on it. Agree with the person and offer additional evidence, ever so kindly or not, of his previous failures or upcoming insurmountable obstacles: "Jack, you are tired, aren't you, buddy? Yes, and just think how beat you'll feel after a few more days and a couple more Challenges!" Paint the darker picture for that person's ears alone. Encourage Jack to do his best on the Challenges for the good of the team (assuming it is still at the team immunity stage of play) but then, when it is safe to do so, nudge his thinking to attributions that negatively affect his mood and increase his perception of fatigue.

In contrast, if you've made an alliance with someone who is starting to feel emotionally or mentally weak or physically tired, gently determine if there is something in how he is thinking about himself that is contributing to this. If so, help him re-frame his attributions to buck up and see another day, assuming you want to keep this alliance. If someone is truly fatigued beyond recovery and hints he may want to go, let him go peacefully and with grace. Use your head about where the balance is but, in my humble opinion, it is not worth over-persuading someone who dramatically and publicly does the "I can't handle it anymore, please vote me off" spiel (Shane, *Survivor: Panama*, and a few others before him). If close allies are speaking privately in a moment of trust, perhaps attempt to encourage them, in order to preserve the alliance. Otherwise let them go (as they did with Stephannie, above).

3. Don't let people jump to conclusions about you.
Now that you understand the fundamental attribution error, you know people are going to attribute anything you do to *you* instead of whatever circumstances you were dealing with. In a game like *Survivor*, they probably won't stop at simply overestimating your personal control and underestimating the situation, they'll probably also make global and stable/permanent conclusions about you—as they did with Stephannie (*Survivor: Cook Islands*), who claimed she wanted to stay despite her self-defeating comments. Don't let this happen. Manage your image by educating them about the situational factors you faced—it was something specific and temporary that caused you to do what you did, not a lack of personal character ("Wow, that rope was covered in algae or something. I'm strong but I just couldn't get a grip on that dang rope"). Mention in passing that this is the first time you ever made that mistake and don't anticipate making it again. How you explain your behavior to others will help persuade them that you either have outlived your usefulness or have just had a momentary lapse.

4. Don't jump to conclusions about others.
Realize that you may be assuming something quite incorrect about others too—that you may have made a fundamental attribution error about them. It is particularly useful to stop and think it through a minute

before you spout off and make broad sweeping generalizations about someone, whether in your thoughts or publicly. You may, upon reflection or conversation, realize there were mitigating situational circumstances that impacted an individual's behavior and stop short of scuttling a good deal with this person.

5. *Lead people to conclude what you wish about others.*
Based on what we've just covered, it follows logically to lead people to conclude negative things about people you don't like. Manipulate attributional awareness to remind of, emphasize, or lead people to uncharitable conclusions about other players, saying quietly to the right people how "Jane makes mistakes at everything and it seems like at every Challenge" (global and stable) or "That guy's a jerk and he's never going to change" (stable and internal). Likewise, don't let others jump to conclusions about someone you want to keep around. Stay alert and you can do some "image management" for someone in your alliance or for someone you are hoping to sway later—completely re-spinning the situation. If someone is speaking negatively about an ally in words that indicate stable, internal, and global attributions, you gently come back with counter-examples that are temporary, external, and specific. For instance, "She's messed up a couple times, sure, but remember that Jane was right on target when she . . ." or "John, a jerk? Not all the time, just when he's lost a Challenge . . ." and so on.

THE WISDOM OF AN ATTRIBUTIONAL APPROACH

Permit me to anticipate and address potential hesitations about this set of tips. You may say, "Wait a minute! Isn't this just making excuses or doing damage control?" or "Isn't this just a spin game?" Well, no and yes. The attribution process and the fundamental attribution error are real aspects of human thinking—it's a big part of how we think about our lives and make sense of others' behavior. Understanding that you and others do this gives you a tool for influencing your own and others' moods and for influencing perception or correcting the mistaken conclusions to which someone may jump. Done poorly it could come off as "making excuses," but done properly it comes off as "offering reasons," as clarifying or explaining. Your attitude, vocal tone, posture, and timing make a difference here. Are these tips "spin game"? They don't have to be, but certainly can be. Read on.

A MATTER OF CONSCIENCE

How you use the attribution and/or the social comparison tips and tactics is up to you and how you choose to play the game of *Survivor*. You can spin something—most would say that's fair, while others would say it isn't. You can bend the truth or outright lie—some would consider that fair as it is, after all, a game that invites if not expects it. Indeed, we could have an entire chapter on lying through commission (what you say) or omission (what you don't say). Three of the *Survivor* winners I mentioned here would likely have a different take on such matters. For instance, Brian (*Survivor: Thailand*) and Chris (*Survivor: Vanuatu*) took what we'll call a less-straightforward approach to winning. Tom (*Survivor: Palau*) was more straightforward—he left himself wiggle-room in how he made or explored what may be considered side deals from his initial alliance. That's the way to make both winning friends and influencing votes easier to do at the same time—take care that you word your conversations to help protect people's perception of you in case something turns out differently than they'd hoped. If you word it well, anticipate and appreciate their perspective, alert them in passing that you've chatted with so-and-so, they are "primed," if you will, to receive a bit better whatever happens at the next shake-up which, in turn, reduces shock, betrayal, and finger-pointing.

So who are you and how do you want to play as you outwit, outplay, and outlast? To which voice do *you* listen more often—the angel on your right shoulder or the devil on your left? How do you blend them to form your conscience—to form your personality?

You could use these tips and tactics, say, to bring someone down in mood and mismanage his image in the eyes of others, you could use your understanding to keep someone's mood up or properly manage or even enhance your own or another's image, or you could simply use these tools when you have a genuine situation to clarify. I present the ideas simply to raise your awareness so you can practice now in seeing these principles at work and how to work with them in yourself and others. Then you'll be all ready when you hit *Survivor*. My personal preference would be to use your knowledge and skills to be positive and supportive of self and others on your way to the win. But whether you use your knowledge or skills for "good" or "evil" is up to you, because behavior is a function of both personality and environment. All the contestants are in an environment that is largely similar (though camp sites and team dynamics will vary) but the personality you go in with will interact with those external influences in a new and interestingly different way than anyone who came before. If you choose to go in planning on using deception like self-named Jonny "Fairplay" (*Survivor: Pearl Islands*, third place) who lied often, planned ahead to get fake news on his grandma's death for sympathy, went in with the intention to be the "dirtiest player ever" and left proclaiming he was proud he "didn't play fair and didn't plan on it," then that's your choice and you'll be using my tips and tactics for manipulation.

Other people will—like most *Survivor* players—choose to go in and play in as aboveboard a way as possible, and then feel considerable guilt if they stray from their principles in any way or misplay their cards. For instance, Ian (*Survivor: Palau*) let missteps and emotions get to him but chose to handle it nobly in the end by quitting the last Immunity Challenge to let the final two whom he felt deserved it (for whatever his public and personal reasons) go forward. Similarly, Rafe (*Survivor: Guatemala*) kindly released Danni from her promise to take him to the final two so he'd have a clean conscience that she had chosen for the right reasons. Well, she chose Stephenie. So did Rafe make a smart move or a dumb move? You decide. Either way, we can respect that his personality led him to act above the situational variables even in the face of the powerful and tempting opportunity to be either the one who will win $1 million or $100,000. I suspect the Ians and Rafes of this world would use the knowledge of these tips in an honorable way to secure stronger relationships when they, hopefully, show up on the next *Survivor: All-Stars*. When they do, or when you, dear reader, win in a future *Survivor*, remember me on my couch thinking up new twists for the yet-to-request-my-input *Survivor* puppet masters, and my living vicariously through you as you used these tips to secure your success.

ACKNOWLEDGMENTS

Many thanks to my friends and colleagues Dr. Linda Luecken, Dr. Stanley Parkinson, Rita Erickson, and Tracy Perkins for commenting on drafts of this work. I appreciate each of them in many unique ways, but special thanks to Linda for being my *Survivor*-watching buddy, season after season.

STEPHANIE R. DELUSÉ, PH.D., psychologist, researcher, author, and teacher, is also associate faculty director of the Bachelor of Interdisciplinary Studies (BIS) program at Arizona State University. Her graduate training emphasized social psychology, priming her appreciation for the group dynamics in *Survivor* and the inherent tensions between personality and environment and between competition and cooperation. Her most recent academic efforts have earned her recognition for her teaching, including selection as one of ASU's Featured Faculty in 2006 and an Outstanding Faculty Award in 2005. In her sparse free time she communes with nature most frequently in the guise of her cat, her trees, and her herb garden replete with insect life and lizards.

Psychologists turn their attention to *The Simpsons*, one of America's most popular and beloved shows, in these essays that explore the function and dysfunctions of the show's characters. Designed to appeal to both fans of the show and students of psychology, this unique blend of science and pop culture consists of essays by professional psychologists drawn from schools and clinical practices across the country. Each essay is designed to be accessible, thoughtful, and entertaining, while providing the reader with insights into both *The Simpsons* and the latest in psychological thought. Every major area of psychology is covered, from clinical psychology and cognition to abnormal and evolutionary psychology, while fresh views on eclectic show topics such as gambling addiction, Pavlovian conditioning, family therapy, and lobotomies are explored.

smartpopbooks.com | BenBella Books

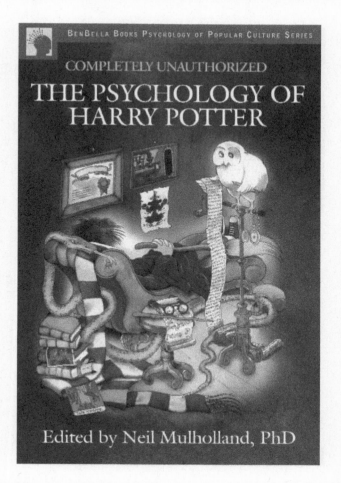

Harry Potter has provided a portal to the wizarding world for millions of readers, but an examination of Harry, his friends, and his enemies will take us on yet another journey: through the psyche of the Muggle (and wizard!) mind. The twists and turns of the series, as well as the psychological depth and complexity of J. K. Rowling's characters, have kept fans enthralled with and puzzling over the many mysteries that permeate Hogwarts and beyond. Now, in *The Psychology of Harry Potter*, leading psychologists delve into the ultimate Chamber of Secrets, analyzing human mind and motivation by examining the themes and characters that make the Harry Potter books the bestselling fantasy series of all time. Grab a spot on the nearest couch, and settle in for some fresh revelations about our favorite young wizard!

smartpopbooks.com | BenBella Books

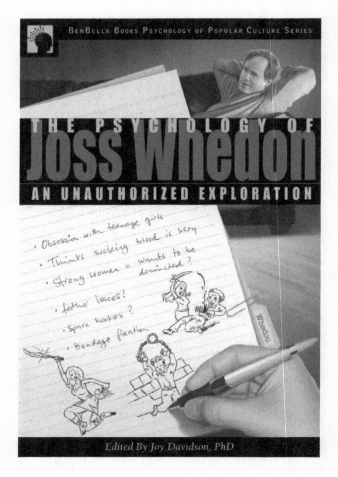

Joss Whedon—creator of the wildly popular *Buffy the Vampire Slayer*, its spin-off *Angel*, the short-lived series Firefly, and the feature film it inspired, *Serenity*—takes a seat on the couch in this in-depth examination of the psychological gravity that has captivated his deeply devoted fan base. Whedon fans will enjoy a discussion of issues that are both funny and profound, from the significance of Angel's mommy issues and the best way to conduct government experiments on vampires to what could drive a man to become a cannibalistic Reaver and the psychological impact of being one girl in all the world chosen to fight the forces of darkness.

Available December 2007

smartpopbooks.com | BenBella Books

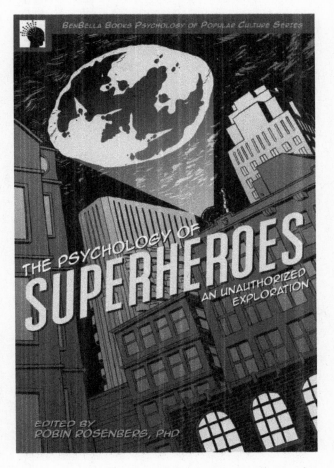

Unmasking superhuman abilities and double lives, this analysis showcases nearly two dozen psychologists as their essays explore the minds of pop culture's most intriguing and daring superheroes, including Spider-Man, Batman, Superman, and the X-Men. Exposing the inner thoughts that these reclusive heroes would only dare share with trained professionals, heady experts give detailed psychoanalyses of what makes specific superheroes tick while answering such questions as Why do superheroes choose to be superheroes? Why is there so much prejudice against the X-Men mutants? What makes Spider-Man so altruistic? and Why are supervillains so aggressive? Additionally, the essays tackle why superheroes have such an enduring effect on American culture.

Available March 2008

smartpopbooks.com | BenBella Books